The Curious Researcher

The Curious Researcher

□ ■ □

A Guide to Writing Research Papers

BRUCE BALLENGER

University of New Hampshire

ALLYN AND BACON

Boston   London   Toronto   Sydney   Tokyo   Singapore

Editor in Chief, Humanities: *Joseph Opiela*
Series Editorial Assistant: *Brenda Conaway*
Editorial-Production Administrator: *Rowena Dores*
Editorial-Production Service: *Denise Hoffman, Alternative Graphics*
Copyeditor: *Susan Freese*
Composition Buyer: *Linda Cox*
Manufacturing Buyer: *Louise Richardson*
Cover Administrator: *Linda K. Dickinson*
Cover Designer: *Suzanne Harbison*

Copyright © 1994 by Allyn and Bacon
A Division of Simon & Schuster, Inc.
160 Gould Street
Needham Heights, Massachusetts 02194

Library of Congress Cataloging-in-Publication Data

Ballenger, Bruce P.
    The curious researcher: a guide to writing research papers / Bruce
    Ballenger.
      p.   cm.
    Includes index.
    ISBN 0-205-13905-1 (pbk.)
    1. Report writing—Handbooks, manuals, etc. 2. Research—
Handbooks, manuals, etc. I. Title
LB2369.B246   1993
808'.02—dc20   93-11200
                                        CIP

Printed in the United States of America

10 9 8 7 6 5 4   98 97 96 95

For Rebecca,
who reminds me to ask Why

□ ■ □

Contents

Chapter 2
The Second Week   55

Chapter 3
The Third Week   77

Chapter 5
The Fifth Week   167

□ ■ □

Preface

A few years ago, I had a student who immediately distinguished herself as a gifted writer. Jayne's first essay, titled "The Sterile Cage," was a touching and insightful piece about what it meant to spend a year of her life in a hospital bed, suspended in a stainless steel cage, recovering from a bone disorder. I still copy the essay for my classes, praising the richness of detail and the subtle way a writer's voice can woo a reader. When it was time to assign a research paper, I looked forward to seeing what Jayne would do. She chose a topic in childhood development, and though she said it was going well, I could tell it was loveless labor for her.

Teaching the research paper was the same for me back then. Though I believed in the assignment, convinced that research is a practical academic skill and that research writing is common in other classes, I disliked how cold the classroom became when the subject came up—the sometimes surly silences and sighs—and quickly longed to return to teaching the essay, something for which my students developed some genuine enthusiasm. We would plow through the five weeks it took for students to research and write their papers, all of us anxious for the unit to be over with.

I finally knew I was doing something wrong in my approach to research when I came across Jayne's paper one evening, halfway through the stack of draft research papers. The paper was awful reading. Though she obviously researched the subject vigorously, demonstrating an impressive bibliography, Jayne's paper was unfocused, her analysis lifeless, and her prose wooden. The voice she had found in her essays was "missing in action," as was her usual talent for getting to the heart of a topic. I distinctly remember the conference we had in my office a week later because it was so unpleasant.

What did she think of the paper? I asked. "Not much."

xvii

Did she find it unfocused? "Sort of."

Did the paper sound lifeless to her? "Yes."

Jayne glared across the desk at me.

"What do you want from me?" she said. "This is a research paper, damnit. It's *supposed* to be this way."

At that moment, Jayne spoke for the many students I've had over the years who've come to believe that the research paper is a vampirish creation that, at a teacher's request, periodically comes back from the dead to suck the life out of them. Some students, thankfully, don't see it that way, but the Jaynes of the world are not to blame for their cynicism. One student spoke for many when he said, "The definition of *research* is 'tiresome studies on a subject that a person does not like.' "

The assignment clearly carries "baggage," much of it filled with weighty misconceptions about what it means to do research. "Research [in high school] was a certain number of pages with a certain number of quotes on a certain topic," wrote Nancy, a college freshman, when asked about her experiences with research papers. Her comments are typical. "I found it very hard to learn much more than how to link quotes together from these papers. We also had a very strict form for the intro., exactly where the sentence would fall and what it should say."

In our rush to teach students the formal elements of the research paper, teachers sometimes forget that, despite its many conventions, the success of research writing depends on the same thing that makes most other kinds of writing successful: the writer's interest in what she's writing about. That research can be a process of discovery, a sometimes mad rush down trails that appear unexpectedly, is not well known, even among college students. That researchers sometimes literally hunger to learn more about some aspect of a subject and that the time looking can be fulfilling, even exciting, are less known yet. The reason is simple: Nobody has pointed out that research is really about *curiosity*.

That's the premise of this book: Research is rooted in curiosity. This is hardly a radical notion, though strangely enough, many books on writing the college research paper limit their discussion of curiosity to short chapters or sections of chapters, usually titled "Choosing a Topic." Being driven by curiosity involves more than choosing a good topic. Curiosity includes a willingness to be open to what you'll find as you immerse yourself in the research as well as a willingness to change your mind, to let go of preconceived notions. Curiosity is an invitation to be confused and a desire to try to straighten things out, first for yourself and then for the people you're writing for. That's an important distinction. So many students come to the research paper with only one question in mind: What exactly does the teacher want?

Pleasing the teacher is an old game, of course, but it's worse with the research paper because so much of the project seems so prescribed—a certain number of pages, particular citation methods, an outline, an introduction, body, and conclusion. What's worse, many students assume things about how to write the paper that may be unstated—that there is a certain formal voice in all research writing; that all research papers are objective; that the longer the bibliography, the better the grade. With all these rules to worry about, it's no surprise that many students believe their own curiosity about what they're writing is beside the point.

The Curious Researcher says otherwise. I'm convinced that teachers can teach the conventions of the college research paper without students' losing their sense of themselves as masters of their own work. We teachers might begin by reminding ourselves of our own moments of enthusiasm, late at night in the college library, when an unexpected source suddenly cracked open a new door on our research topic and the light poured in, helping us to see the topic in a new way. I have found new enthusiasm for the research paper—in fact, I love teaching it—by renewing my excitement about research as a means of satisfying my own curiosity. It made sense to me to share that enthusiasm with the student readers of this book by relating my own experiences with research, including the research that went into writing this book. In a break with the usual "I'm the flawless expert" tone of many textbooks, I will also share my own occasional frustrations with the research process. All writers struggle sometimes, including this one.

Despite the obvious differences between the author of this book and its readers, I hope that, by sharing the research trails I've followed—dead ends and all—students will see that the research process, like the writing process, is never neat, never as simple as some textbooks imply. Thank God! That's what makes research interesting.

One of the things Jayne was trying to say to me that day in my office was that everything she learned about being a good writer and writing strong prose seemed irrelevant when the research paper assignment came along. Somehow, my students got the message that, in the research paper, the writing and the writer don't really matter. In the rigid little world of the research paper, what mattered was getting it right.

This book aims to challenge that assumption by helping students see how integrally the *research* process and the *writing* process are bound. While acknowledging that the research paper does have its own distinct conventions, *The Curious Researcher* promotes the idea that research papers can, in fact, be interesting to write and to read. It accomplishes that, in part, by featuring examples of research writing that are compelling and by encouraging student writers to consider alternatives to the strict forms of the research paper they learned in high school.

I am often amazed at what students do with this new freedom. I believe little is lost in not prescribing a formal research paper, particularly in an introductory composition course. As students move on from here to their declared majors, they will learn the scholarly conventions of their disciplines from those best equipped to teach them. In the meantime, students will master valuable library skills and learn many of the technical elements of the research paper, such as citation methods and evaluating sources. But most important, students will discover, often for the first time, what college research is really about: *using the ideas of others to shape ideas of their own.*

Since procrastination ails many student researchers, this book is uniquely designed to move them through the research process, step by step and week by week, for five weeks, the typical period allotted for the assignment. The structure of the book is flexible, however; students should be encouraged to compress the sequence if their research assignment will take less time or ignore it altogether and use the book to help them solve specific problems as they arise.

If you do encourage your students to follow the five-week sequence, I think you'll find that they'll like the way *The Curious Researcher* doesn't deluge them with information, as do so many other research paper texts, but doles it out, week by week, when the information is most needed.

The Introduction, "Rethinking the Research Paper," challenges students to reconceive the research paper assignment. For many of them, this will amount to a "declaration of independence." During "The First Week," students are encouraged to discover a topic that they're genuinely curious about and to learn to navigate the reference section of the library through a unique self-teaching exercise. In "The Second Week," students focus the topic of the paper and develop a research strategy. In "The Third Week," students learn notetaking techniques, the dangers of plagiarism, and tips on how to conduct a search that challenges them to dig more deeply for information. During "The Fourth Week," students begin writing and review documentation conventions of the Modern Language Association (MLA). In "The Fifth Week," students are guided through the final revision, including how to prepare the bibliography page and format of the paper.

Four appendixes present sample research papers by students, which illustrate many of the approaches taught in the book. The samples range from a highly personal and informal research essay ("Lemming Death," Appendix A) to a somewhat less personal and more formal paper ("Metamorphosis, the Exorcist, and Oedipus," Appendix D). Also included are two papers that fall somewhere between the two mentioned: an unrevised draft on the children's program "Sesame Street" (Appendix B), written in MLA style, and a more polished paper on spouse abuse and alcoholism, using APA conventions (Appendix C). Though each of these papers has notable strengths, none is by any means flawless. That's what makes them useful examples. I've annotated each sample essay with comments about strengths and options for further revision.

Unlike other textbooks, which relegate exercises to the ends of chapters, *The Curious Researcher* makes them integral to the process of researching and writing the paper. Though techniques such as fastwriting and brainstorming—featured in some of the writing exercises—are now commonplace in many composition classes, they have rarely been applied to research writing and certainly not as extensively as they have been here. Fastwriting is an especially useful tool, not just for prewriting but for open-ended thinking throughout the process of researching and writing the paper. The exercises are also another antidote to procrastination, challenging students to stay involved in the process as well as providing instructors with a number of short assignments throughout the five weeks that help them monitor students' progress.

But I'm convinced that the value of any text on research writing, no matter how clever its design, is dependent on the fire ignited by students' topics. Students must be curious researchers. When they take charge of discovering what they want to know, students like Jayne begin to get their voices back, eager to share what they've learned. I believe this book will help.

ACKNOWLEDGMENTS

Teaching writing is often a deeply personal experience. Because students often write from their hearts as well as their minds, I've been privileged to read work that genuinely matters to them. More often than they realize, students teach the teacher, and they have especially tutored me in how to rethink the research paper.

Because students move so quickly in and out of my life, I rarely get the chance to acknowledge their lessons. I'd like to take that opportunity now. Jayne Wynters, whose story begins this book, was a student of mine a decade ago, and she deserves much credit for challenging my ideas about the college research paper that lead to *The Curious Researcher*. Other students who either contributed directly to this text or helped me to conceive it include Kim Armstrong, Christine Berquist, Daniel Jaffurs, Heather Dunham, Candace Collins, Jason Pulsifer, Jennifer White, and Karoline Ann Fox.

Many of my colleagues at the University of New Hampshire have been instrumental in the genesis of this book. I am especially grateful to three of them. Thomas Newkirk has been my mentor for some years now, and it was his belief that I had something useful to say about the freshman research paper that inspired me to write this text. Robert Connors is not only a preeminent composition scholar but a friend, and his early encouragement and advice were also extremely valuable. And Donald Murray, my first writing teacher, continues to cast his long and welcome shadow on everything I do in the field.

Other writers and writing teachers who contributed directly to *The Curious Researcher* or gave me valuable ideas include Robin Lent, Brock Dethier, Barbara Tindall, Donna Qualley, Barry Lane, Nora Nevin, Diane McAnaney, Sue Hertz, Jane Harrigan, Tamara Niedlsowski, Greg Bowe, and Bronwyn Williams.

I am also grateful to my editor at Allyn and Bacon, Joseph Opiela, who believed in this project from the very beginning, and also to his talented assistant, Brenda Conaway. Susan Freese did a masterful job reining in my sometimes unruly prose.

I would also like to thank those individuals who reviewed the book for Allyn and Bacon:

Joseph T. Barwick, Central Piedmont Community College
Arnold J. Bradford, Northern Virginia Community College
Jack Branscomb, East Tennessee State University
Patricia E. Connors, Memphis State University
A. Cheryl Curtis, University of Hartford
John Fugate, J. Sargeant Reynolds Community College
Walter S. Minot, Gannon University
Michele Moragne e Silva, St. Edwards University
Al Starr, Essex Community College
Henrietta S. Twining, Alabama A&M
Matthew Wilson, Rutgers University

And finally, I am most indebted to my wife, Karen Kelley, who helped me see this project through during a difficult time in our lives.

INTRODUCTION

□ ■ □

Rethinking
the Research Paper

Unlike most textbooks, this one begins with your writing, not mine. Find a fresh page in your notebook, grab a pen, and spend fifteen minutes doing the following exercise.*

□ *EXERCISE 1*
Reflecting on Research

Most of us were taught to think before we write, to have it all figured out in our heads before we pick up our pens. This exercise asks you to think *through* writing rather than *before,* letting the words on the page lead you to what you want to say. With practice, that's surprisingly easy using a technique called *fastwriting*. Basically, you just write down whatever comes into your head, not worrying about whether you're being eloquent, grammatical, or even very smart. It's remarkably like talking to a good friend, not trying to be brilliant and even blithering a bit, but along the way discovering what you think. If the writing stalls, write about that, or write about what you've already written until you find a new trail to follow. Just keep your pen moving.

---

* This exercise uses a technique called *loop writing.* For more information on *looping,* see Peter Elbow and Pat Belanoff, *A Community of Writers* (New York: Random House, 1989), 53–60.

1

Try a fastwrite that focuses on your thoughts about the subject of this book. On the top of the page, write these words: "Research and Research Papers." Skip a line and then write, "First Thoughts." Now spend five minutes (time yourself) fastwriting about what comes into your mind when you think of research and research papers. What occurs to you when you first hear those words? Then what? What are your prejudices and preconceptions about them? Remember to keep your pen moving, and don't worry about grammar or coherence.

After five minutes, skip a line and write, "People, Stories, and Moments." Now fastwrite for another five minutes, concentrating again on research and research papers, but this time think about specific people, papers, assignments, scenes, situations, or stories you associate with those words. Perhaps recall a paper you wrote for Mr. Wills in your sophomore year, or that evening in the library when you pored over the *Encyclopaedia Britannica* for information on China, or the class in which you learned about writing college papers.

Finally, skip another line and write, "Lies, Expectations, and Sayings." Spend five more minutes *brainstorming* a list of phrases, clichés, sayings, ideas, and beliefs about research and research papers you've picked up along the way, even if you know they're silly or untrue. A *brainstorm* is like a fastwrite, except that you make a quick, uncensored list of things instead of trying to write sentences. Jot down anything that comes to mind: for example, "The most important thing about a research paper is the thesis statement," or "All research is dry and boring," or "The best source of information is the encyclopedia."

□ ■ □

Very few of us recall the research papers we wrote in high school, and if we do, what we remember is not what we learned about the topic but what a bad experience it was. Joe was an exception. "I remember one assignment was to write a research paper on a problem in the world, such as acid rain, and then come up with your own solutions and discuss moral and ethical aspects of your solution, as well. It involved not just research but creativity and problem solving and other stuff."

For the life of me, I can't recall a single research paper I wrote in high school, but like Joe, I remember the one that I finally enjoyed doing a few years later in college. It was a paper on the whaling industry, and what I remember best was the introduction. I spent a lot of time on it, describing in great detail exactly what it was like to stand at the bow of a Japanese whaler, straddling an explosive harpoon gun, taking aim, and blowing a bloody hole in a humpback whale.

I obviously felt pretty strongly about the topic.

Unfortunately, many students feel most strongly about getting their research papers over with. So it's not surprising that when I tell my Freshman English course that one of their writing assignments will be an eight- to ten-page research paper, there is a collective sigh. They knew it was coming. For years, their high school teachers prepared them for the College Research Paper, and it loomed ahead of them as one of the torturous things you must do, a five-week sentence of hard labor in the library, picking away at cold, stony facts. Not surprisingly, students' eyes roll in disbelief when I add that many of them will end up liking their research papers better than anything they've written before.

I can understand why Joe was among the few in the class inclined to believe me. For many students, the library is an alien place, a wilderness to get lost in, a place to go only when forced. Others carry memories of research paper assignments that mostly involved taking copious notes on index cards, only to transfer pieces of information into the paper, sewn together like patches of a quilt. There seemed little purpose to it. "You weren't expected to learn anything about yourself with the high school research paper," wrote Jenn, now a college freshman. "The best ones seemed to be the ones with the most information. I always tried to find the most sources, as if somehow that would automatically make my paper better than the rest." For Jenn and others like her, research was a mechanical process and the researcher a lot like those machines that collect golf balls at driving ranges. You venture out to pick up information here and there, and then deposit it between the title page and the bibliography for your teacher to take a whack at.

GOOD RESEARCH AND GOOD WRITING

It should be no surprise that student research papers can be lifeless things. Many students believe that the quickest way to kill a piece of writing is to use *facts* and that there's nothing at all *creative* about the research process. Many instructors must believe this, too, since they often dread assigning research papers and then dread reading them. Fortunately, that's changing. More and more college instructors—and their students—are beginning to recognize this simple fact: *Good research doesn't have to mean bad writing.*

The deadline for your paper is around five weeks away. Though you have some hard work ahead, I do hope that by the time you finish your paper and this book, you will see the research process at least a little differently. I hope you will see the library as an ally, not an adversary, and not as a wilderness but familiar territory where you know how to find what you need. I hope you will see the research paper as a piece of writing that has as much to do with what you think and how you see things as the personal essay you wrote in English or the poem you jotted down in your journal last night. I hope you will see that a research paper can be engaging to read as well as to write and that facts are another kind of detail that, when used purposefully, can bring research writing to life. Maybe most important, I hope you will see the research paper as a means of satisfying your own curiosity, a curiosity that will drive you to dig deeper into your topic, even late at night when the library is deserted and you have a 7 A.M. class the next day.

USING THIS BOOK

The Exercises

Throughout this book, you'll be asked to do exercises that either help you prepare your research paper or actually help you write it. You'll need a research notebook in which you'll do the exercises and perhaps compile your notes for the paper. Any notebook will do, as long as there are sufficient pages and left margins. Your instructor may ask you to hand in the work you do in response to the exercises, so it would be useful to use a notebook with detachable pages.

Several of the exercises in this book ask that you use techniques like fastwriting and brainstorming. This chapter began with one, so you've already had a little practice with the two methods. Both fastwriting and brainstorming ask that you suspend judgment until you see what you come up with. That's pretty hard for most of us because we are so quick to criticize ourselves, particularly about writing. But if you can learn to get comfortable with the sloppiness that comes with writing almost as fast as you think, not bothering about grammar or punctuation, then you will be rewarded with a new way to think, letting your own words lead you in sometimes surprising directions. Though these so-called creative techniques seem to have little to do with the serious business of research writing, they can actually be an enormous help throughout the process. Try to ignore that voice in your head that wants to convince you that you're wasting your time using fastwriting or brainstorming. When you do, they'll start to work for you.

The Five-Week Plan

But more about creative techniques later. You have a research paper assignment to do. If you're excited about writing a research paper, that's great. You probably already know that it can be interesting work. But if you're dreading the work ahead of you, then your instinct might be to procrastinate, put it off until the week it's due. That would be a mistake, of course. If you try to rush through the research and the writing, you're absolutely guaranteed to hate the experience and add this assignment to the many research papers in the garbage dump of your memory. It's also much more likely that the paper won't be very good. Because procrastination is the enemy, this book was designed to help you budget your time and move through the research and writing process in five weeks. It may take you a little longer, or you may be able to finish your paper a little more quickly. But at least initially, use the book sequentially.

This book can also be used as a reference to solve problems as they arise. For example, suppose you're having a hard time finding enough information on your topic or you want to know how to plan for an interview. Use the Table of Contents as a key to typical problems and where in the book you can find some practical help with them.

THE RESEARCH PAPER AND THE RESEARCH REPORT

Anyone who spent a few years in high school clutching index cards and making a beeline for the *Encyclopaedia Britannica* or *Reader's Guide* every time a research paper assignment was given will probably be glad that the college-level research paper will be a different experience. It's a little hard to get excited about paraphrasing an encyclopedia or the December issue of *Time* onto notecards and then inserting that information into the paper. But that's what seemed the logical thing to do when the assignment was to write a paper that reflects what's known about your topic. That's called a *research report,* and it's a fairly common assignment in the first few years of high school.

Discovering Your Purpose

For the paper you're about to write, the information you collect must be used much more *purposefully* than simply reporting what's known about a particular topic. Most likely, you will define what that purpose is. For example, you may end up writing a paper whose purpose is to argue a point—say, eating meat is morally suspect because of the way stock animals are treated at slaughterhouses. Or your paper's purpose may be to reveal some less-known or surprising aspect of a topic—say, how the common housefly's eating habits are not unlike our own. Or your paper may set out to explore a thesis, or idea, that you have about your topic—for example, your topic is the cultural differences between men and women, and you suspect the way girls and boys play as children reflects the social differences evident between the genders as adults.

Whatever the purpose of your paper turns out to be, the process all usually begins with something you've wondered about, some itchy question about an aspect of the world you'd love to know the answer to. It's the writer's curiosity—not the teacher's—that is at the heart of the college research paper.

In some ways, frankly, *research reports* are easier. You just go out and collect as much stuff as you can, write it down, organize it, and write it down again in the paper. Your job is largely mechanical and often deadening. In the *research paper,* you take a much more active role in *shaping and being shaped by* the information you encounter. That's harder because you must evaluate, judge, interpret, and analyze. But it's also much more satisfying because what you end up with says something about who you are and how you see things.

HOW FORMAL SHOULD IT BE?

When I got a research paper assignment, it often felt as if I was being asked to change out of blue jeans and a wrinkled oxford shirt and get into a stiff tuxedo. Tuxedos have their place, such as at the junior prom or the Grammy Awards, but they're just not me. When I first started writing research papers, I used to think that I *had* to be formal, that I needed to use big words like *myriad* and *ameliorate* and to use the pronoun *one* instead of *I.* I thought the paper absolutely needed to have an introduction, body, and conclusion—say what I was going to say, say it, and say what I said. It's no wonder that the first college research paper I had to write—on Plato's *Republic* for a philosophy class—seemed to me as though it were written by someone else. I felt at arm's length from the topic I was writing about.

You may be relieved to know that not all research papers are necessarily rigidly formal or dispassionate. Some are. Research papers in the sciences, for example, often have very formal structures, and the writer seems more a reporter of results than someone who is passionately engaged in making sense of them. This *formal stance*

QUESTIONS TO ASK YOUR INSTRUCTOR ABOUT THE RESEARCH ASSIGNMENT

It's easy to make assumptions about what your instructor expects for the research paper assignment. After all, you've probably written such a paper before and may have had the sense that the "rules" for doing so were handed down by God. Unfortunately, those assumptions may get in the way of writing a good paper, and sometimes they're dead wrong. If you got a handout describing the assignment, it may answer the questions below, but if not, make sure you raise them with your instructor when he gives the assignment.

- How would you describe the audience for this paper?
- Do you expect the paper to be in a particular form or organized in a special way? Or can I develop a form that suits the purpose of my paper?
- Do you have guidelines about format (margins, title page, outline, bibliography, citation method, etc.)?
- Can I use other visual devices (illustrations, subheadings, bulleted lists, etc.) to make my paper more readable?
- Can I use the pronoun *I* when appropriate?
- Can my own observations or experiences be included in the paper if relevant?
- Can I include people I interview as sources in my paper? Would you encourage me to use "live" sources as well as published ones?
- Should the paper *sound* a certain way, have a particular tone, or am I free to use a writing voice that suits my subject and purpose?

puts the emphasis where it belongs: on the validity of the data in proving or disproving something, rather than on the writer's individual way of seeing something. Some papers in the social sciences, particularly scholarly papers, take a similarly formal stance, where the writer not only seems invisible but seems to have little relation to the subject. There are many reasons for this approach. One is that *objectivity*—or as one philosopher put it, "the separation of the perceiver from the thing perceived"—is traditionally a highly valued principle, particularly among scholars and researchers. For example, if I'm writing a paper on the effectiveness of Alcoholics Anonymous (AA), and I confess that my father—who attended AA—drank himself to death, can I be trusted to see things clearly?

Yes, *if* my investigation of the topic seems thorough, balanced, and informative. And I think it may be an even better paper because my passion for the topic will encourage me to look at it more closely. Though reading their papers may suggest otherwise, most scholars are not nearly as dispassionate about their topics as they seem. They are driven by the same thing that will send you to the library over the next few weeks—their own curiosity—and most recognize that good research often involves both objectivity and subjectivity. As the son of an alcoholic, I am motivated to explore my own perceptions of his experience in AA, yet I recognize the need to verify those against the perceptions of others with perhaps more knowledge.

Your instructor may want you to write a formal research paper. You should determine if a formal paper is required when you get the assignment. (See the box, "Questions to Ask Your Instructor About the Research Assignment.") Also make sure that you understand what the word *formal* means. Your instructor may have a specific format you should follow or tone you should keep. But more likely, she is much more interested in your writing a paper that reflects some original thinking on your part and that is also lively and interesting to read. Though this book will help you write a formal research paper, it encourages what might be called a *research essay,* a paper that does not have a prescribed form, though it is as carefully researched and documented as a more formal paper.

BECOMING AN AUTHORITY
BY USING AUTHORITIES

Whether formal or less so, all research papers do attempt to be *authoritative.* That is, they rely heavily on a variety of credible sources beyond the writer who helped shape the writer's point of view. Those sources are mostly already published material, but they can also be other people, usually experts in relevant fields whom you interview for their perspectives. Don't underestimate the value of "live" and other nonlibrary sources. Authorities don't just live in books. One might live in the office next door to your class.

Though in research papers the emphasis is on using credible outside sources, that doesn't mean that your own experiences or observations should necessarily be excluded from your paper when they're relevant. In fact, in some papers, they are essential. For example, if you decide to write a paper on Alice Walker's novel *The Color Purple,* your own reading of the book—what strikes you as important—should be at the heart of your essay. Information from literary critics you discover in your research will help you develop and support the assertions you're making about the novel. That support from people who are considered experts—that is, scholars, researchers, critics, and practitioners in the field you're researching—will rub off on you, making your assertions more convincing, or authoritative.

Reading and talking to these people will also change your thinking, which is part of the fun of research. You will actually learn something, rather than remain locked into preconceived notions.

FACTS DON'T KILL

You probably think the words *research paper* and *interesting* are mutually exclusive. The prevalent belief among my students is that the minute you start having to use facts in your writing, then the prose wilts and dies like an unwatered begonia. It's an understandable attitude. There are many examples of informational writing that is dry and wooden, and among them, unfortunately, may be some textbooks you are asked to read for other classes.

But factual writing doesn't have to be dull. You may not consider the article "Why God Created Flies" (see the following exercise) a research paper. It may be unlike the research papers you've been assigned in some ways; it has no citation of sources, a heavy use of the author's personal experiences, and an informal structure. But it is a piece that's research based, containing plenty of facts about flies. It has a clear purpose and a thesis. Yet despite that, it's a pretty good read.

☐ EXERCISE 2
Bringing "Flies" to Life

Read Conniff's "Why God Created Flies" first for pure enjoyment. Then reread the article with your pen in hand, and, in your research notebook, list what you think makes the article interesting. Be specific. What devices or techniques does Conniff use to hold your interest? Your instructor may want you to bring your list to class for discussion.

Other questions for class discussion:

- In what ways is this article unlike any research paper you've ever written?
- How does Conniff handle the factual material? How is it woven into the article?
- What kinds of facts does he use? Are they memorable? Why?
- What is Conniff's main point, or thesis? Where is it stated most clearly?
- Does the humor in the article make it less authoritative? Does the author's use of personal experiences and observations strengthen or weaken the research?
- Is this article *objective*? In what ways? In what ways is it *subjective*? Can a good research paper be both without sacrificing its authority?
- Compare "Why God Created Flies" with the student essay "Lemming Death" in Appendix A. How are they similar? How are they different?

□ ■ □

Why God Created Flies
by Richard Conniff

THOUGH I HAVE been killing them for years now, I have never tested the folklore that, with a little cream and sugar, flies taste very much like black raspberries. So it's possible I'm speaking too hastily when I say there is nothing to like about houseflies. Unlike the poet who welcomed a "busy, curious, thirsty fly" to his drinking cup, I don't cherish them for reminding me that life is short. Nor do I much admire them for their function in clearing away carrion and waste. It is, after all, possible to believe in the grand scheme of recycling without liking undertakers.

A fly is standing on the rim of my beer glass as I write these words. Its vast, mosaic eyes look simultaneously lifeless and mocking. It grooms itself methodically, its forelegs entwining like the arms of a Sybarite luxuriating in bath oil. Its hind legs twitch across the upper surface of its wings. It pauses, well fed and at rest, to contemplate the sweetness of life.

Reprinted by permission of writer Richard Conniff, from *Audubon Magazine*, July, 1989.

We are lucky enough to live in an era when scientists quantify such things, and so as I type and wait my turn to drink, I know that the fly is neither busy nor curious. The female spends 40.6 percent of her time doing nothing but contemplating the sweetness of life. I know that she not only eats unspeakable things, but spends an additional 29.7 percent of her time spitting them back up and blowing bubbles with her vomit. The male is slightly less assiduous at this deplorable pastime but also defecates on average every four and a half minutes. Houseflies seldom trouble us as a health threat anymore, at least in this country, but they are capable of killing. And when we are dead (or sooner, in some cases), they dine on our corrupted flesh.

It is mainly this relentless intimacy with mankind that makes the housefly so contemptible. Leeches or dung beetles may appall us, but by and large they satisfy their depraved appetites out of our sight. Houseflies, on the other hand, routinely flit from diaper pail to dinner table, from carrion to picnic basket. They are constantly among us, tramping across our food with God-knows-what trapped in the sticky hairs of their half-dozen legs.

Twice in this century, Americans have waged war against houseflies, once in a futile nationwide "swat the fly" campaign and again, disastrously, with DDT foggings after World War II. The intensity of these efforts, bordering at times on the fanatic, may bewilder modern Americans. "Flies or Babies? Choose!" cried a headline in the *Ladies' Home Journal* in 1920. But our bewilderment is not due entirely to greater tolerance or environmental enlightenment. If we have the leisure to examine the fly more rationally now, it is primarily because we don't suffer its onslaughts as our predecessors did. Urban living has separated us from livestock, and indoor plumbing has helped us control our own wastes and thus control houseflies. If that changed tomorrow, we would come face to face with the enlightened, modern truth: With the possible exception of *Homo sapiens,* it is hard to imagine an animal as disgusting or improbable as the housefly. No bestiary concocted from the nightmares of the medieval mind could have come up with such a fantastic animal. If we want to study nature in its most exotic permutations, the best place to begin is here, at home, on the rim of my beer glass.

IN THIS COUNTRY, more than a dozen fly species visit or live in the house. It is possible to distinguish among some of them only by such microscopic criteria as the pattern of veins in the wings, so all of them end up being cursed as houseflies. Among the more prominent are the blue- and greenbottle flies, with their iridescent abdomens, and the biting stable flies, which have served this country as patriots, or at least provocateurs. On July 4, 1776, their biting encouraged decisiveness among delegates considering the Declaration of Independence. "Treason," Thomas Jefferson wrote, "was preferable to discomfort."

The true housefly, *Musca domestica,* does not bite. (You may think this is something to like about it, until you find out what it does instead.) *M. domestica,* a drab fellow of salt-and-pepper complexion, is the world's most widely distributed insect species and probably the most familiar, a status achieved through its pronounced fondness for breeding in pig, horse, or human excrement. In choosing at some point in the immemorial past to concentrate on the wastes around human habitations, *M. domestica* made a major career move. Bernard Greenberg of the University of Illinois at Chicago has traced human representations of the housefly back to a Mesopotamian cylinder seal from 3000 B.C. But houseflies were probably with us even before we had houses, and they spread with human culture.

Like us, the housefly is prolific, opportunistic, and inclined toward exploration. It can adapt to a diet of either vegetables or meat, preferably somewhat ripe. It will lay its eggs not just in excrement but in rotting lime peels, birds nests, carrion, even flesh wounds that have become infected and malodorous. Other flies aren't so flexible. For instance, *M. autumnalis,* a close relative, prefers cattle dung and winds up sleeping in pastures more than in houses or yards.

Although the adaptability and evolutionary generalization of the housefly may be admirable, they raise one of the first great questions about flies: Why is there this dismaying appetite for abomination?

Houseflies not only defecate constantly but do so in liquid form, which means they are in constant danger of dehydration. The male can slake his thirst and get most of the energy he needs from nectar. But fresh manure is a good source of water, and it contains the dissolved protein the female needs to make eggs. She also lays her eggs in excrement or amid decay so that when the maggots hatch, they'll have a smorgasbord of nutritious microorganisms on which to graze.

Houseflies bashing around the kitchen or the garbage shed thus have their sensors attuned to things that smell sweet, like flowers or bananas, and to foul-smelling stuff like ammonia and hydrogen sulfide, the products of fermentation and putrefaction. (Ecstasy for the fly is the stinkhorn fungus, a source of sugar that smells like rotting meat.)

The fly's jerky, erratic flight amounts to a way of covering large territories in search of these scents, not just for food but for romance and breeding sites. Like dung beetles and other flying insects, the fly will zigzag upwind when it gets a whiff of something good (or, more often, bad) and follow the scent plume to its source.

HENCE THE SECOND question about the housefly: How does it manage to fly so well? And the corollaries: Why is it so adept at evading us when we swat it? How come it always seems to land on its feet, usually upside-down on the ceiling, having induced us to plant a fist on the spot where it used to be, in the middle of the strawberry trifle, which is now spattered across the tablecloth, walls, loved ones, and honored guests?

The housefly's manner of flight is a source of vexation more than wonder. When we launch an ambush as the oblivious fly preens and pukes, its pressure sensors alert it to the speed and direction of the descending hand. Its wraparound eyes are also acutely sensitive to peripheral movement, and they register changes in light about ten times faster than we do. (A movie fools the gullible human eye into seeing continuous motion by showing it a sequence of twenty-four still pictures a second. To fool a fly would take more than 200 frames a second.) The alarm flashes directly from the brain to the middle set of legs via the largest, and therefore fastest, nerve fiber in the body. This causes so-called starter muscles to contract, simultaneously revving up the wing muscles and pressing down the middle legs, which catapult the fly into the air.

The fly's wings beat 165 to 200 times a second. Although this isn't all that fast for an insect, it's more than double the wingbeat of the speediest hummingbird and about twenty times faster than any repetitious movement the human nervous system can manage. The trick brought off by houseflies and many other insects is to remove the wingbeat from direct nervous system control, once it's switched on. Two systems of muscles, for upstroke and downstroke, are attached to the hull of the fly's midsection, and they trigger each other to work in alternation. When one set contracts, it deforms the hull, stretching the other set of muscles and making it contract automatically a fraction of a second later. To keep this seesaw rhythm going, openings in the midsection stoke the muscles with oxygen that comes directly from the outside (flies have no lungs). Meanwhile the fly's blood (which lacks hemoglobin and is therefore colorless) carries fuel to the cells fourteen times faster than when a fly is at rest. Flies can turn a sugar meal into useable energy so fast that an exhausted fly will resume flight almost instantly after eating. In humans . . . but you don't want to know how ploddingly inadequate humans are by comparison.

An airborne fly's antennae, pointed down between its eyes, help regulate flight, vibrating in response to airflow. The fly also uses a set of stubby wings in back, called halteres, as a gyroscopic device. Flies are skillful at veering and dodging—it sometimes seems that they are doing barrel rolls and Immelmann turns to amuse themselves while we flail and curse. But one thing they cannot do is fly upside-down to land on a ceiling. This phenomenon puzzled generations of upward-glaring, strawberry-trifle-drenched human beings, until high-speed photography supplied the explanation. The fly approaches the ceiling rightside up, at a steep angle. Just before impact, it reaches up with its front limbs, in the manner of Superman exiting a telephone booth for takeoff. As these forelegs get a grip with claws and with the sticky, glandular hairs of the footpads, the fly swings its other leg up into position. Then it shuts down its flight motor, out of swatting range and at ease.

While landing on the ceiling must be great fun, humans tend to be more interested in what flies do when they land on food. To find out, I trapped the fly on the rim of my beer glass. (Actually, I waited till it found a less coveted perch, then slowly lowered a mayonnaise jar over it.) I'd been reading a book called *To Know a Fly,* in which author Vincent Dethier describes a simple way of seeing how the fly's proboscis works. First I refrigerated the fly to slow it down and anesthetize it. Then I attempted to attach a thin stick to its wing surface with the help of hot candlewax. It got away. I brought it back and tried again. My four-year-old son winced and turned aside when I applied the wax. "I'm glad I'm not a fly," he said, "or you might do that to me." I regarded him balefully but refrained from mentioning the ant colony he had annihilated on our front walk.

Having finally secured the fly, I lowered its feet into a saucer of water. Flies have taste buds in their feet, and when they walk on something good (bad), the proboscis, which is normally folded up neatly inside the head, automatically flicks down. No response. I added sugar to the water, an irresistible combination. Nothing. More sugar. Still nothing. My son wandered off, bored. I apologized to the fly, killed it, and decided to look up the man who had put me in the awkward position of sympathizing with a fly, incidentally classing me in my son's eyes as a potential war criminal.

DETHIER, A BIOLOGIST at the University of Massachusetts at Amherst, turned out to be a gentle, deferential fellow in his mid-seventies, with weathered, finely wrinkled skin and gold-rimmed oval eyeglasses on a beak nose. He suggested mildly that the fly might not have responded because it was outraged at the treatment it received. It may also have eaten recently, or it may have been groggy from hibernation. (Some flies sit out the winter in diapause, in which hormones induce inactivity in response to shortened day length. But cold, not day length, is what slows down hibernating species like the housefly, and the sudden return of warmth can start them up again. This is why a fly may miraculously take wing on a warm December afternoon in the space between my closed office window and the closed storm window outside, a phenomenon I had formerly regarded as new evidence for spontaneous generation.)

Dethier has spent a lifetime studying the fly's sense of taste, "finding out where their tongues and noses are, as it were." He explained the workings of the proboscis to me.

Fly taste buds, it seems, are vastly more sensitive than ours. Dethier figured this out by taking saucers of water containing steadily decreasing concentrations of sugar. He found the smallest concentration a human tongue could taste. Then he found the smallest concentration that caused a hungry fly to flick out its proboscis. The fly, with 1,500 taste hairs arrayed on its feet and in and around its mouth, was ten million times more sensitive.

When the fly hits pay dirt, its proboscis telescopes downward and the fleshy lobes at the tip puff out. These lips can press down tight to feed on a thin film of liquid, or they can cup themselves around a droplet. They are grooved crosswise with a series of parallel gutters, and when the fly starts pumping, the liquid is drawn up through these gutters. Narrow zigzag openings in the gutters filter the food, so that even when it dines on excrement, the fly can "choose" some morsels and reject others.

A drop of vomit may help dissolve the food, making it easier to lap up. Scientists have also suggested that the fly's prodigious vomiting may be a way of mixing enzymes with the food to aid digestion.

If necessary, the fly can peel its lips back out of the way and apply its mouth directly to the object of its desire. Although a housefly does not have true teeth, its mouth is lined with a jagged, bladelike edge that is useful for scraping. In his book *Flies and Disease,* Bernard Greenberg writes that some blowflies (like the one on the rim of my beer glass, which turned out to be a *Phormia regina*) "can bring 150 teeth into action, a rather effective scarifier for the superficial inoculation of the skin, conjunctiva, or mucous membranes."

HENCE THE FINAL great question about flies: What awful things are they inoculating us with when they flit across our food or land on our sleeping lips to drink our saliva? Over the years, authorities have suspected flies of spreading more than sixty diseases, from diarrhea to plague and leprosy. As recently as 1951, the leading expert on flies repeated without demurring the idea that the fly was "the most dangerous insect" known, a remarkable assertion in a world that also includes mosquitoes. One entomologist tried to have the housefly renamed the "typhoid fly."

The hysteria against flies earlier in the century arose, with considerable help from scientists and the press, out of the combined ideas that germs cause disease and that flies carry germs. In the Spanish-American War, easily ten times as many soldiers died of disease, mostly typhoid fever, as died in battle. Flies were widely blamed, especially after a doctor observed particles of lime picked up in the latrines still clinging to the legs of flies crawling over army food. A British politician argued that flies were not "dipterous angels" but "winged sponges speeding hither and thither to carry out the foul behests of Contagion." American schools started organizing "junior sanitary police" to point the finger at fly breeding sites. Cities sponsored highly publicized "swat the fly" campaigns. In Washington, D.C., in 1912, a consortium of children killed 343,800 flies and won a $25 first prize. (This is a mess of flies, 137.5 swatted for every penny in prize money, testimony to the slowness of summers then and the remarkable agility of children—or perhaps to the overzealous imagination of contest sponsors. The figure does not include the millions of dead flies submitted by losing entrants.)

But it took the pesticide DDT, developed in World War II and touted afterwards as "the killer of killers," to raise the glorious prospect of "a flyless millennium." The fly had by then been enshrined in the common lore as a diabolical killer. In one of the "archy and mehitabel" poems by Don Marquis, a fly visits garbage cans and sewers to "gather up the germs of typhoid, influenza, and pneumonia on my feet and wings" and spread them to humanity, declaring that "it is my mission to help rid the world of these wicked persons/i am a vessel of righteousness."

Public health officials were deadly serious about conquering this arch fiend, and for them DDT was "a veritable godsend." They recommended that parents use wallpaper impregnated with DDT in nurseries and playrooms to protect children. Believing that flies spread infantile paralysis, cities suffering polio epidemics frequently used airplanes to fog vast areas with DDT. Use of the chemical actually provided some damning evidence against flies, though not in connection with polio. Hidalgo County in Texas, on the Mexican border, divided its towns into two groups and sprayed one with DDT to eliminate flies. The number of children suffering and dying from acute diarrheal infections caused by *Shigella* bacteria declined in the sprayed areas but remained the same in the unsprayed zones. When DDT spraying was stopped in the first group and switched to the second, the dysentery rates began to reverse. Then the flies developed resistance to DDT, a small hitch in the godsend. In state parks and vacation spots, where DDT had provided relief from the fly nuisance, people began to notice that songbirds were also disappearing.

IN THE END, the damning evidence was that we were contaminating our water, ourselves, and our affiliated population of flies with our own filth (not to mention DDT). Given access to human waste through inadequate plumbing or sewerage treatment, flies can indeed pick up an astonishing variety of pathogens. They can also reproduce at a godawful rate: In one study, 4,042 flies hatched from a scant shovelful, one-sixth of a cubic foot, of buried night soil. But whether all those winged sponges can transmit the contaminants they pick up turns out to be a tricky question, the Hidalgo County study being one of the few clearcut exceptions. Of polio, for instance, Bernard Greenberg writes, "There is ample evidence that human populations readily infect flies . . . But we are woefully ignorant whether and to what extent flies return the favor."

Flies probably are not, as one writer declared in the throes of hysteria, "monstrous" beings "armed with horrid mandibles . . . and dripping with poison." A fly's body is not, after all, a playground for microbes. Indeed, bacterial populations on its bristling, unlovely exterior tend to decline quickly under the triple threat of compulsive cleaning, desiccation, and ultraviolet radiation. (Maggots actually produce a substance in their gut that kills off whole populations of bacteria, which is one reason doctors have sometimes used them to clean out infected wounds.) The fly's "microbial cargo," to use Greenberg's phrase, reflects human uncleanliness. In one study, flies from a city neighborhood with poor facilities carried up to 500 million bacteria, while flies from a prim little suburb not far away yielded a maximum count of only 100,000.

But wait. While I am perfectly happy to suggest that humans are viler than we like to think, and flies less so, I do not mean to rehabilitate the fly. Any animal that kisses offal one minute and dinner the next is at the very least a social abomination. What I am coming around to is St. Augustine's idea that God created flies to punish human arrogance, and not just the calamitous technological arrogance of DDT. Flies are, as one biologist has remarked, the resurrection and the reincarnation of our own dirt, and this is surely one reason we smite them down with such ferocity. They mock our notions of personal grooming with visions of lime particles, night soil, and dog leavings. They toy with our delusions of immortality, buzzing in the ear as a memento mori (a researcher in Greenberg's lab assures me that flies can strip a human corpse back to bone in about a week, if the weather is fine). Flies are our fate, and one way or another they will have us.

It is a pretty crummy joke on God's part, of course, but there's no point in getting pouty about it and slipping into unhealthy thoughts about nature. What I intend to do, by way evening the score, is hang a strip of flypaper and cultivate the local frogs and snakes, which have a voracious appetite for flies (flycatchers don't, by the way; they seem to prefer wasps and bees). Perhaps I will get the cat interested, as a sporting proposition. Meanwhile, I plan to get a fresh beer and sit back with my feet up and a tightly rolled newspaper nearby. Such are the consolations of the ecological frame of mind.

I love "Why God Created Flies" partly because it never occurred to me when I first read it that I was reading research. Elmore Leonard, a distinguished fiction writer, says that when his writing *sounds* like writing, he needs to rewrite it. His prose, which is lean, efficient, yet powerful, reflects that philosophy. It doesn't call attention to itself. Much research writing does. It lumbers along from fact to fact and quote to quote, saying "Look at how much I know!"

Demonstrating knowledge is not nearly as impressive as *using* it toward some end. Conniff does just that, masterfully weaving surprising information about the common housefly with his longing to determine where in God's plan the pest might fit in.

It's informative, it's funny, and yes, it's research. Richard Conniff is not a bug expert. (If he were, he'd probably be published in the *Journal of Entomology*.) He's just a guy who noticed a fly on his beer glass and wondered, What is it doing there? The best research often starts that way, with what at first seems to be a simple question. Like a lucky archaeologist, the researcher often finds more than he expects just below the surface of even the simplest questions. But first, he's got to want to dig.

1

□ ■ □

The First Week

THE IMPORTANCE OF
GETTING CURIOUS

A few years back, I wrote a book about lobsters. At first, I didn't intend it to be a book. I didn't think there was that much to say about lobsters. But the more I researched the subject, the more questions I had and the more places I found to look for answers. Pretty soon, I had 300 pages of manuscript.

My curiosity about lobsters began one year when the local newspaper printed an article about what terrible shape the New England lobster fishery was in. The catch was down 30 percent, and the old-timers were saying it was the worst year they'd seen since the thirties. Even though I grew up in landlocked Chicago, I'd always loved eating lobsters after being introduced to them at age eight at my family's annual Christmas party. Many years later, when I read the article in my local newspaper about the vanishing lobsters, I was alarmed. I wondered, Will lobster go the way of caviar and become too expensive for people like me?

That was the question that triggered my research, and it soon led to more questions. What kept me going was my own curiosity. It's the same curiosity that motivated Richard Conniff to research and then write about the houseflies landing on the lip of his beer glass. If your research assignment is going to be successful, you need to get curious, too. If you're bored by your research topic, your paper will almost certainly be boring, as well, and you'll end up hating writing research papers as much as ever.

Learning to Wonder Again

Maybe you're naturally curious, a holdover from childhood when you were always asking Why? Or maybe your curiosity paled as you got older, and you forgot that being curious is the best reason for wanting to learn things. Whatever condition it's in, your curiosity must be the driving force behind your research paper. It's the most essential ingredient. The important thing, then, is this: *Choose your research topic carefully. If you lose interest in it, change your topic to one that does interest you or find a different angle.*

In most cases, instructors give students great latitude in choosing their research topics. (Some instructors narrow the field, asking students to find a focus within some broad, assigned subject. When the subject has been assigned, it may be harder for you to discover what you are curious about, but it won't be impossible, as you'll see.) Some of the best research topics grow out of your own experience (though they certainly don't have to), as mine did when writing about lobster overfishing or Conniff's did when writing about houseflies. Begin searching for a topic by asking yourself this question: What have I seen or experienced that raises questions that research can help answer?

Getting the Pot Boiling

A subject might bubble up immediately. For example, I had a student who was having a terrible time adjusting to her parents' divorce. Janabeth started out wanting to know about the impact of divorce on children and later focused her paper on how divorce affects father-daughter relationships.

Kim remembered spending a rainy week on Cape Cod with her father, wandering through old graveyards, looking for the family's ancestors. She noticed patterns on the stones and wondered what they meant. She found her ancestors as well as a great research topic.

For years, Wendy loved J. D. Salinger's work but never had the chance to read some of his short stories. She jumped at the opportunity to spend five weeks reading and thinking about her favorite author. She later decided to focus her research paper on Salinger's notion of the misfit hero.

Sometimes other people, often unwittingly, will give you great topic ideas. Recently, a student in my composition class had a conversation with her friends in the wee hours of the morning about the

Public Media Resource Center (PMRC), a Washington, D.C.–based group that is pushing for labeling music with pornographic or violent content. In the midst of the discussion, she realized how strongly she felt about the potential for censorship. She had a topic.

Sometimes, one topic triggers another. Chris, ambling by Thompson Hall, one of the oldest buildings on campus, wondered about its history. After a little initial digging, he found some 1970 newsclips from the student newspaper, describing a student strike that paralyzed the school. The controversy fascinated him more than the building did, and he pursued the topic. He wrote a great paper.

If you're still drawing a blank, try the following exercise in your notebook.

☐ *EXERCISE 1-1*
Finding Out What You Want to Know

Make an "authority" list. In five minutes, brainstorm a list of things about which you already know something but would like to learn more. But first, a little more on how to make brainstorming work for you.

Essentially, you'll be making a fast list of whatever comes to mind. Don't censor yourself. Write down things even if they seem stupid. Don't worry if you build a list of words and phrases that only you can decipher; the list is meant exclusively for you. You'll probably find that your list comes in waves—you'll jot down four or five things, then draw a blank, and you'll think of four more. Just relax and enjoy your wandering mind. Ready? Begin.

Now make a "nonauthority" list. Take another five minutes, and brainstorm a list of things you don't know much about but would like to learn more.

Look at both lists, reviewing all the items you've jotted down. Circle one item you'd like to look at more closely, that makes you wonder.

Finally, take another five minutes and build a list of questions about your subject that you'd love to learn the answers to. Write down any questions that come to mind.

If you are getting nowhere with your subject, try another from the list. Repeat the last few steps with another subject until you produce a good list of questions. Save them for later.

Following are the lists I made recently when I did this exercise.

Things I know something about:

dinghy sailing
St. John
trout fishing
western Montana
teaching writing
Joan Didion
Wallace Stegner
Robert Bly
environmental movement
woodstoves
finish carpentry
Earth Day
plant taxonomy
ecology
birdwatching
Great Lakes

Lake Michigan
lobsters
Maine coast
tying flies
keeping a journal
publishing industry
Alaskan pipeline
draft for Vietnam War
gardening
Robinson Jeffers
public relations
nonprofit organizations
Boundary Waters Canoe Area
    (BWCA)
direct mail fund-raising

Things I don't know much about but would like to learn more:

fatherhood
masculinity
masculine myths
Joseph Campbell
astronomy
building telescopes
New Zealand
cabinet making
restoration of Atlantic salmon
trout fishing in New England
decline of mills in New England
labor history in the mills
International Workers of the
    World (IWW)
offshore groundfish fishery
Piscataqua River
literary nonfiction

childhood development
making money in publishing
macroeconomics
how the Federal Reserve works
operating large sailing ships
writing poetry
freewriting
research writing
invertebrate zoology
garbage
new recycling techniques
playwriting
art history
photography
rain forests
greenhouse effect
ice skating

One item selected from both lists:

Great Lakes

Questions about my selected item:

Why do the lake levels seem to fluctuate so mysteriously?

How did the Army Corp of Engineers reverse the direction of the Chicago River?

Do the lakes have a rich commercial fishing industry?

Where are most of the lakes' shipwrecks concentrated?

Where are the most dangerous waters?

Is Lake Superior still pristine?

What distinguishes the lakes from each other?

Which lakes are most polluted?

What's the nature of the pollution?

Is it true that fish caught in most of the lakes should not be eaten because of toxins in their fatty tissues?

How did the St. Lawrence Seaway and canals connecting the lakes to the sea affect the ecology?

Did the transplantation of salmon in the late 1960s affect the ecology?

What happened to the massive alewife die-offs I remember hearing about when I was a kid?

Are the lakes less polluted now than in the 1960s?

Has there ever been a massive oil spill on any of the Great Lakes?

Whatever happened to the Erie Canal?

Do the lakes ever completely freeze?

Which industry is most responsible for pollution of the Great Lakes?

Which is the most polluted tributary?

□ ■ □

This exercise was useful if it helped you inventory some of the things you're curious about. It was even more useful if you found something on your list that raised interesting questions for you. You might have a tentative research topic. I found an item—the Great Lakes—in the list of "things I know something about." I grew up a quarter mile from Lake Michigan, and it became a fixture in my life. It still is, though I now live 700 miles away. I wasn't quite sure what

I wanted to know about the Great Lakes, but when I made my list of questions, my curiosity grew along with it. Any one of these "trailhead" questions might lead me into a great research project.

Other Ways to Find a Topic

If you're still stumped about a tentative topic for your paper, consider the following:

■ *Search an index.* Wander over to the library and use InfoTrac or the computerized card catalog to hunt for topic ideas in broad subject areas that interest you. For example, type in PSYCHOLOGY, and you'll get a long list of "see also" prompts that will narrow the subject further. Choose one subject (e.g., forensic psychology) that sounds interesting to you, and follow the prompts. The topic will be further narrowed (e.g., forensic toxicology). Keep shaving away at the subject until you get a narrow topic that intrigues you.

■ *Browse through an encyclopedia.* A general encyclopedia, like the *World Book* or *Encyclopaedia Britannica,* can be fertile ground for topic ideas. Start with a broad subject (e.g., the Great Lakes), and read the entry, looking for an interesting angle that appeals to you, or just browse through several volumes, alert to interesting subjects.

■ *Consider essays you've already written.* Could the topics of any of these essays be further developed as research topics? For example, Diane wrote a personal essay about how she found the funeral of a classmate alienating, especially the wake. Her essay asked what purpose such a ritual could serve, a question, she decided, that would best be answered by research. Other students wrote essays on the difficulty of living with a hyperactive brother or an alcoholic parent, topics that yielded wonderful research papers. A class assignment to read Ken Kesey's *One Flew Over the Cuckoo's Nest* also inspired Li to research the author.

■ *Pay attention to what you've read recently.* What newspaper articles have sparked your curiosity and raised interesting questions? Rob, a hunter, encountered an article that reported the number of hunters was steadily declining in the United States. He wondered why. Karen read an account of a particularly violent professional hockey game. She decided to research the Boston Bruins, a team with a history of violent play, and examine how violence has affected the sport. Don't limit yourself to the newspaper. What else have you read recently—perhaps magazines or books—or seen on TV that has made you wonder?

■ *Consider practical topics.* Perhaps some questions about your career choice might lead to a promising topic. Maybe you're thinking about teaching but wonder about current trends in teacher salaries. One student, Anthony, was being recruited by a college to play basketball and researched the tactics coaches use to lure players. What he learned helped prepare him to make a good choice.

■ *Think about issues, ideas, or materials you've encountered in other classes.* Have you come across anything that intrigued you, that you'd like to learn more about?

■ *Look close to home.* An interesting research topic may be right under your nose. Does your hometown (or your campus community) suffer from a particular problem or have an intriguing history that would be worth exploring? Jackson, tired of dragging himself from his dorm room at 3:00 A.M. for fire alarms that always proved false, researched the readiness of the local fire department to respond to such calls. Ellen, whose grandfather worked in the aging woolen mills in her hometown, researched a crippling strike that took place there sixty years ago. Her grandfather was an obvious source for an interview.

What Is a Good Topic?

Most writing—be it a personal essay, a poem, or an instruction sheet for a swing set—is trying to answer questions. That's especially true of a research paper. The challenge in choosing the right topic is to find one that raises questions to which you'd really like to learn the answers. Later, the challenge will be limiting the number of questions your paper tries to answer. For now, look for a topic that makes you at least a little hungry to learn more.

Also consider the intellectual challenge your topic poses and where you will be able to find information about it. You might really want to answer the question, Is Elvis dead? It may be a burning question for you. But you will likely find that you must rely on sources like the *National Enquirer* or a book written by a controversial author who's a regular guest on Geraldo. Neither source would carry much weight in a college paper. If you're considering several topic ideas, favor the one that might offer the most intellectual challenge and possibly the most information. At this point, you may not really know whether your tentative topic meets those criteria. The rest of this week, you'll take a preliminary look at some library sources to find out whether you have selected a workable topic.

Checking Out Your Tentative Topic

Consider the potential of the tentative topic you've chosen by using this checklist:

- Does it raise questions I'd love to learn the answers to? Does it raise a lot of them?
- Do I feel strongly about it? Do I already have some ideas about the topic that I'd like to explore?
- Can I find authoritative information to answer my questions? Does the topic offer the possibility of interviews? An informal survey?
- Will it be an intellectual challenge? Will it force me to reflect on what *I* think?
- Are a lot of people researching this topic or a similar one? Will I struggle to find sources in the library because other students have them?

Don't worry if you can't answer "yes" to all of these questions or if you can't answer some yet. Being genuinely curious about your topic is the most important consideration of all.

Making the Most of an Assigned Topic

If your instructor limits your choice of topics, then it might be a little harder to find one that piques your curiosity, but it will not be nearly as hard as it seems. It is possible to find an interesting angle on almost any subject if you're open to the possibilities. If you're not convinced, try this exercise in class.

☐ *EXERCISE 1-2*
The Myth of the Boring Topic

On a piece of paper, write down the most boring topic you can think of. Anything. Exchange papers with someone else in class. Brainstorm a list of questions about your partner's proposed topic that might, in fact, be really interesting to explore. Play with as many angles as you can. Discuss in class what you came up with.

☐ ■ ☐

Last time I tried this exercise, my partner's boring topic idea was dolls. I thought it was a brilliantly boring choice. But it didn't take me long to come up with some angles that were intriguing.

Why do some dolls, like the Cabbage Patch, suddenly soar in popularity and then seem to fizzle?

Why are some dolls, like Barbie and GI Joe, so enduring?

How are new doll designs conceived?

Why is my one-year-old daughter so bonded with the rattiest-looking doll in her collection?

What's the nature of that bond?

Would it be different for a one-year-old boy?

Suddenly, I was starting to getting excited about a topic I would have dismissed without a second thought.

If you've been asked to write on an assigned topic or choose from a limited list of ideas, don't despair. Instead, brainstorm a long list of questions, hunting for an angle you can get enthusiastic about.

If at first, you seem to have little interest or knowledge about an assigned topic, try bringing it into your world, as I did when I reflected on what I've noticed or experienced with dolls. Pay attention to what aspects of the topic get a rise out of you, if any. If you're asked to write a paper on an assigned novel, for example, which characters struck you? Which moments or scenes moved you? Why? Could your paper explore the answer to one of those questions?

Another way to discover what makes you curious about an assigned topic is simply to do some preliminary reading on it. Find some books and articles on the topic, and scan them for interesting angles or intriguing bits of information. What did you encounter that made you want to read more?

If all else fails, examine your assigned topic through the following "lenses." One might give you a view of your topic that seems interesting.

- *People.* Who has been influential in shaping the ideas in your topic area? Do any have views that are particularly intriguing to you? Could you profile that person and her contributions?
- *Trends.* What are recent developments in this topic? Are any significant? Why?
- *Controversies.* What do experts in the field argue about? What aspect of the topic seems to generate the most heat? Which is most interesting to you? Why?
- *Impact.* What about your topic currently has the most affect on the most people? What may in the future? How? Why?

Admittedly, it is harder to make an assigned topic your own. But you can still get curious if you approach the topic openly, willing to see the possibilities by finding the questions that bring it to life for you.

BEFRIENDING THE LIBRARY

I'm not exactly sure when I got my first library card, but I remember using it often. The children's section of my hometown library was a small wing, off to the side, with bright carpeting and midget fiberglass tables and chairs in orange and green; even the bookshelves were pint sized. On long, boring summer days, I would wander into the library and through the shelves of books, pulling this one then that, each covered in protective plastic. I would settle into one of those small chairs and spend an hour quietly turning pages. The librarians, always busy with official business behind the desk—stamping cards, flicking through files, taping those protective plastic covers on new books—would smile pleasantly at me now and then. I liked the children's library, and it seemed to like me.

The adult section, visible from the children's library through a glass door, was another matter. The shelves towered to the ceiling, and the tables and chairs were large, lumbering, wooden things that I could barely move. I was lost in the place. The books were out of reach, there were too many of them, and my sneakers squeaked on the bare, polished floor. The librarians, sentries of silence, seemed to watch my every move. The adult library seemed a solemn place, as if the business of containing so much knowledge was a serious affair.

Faced with spending the next five weeks in your college library, you may feel a little like I did as a child, wandering through that glass door to the adult section. Your college library may seem to be a wilderness, waiting to swallow you up. This apprehension is easy to understand. Some large universities have a dozen or more libraries on campus, each specializing in a field or discipline. The central library may contain vast collections of books, numbering in the millions. In addition to the familiar card catalog, there are computer terminals for accessing sources and a large section of specialized indexes and other reference materials. Everywhere you look, scholarly looking people sit before mounds of thick books, confidently flipping pages. A scene such as this may make you long for the days when writing a research paper involved buying a packet of 3" × 5" notecards and going directly to the *Encyclopaedia Britannica,* or maybe, if it was a serious research paper, the *Reader's Guide to Periodical Literature.*

When I poll my students every semester about their feelings toward the library, the result is always the same and almost unanimous: The college students I teach, freshmen and seniors alike, dread spending time in the library. Some are almost phobic about it. If you share some of these feelings about library work, then you're in for a rough time the next five weeks. Why do so many of us view the library with such loathing? It's worthwhile talking about that in class this week. But first, explore your own library experiences, as I did, in the following short exercise.

☐ *EXERCISE 1-3*
Loving or Loathing the Library

Take your research notebook, and go over to your library. Find a comfortable place to sit. Now spend seven minutes fastwriting about your experiences in libraries. Try beginning with your hometown library, where you spent time researching the paper on China in the seventh grade. Think about librarians you've known or where in the library you used to hang out. Maybe reflect on how you feel and what you think now, sitting in this library. Write about what excites you about doing research there and what you dread.

A reminder about fastwriting: Like brainstorming, fastwriting requires that you suspend judgment about what you think until you see what you say. Give yourself permission to write badly. You will be able to if you write quickly. Don't worry about grammar or even staying focused. Just keep your pen moving for seven minutes, thinking *through* writing rather than *before* it.

Discuss your fastwrite in class this week or with your instructor in conference.

☐ ■ ☐

Inevitably, anyone who has been given a research assignment has had the experience of not finding a source that should have been there. In your fastwrite, you may have remembered researching a topic only to discover that the book you really needed was missing from the shelves or that the magazine with the essential article had key pages torn out of it. You may have written about the harsh glare of the fluorescent lights or how the heat was always turned up too high in your local library. You may have reminisced about carrying bundles of index cards for that paper on *The Scarlet Letter* and using one of them to pass love notes to Lori Jo Flink, only to discover later that the card contained information you needed.

But maybe you also wrote about the smell of new books, or the time you discovered the works of a favorite writer, or the kind librarian who first introduced you to *Charlotte's Web*. Maybe you wrote about some dark corner of the library where you pulled your chair up to a small table near the window, opened a good book, and lost yourself in another world some writer created.

For many of us, libraries that were once welcoming places during childhood become less so as we grow older. The disenchantment often begins in high school, when we are given research assignments that don't interest us or are asked to use sources that we don't know how to find. Pretty soon, the library becomes identified as the place where we toil over things we don't care about.

As I pointed out earlier, a successful research paper most often results from a good experience with the process of researching. Making it a good experience depends partly on finding a way to engage your topic, to make it your own, and to be motivated largely by your own curiosity. In essence, you need to get control over your topic by discovering the questions *you* most want answers to and by letting them guide your search. In the same way, you must learn to get control of the library and what it offers, rather than let the library keep control over you. Learn to see the library as an ally, rather than an adversary, in helping you to find out what you want to know.

Exercise 1-3 gave you a chance to air your feelings about research and libraries. This week, you also need to get down to the task of understanding how your library works, especially where to begin looking for the answers to your questions.

The Basic Plan of the College Library

Most university libraries are similarly organized. There's a *circulation desk* where you check out material, pay fines, ask for change for the photocopy machines, and so on. One valuable service the circulation desk provides the researcher is determining whether a needed book has been loaned and if so, when it's due back. The *stacks* is another name for a room full of bookshelves. A few stacks may be closed to students, which means the library staff will have to retrieve material for you; but most stacks are open, and you will be free to wander about. A *reserve desk* holds material, often at an instructor's request, for use by students for a few hours at a time. A room may also be set aside for *special collections,* or material that is valuable or unique.

The *reference section* is the research writer's most important resource. If research is like detective work, then the reference section is the FBI archives. The reference section is rich with helpful leads and information about what you want to know and where you can find it. Knowing just where to look will make an enormous difference in how you feel about the library. It may never be a place where you want to camp out, but once you've mastered the basics of the reference section, the library may finally become familiar territory.

Fortunately, there are people who can help. Most university libraries have staff who are specialists in reference materials, and there's often a separate reference desk where these librarians dwell, surrounded by computer terminals. Most librarians are experts at helping students with their research papers. For years, I was too shy to ask for help or afraid my questions would seem dumb. I now realize how much time I wasted, looking in the wrong places, and how much useful information I never found because of my reluctance to ask for help. Don't make the same mistake.

The Computer Revolution

Whether you love libraries or loathe them, by now, you likely know the basics of how to use them. You know about the general encyclopedias, the *Reader's Guide,* and the card catalog. You may even have tangled with microfilm or a computer database. But what you probably don't appreciate yet is that the reference room is an incredibly rich place to mine for information. And this resource keeps getting better as new reference materials are developed, along with new ways to access them. The computer revolution has transformed the reference room. In the past two years, for example, my own university library has added ten new computer stations and completely converted the card catalog to a new computer system that not only allows me to call up books by author, subject, and title but will tell me whether the book I want is available and if not, when it's due back.

CD-ROM

Compact disc (CD) technology, which has revolutionized the music industry, has done exactly the same thing for the library. The CD-ROM (compact disc with read-only memory) is now a standard fixture in most college libraries, and it's not difficult to use. Once you learn how to search for books and articles on your topic using the CD-ROM, you'll be hooked.

The typical CD−ROM is a 4.72 inch plastic disc that looks exactly like the latest issue from the Rolling Stones, but in some ways, it's even more impressive. Each disc can hold over 500 megabytes of information, the equivalent of 250,000 pages of text.

CDs run on standard personal computers. CDs are available in many fields of study, from general science to business, indexing articles and books on virtually any topic. Using a CD, you can do a search in minutes that would take an hour or more using conventional, bound reference sources. For example, imagine searching ten years' worth of the *Reader's Guide* for articles on manic depression. You'd have to go through each year, volume by volume, jotting down promising article citations. The CD−ROM equivalent of the *Reader's Guide* (the most popular version is InfoTrac) would do the same search in about sixty seconds, and if it were linked to a printer, output the citations you select. You wouldn't have to pick up a pen.

There's a good chance that your college library is quite different than the library you began to master back home, especially in terms of size and sophistication. Before you plunge into researching your paper, get some practice in the reference room, using key sources and discovering new ones. The exercise that follows will introduce you to some of the basic references and how they can contribute to your paper. At the same time, you'll do some preliminary research on your tentative topic, which may help you narrow your focus. Later, you'll get some practice with more unusual sources that you may not have known existed; such sources can really help if you're having a hard time finding information.

☐ *EXERCISE 1-4*
Navigating the Reference Section

Navigate is the key word when it comes to working with the vast selection of reference materials. There are literally thousands of encyclopedias and indexes and almanacs and directories and databases and catalogs and bibliographies in the reference room. As you make your way through this cluttered landscape, it's easy to get lost. Start with the basics, the reference sources most often consulted by writers of college research papers.

This exercise will give you a workout in the basics. It's a self-teaching exercise. You should work at your own pace; most students complete the work in about two to three hours. You'll need your research notebook to jot down the answers to the questions or the results of each step. If your instructor wants you to hand in the results of this exercise, you might want to do it on a separate piece of paper or perhaps he will give you a separate copy of the exercise to write on. Your instructor will also alert you to any special instructions regarding your own library.

If possible, use this exercise to begin researching your tentative research topic, if you have one. For some topics, however, that won't be possible, since this exercise is intended to introduce a range of reference materials, some of which may not be relevant to certain topics.

Knowing What to Look For

Step 1: If you have a topic, describe it in a few words here.

_____

_____

_____

_____

_____

_____

_____

Step 2: Now find the book entitled *Library of Congress Subject Headings (LCSH)*. It may be available at the reference desk. Otherwise, ask the librarian where it's shelved, or check the card catalog. The *LCSH* lists the standard headings used by most libraries to catalog information. It's an easy way to find one or more headings that will quickly yield useful sources on your subject (see Figure 1-1). Consult the *LCSH* with your topic in mind, and jot down several headings that seem promising.

_____

_____

_____

_____

_____

_____

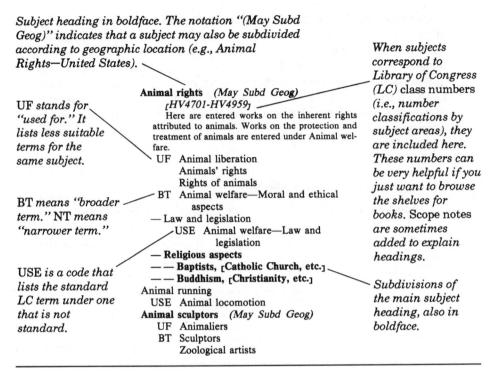

Subject heading in boldface. The notation "(May Subd Geog)" indicates that a subject may also be subdivided according to geographic location (e.g., Animal Rights—United States).

UF stands for "used for." It lists less suitable terms for the same subject.

BT means "broader term." NT means "narrower term."

USE is a code that lists the standard LC term under one that is not standard.

When subjects correspond to Library of Congress (LC) class numbers (i.e., number classifications by subject areas), they are included here. These numbers can be very helpful if you just want to browse the shelves for books. Scope notes are sometimes added to explain headings.

Subdivisions of the main subject heading, also in boldface.

Animal rights   *(May Subd Geog)*
[HV4701-HV4959]
    Here are entered works on the inherent rights attributed to animals. Works on the protection and treatment of animals are entered under Animal welfare.
    UF   Animal liberation
         Animals' rights
         Rights of animals
    BT   Animal welfare—Moral and ethical
         aspects
    — Law and legislation
         USE   Animal welfare—Law and
               legislation
    — **Religious aspects**
    — — **Baptists, [Catholic Church, etc.]**
    — — **Buddhism, [Christianity, etc.]**
Animal running
    USE   Animal locomotion
Animal sculptors   *(May Subd Geog)*
    UF   Animaliers
    BT   Sculptors
         Zoological artists

FIGURE 1-1   There's no need to guess what subject headings to use when searching on your topic. The *Library of Congress Subject Headings* will get you off to the right start. Here a student looking for sources on animal liberation will discover that "Animal rights" is the heading to use.

General Encyclopedias:
Getting the Lay of the Land

I know you probably used encyclopedias extensively in high school. They're not nearly as useful for college papers, but they can be a good starting point to see the landscape of a subject, particularly if you're trying to narrow the focus.

The *Encyclopaedia Britannica* indexing system is in several sections: Micropaedia (ten volumes), Macropaedia (nineteen volumes), Propaedia, and Index. Some Micropaedia articles are complete in themselves, but others refer to one or more places in other Macropaedia volumes, which often expand on the subject. The Propaedia, among other things, explains how knowledge is organized in the encyclopedia and lists authors of articles in it.

Step Three: Find the *Encyclopaedia Britannica* index, and locate one or more listings that best match your topic. Look up the articles listed, and read each quickly. Select the article that seems most useful, and write down the title and something intriguing you gleaned from reading.

Title: _____

Intriguing thing: _____

_____

Make sure to check the bibliography at the end of each encyclopedia article for other useful sources on your topic. If some citations seem promising, write them down below. Be certain to get all the bibliographic information you'll need, in case you need to document the source in your paper (author, title, publication information).

Promising citations in bibliography (if any): _____

_____

_____

Surveying the Reference Landscape

Using a general encyclopedia is a little like looking through the wrong end of binoculars. You get the long view of a subject. That can be helpful, particularly if you are trying to further focus on some aspect of the topic. But in a college paper, pretty soon you'll find that the information in the encyclopedia does not provide the detailed glimpse at your topic that you need. The next step, consulting Sheehy's *Guide to Reference Books,* may move you much closer to that detailed information by directing you to more specialized reference materials.

The *Guide* will reveal to you—maybe for the first time—the incredible variety of references that are available these days. In the *Guide,* organized by field of study (e.g., humanities, social and behavioral sciences, history, science and technology, etc.), you will find listings for specialized encyclopedias, almanacs, directories, indexes, handbooks, dictionaries, and bibliographies. Some of these sources—including almanacs, encyclopedias, and dictionaries—may directly provide information on your topic. But the most useful sources—such as bibliographies and indexes—contain citations for other books and articles that may have information you need.

Step 4: Find the *Guide to Reference Books* in the reference room of your library. Check the index in the back of the book, using the topic headings you found in the *LCSH* or any others that you think might work. Alternatively, look in the front of the book at the more general subject headings, and try to match one to your topic. After deciding what headings to use, browse through the appropriate sections in the *Guide* (see Figure 1-2). Note any reference sources (e.g., an index, almanac, bibliography, dictionary, encyclopedia, etc.) that you find in the *Guide* that seem promising, and list the title of one below. Make sure you get the complete bibliographic citation and comment on what you hope to find in that source. (Don't bother to try to find any sources yet.)

Type of Source (circle):   Index   Almanac   Bibliography

        Dictionary   Encyclopedia   Directory   Handbook   Other

Author: _____

Title: _____

Publication information: _____

_____

Comment: _____

_____

Finding Books

It may seem as if you've already put in your time thumbing through card catalogs, looking for books. You likely know the basics of this task. But because of the massive number of books in your college library and the new technologies for cataloging them, you could probably use some practice. First, some background on how books are classified and shelved.

FIGURE 1-2 A student researching violence on television in the *Guide to Reference Books* might check the index at the back of the book under "Television" and be referred to this page. Note the wide range of possible references that might be useful, especially the bibliographies. The student would then check to see which of the pertinent sources are in his library's collection.

Source: Reprinted with permission of ALA from *Guide to Reference Books,* 10th edition.

See also BG229–BG230, BG233.

Guides

Schreibman, Fay C. Broadcast television: a research guide. Ed. by Peter J. Bukalski. Los Angeles, Calif., American Film Inst., Education Services, 1983. 62p. (Factfile, no.15)
BG290

A useful guide for an area not well covered bibliographically.

Bibliography

McCavitt, William E. Radio and television: a selected, annotated bibliography. Metuchen, N.J., Scarecrow Pr., 1978. 229p.; Suppl. one, 1977–81. Metuchen, N.J., 1982. 155p. **BG291**

For full information *see* CH503.

NAB broadcasting bibliography: a guide to the literature of radio & television. Comp. by the staff of the NAB Library and Information Center, Public Affairs Dept. 2d ed. Wash., Nat. Assoc. of Broadcasters, [1984]. 66p. **BG292**

1st ed. 1982.

Lists 360 books, most of them published since 1975, under seven categories (with numerous subdivisions): fundamentals of broadcasting, the business of broadcasting, broadcasting and the law, the technology and technique of broadcasting, broadcasting and society, comparative broadcasting, related technologies. Also includes a list of periodicals and a publishers directory. Author/title index.

Dissertations

Kittross, John M. A bibliography of theses & dissertations in broadcasting, 1920–1973. Wash., Broadcast Education Assoc., 1978. [238]p. **BG293**

An author listing of some 4,300 dissertations and master's theses completed at American universities, with keyword-in-title index plus an index by year of completion and another by broad topics.

Sparks, Kenneth R. A bibliography of doctoral dissertations in television and radio. [3d ed.] Syracuse, N.Y., School of Journalism, Syracuse Univ., [1971]. 119p. **BG294**

A classified listing of some 900 dissertations completed through June 1970. Author index. Z7221.S65

Indexes

International index to television periodicals; an annotated guide. 1979/80– . London, Internat. Federation of Film Archives, [1983]– . Biennial. **BG295**

Michael Moulds, ed.

There are two systems for classifying books: the *Dewey Decimal* and the *Library of Congress* systems. Each is quite different. The Dewey system, reportedly conceived in 1873 by an Amherst College undergraduate while daydreaming in church, is numerical, dividing all knowledge into ten broad areas and further subdividing each of these into one hundred additional classifications. Adding decimal points allows librarians to subdivide things even further. Just knowing the *call number* of a book will tell you its subject.

Here's the most basic division of Dewey numbers by subject:

000–099	General Works
100–199	Philosophy
200–299	Religion
300–399	Social Science
400–499	Language
500–599	Pure Science
600–699	Applied Science and Technology
700–799	Fine Arts
800–899	Literature
900–999	History

In the Dewey system, there's also a second number (or *Cutter number*) assigned to each book, which begins with the first letter of the author's last name. You don't need to know the significance of that number; just make sure you carefully copy it down when you're interested in the book.

The *Library of Congress* system, which uses both letters and numbers, is much more common in college libraries. Each call number begins with one or two letters, signifying a category of knowledge, which is followed by a whole number between 1 and 9,999. A decimal and one or more Cutter numbers sometimes follows. The Library of Congress system is pretty complex, but it's not hard to use. As you get deeper in your research, you'll begin to recognize call numbers that consistently yield useful books. It is sometimes helpful to simply browse those shelves for other possibilities.

Here is a list by subject of Library of Congress classifications:

A	General Works
B-BJ	Philosophy, Psychology
BL-BX	Religion
C	Auxiliary Sciences of History
D	History: General and Old World
E-F	History: America
G	Geography
H	Social Sciences

J	Political Science
K	Law
KD	Law of the United Kingdom and Ireland
KE	Law of Canada
KF	Law of the United States
L	Education
M	Music
N	Fine Arts
P-PA	General Philology and Linguistics; Classical Languages and Literatures
PB-PH	Modern European Languages
PG	Russian Literature
PJ-PM	Languages and Literature of Asia, Africa, Oceania, American Indian; Artificial Languages
PN, PR, PS, PZ	General Literature: English and American
PQ	French, Italian, Spanish, and Portuguese Literature
PT	German, Dutch, and Scandinavian Literature
Q	Science
R	Medicine
S	Agriculture
T	Technology
U	Military Science
V	Naval Science
Z	Bibliography, Library Science, Reference

Your library probably still has an active card catalog, and you already know how to use that. Remember that cards are organized by subject, author, and title. At this point, you'll likely look under promising subject headings, perhaps suggested by what you found in the *LCSH*. Make sure you pay attention to "see" and "see also" cards; they'll suggest other useful headings to check.

But maybe your college library, like mine, has begun to retire its 3" × 5" cards and replace them with an *online card catalog*. This on-line system uses a computer to do the same thing that you used to do, thumbing through the card catalog. And of course, the computer is much faster. Search on a subject, author, or title, or on a *keyword* that explains the topic you want to find.

Even if your library does have an online card catalog, don't necessarily abandon those old catalog cards. Conversion from the old system to the new one is expensive and laborious, and you may find some sources, particularly older ones, that have not yet been logged into the computer system. Ask the library staff about how current the online catalog is.

Step Five: Give your card catalog or online system a try. Look up your tentative topic under one or several promising subject headings, and note at least one book that seems useful. (Be sure to list all the bibliographic information, in case you end up citing this source in your paper.) If your topic is current or doesn't otherwise lend itself to treatment in books, find a book on a subject that does interest you, say, fiberglass repair. (To be sure, there aren't many topics that can't be researched in books).

Call number: _____

Author(s): _____

Title: _____

Place of publication: _____

Publisher: _____

Date of publication: _____

Now go retrieve the book from the stacks. Look for a wallchart that lists on what floor each category of call number is shelved, or ask the reference librarian for help. At a larger university, you may discover that the book you need is in another library on campus. For example, my college has separate physics, engineering, bioscience, and nursing libraries. Getting a book from one of them involves a short hike.

If the book is missing, check to see if it was misshelved or may be on the "waiting shelves," which are where books that have recently been returned are held before they're reshelved by the library staff. Finally, consult someone at the circulation desk to find out if he knows where the book might be.

If you have found your book, write down the first sentence of the first full paragraph on page 10:

Sentence on page 10: _____

_____

If you haven't found your book, explain what you discovered about its fate at the circulation desk (when it's due back, whether it's being rebound, if it's lost, etc.).

Status of the missing book: _____

_____

Interlibrary Loan

If the library doesn't have the book (or journal article) you want, don't despair. If you have got enough lead time (a few weeks), the library can get the book from another library through interlibrary loan, a service provided at most college libraries through the reference desk. It's usually free and simply involves filling out a search form.

Checking Bibliographies

At the backs of many books are bibliographies, or lists of sources that contributed to the work. Sometimes bibliographies can be mined for additional sources that might be useful to you.

If the book you found has a bibliography, scan the titles and write down at least one promising source you find.

Source(s) from Bibliography: _____

_____

_____

Finding Magazine and Journal Articles

It used to be that the table where the *Reader's Guide to Periodical Literature* was located was one of the busiest in the reference room. You likely remember the *Reader's Guide* from high school—it and the encyclopedia were often the major reference sources for almost every paper. The *Reader's Guide* is still useful, especially if you're hunting for popular magazine articles published four or more years ago, which may not be included in the new computer indexes. The *Reader's Guide* is also helpful for locating citations of magazines published last month, which are listed in monthly supplements.

Perhaps the real weakness of the *Reader's Guide* for college papers is that it's mostly an index to nonscholarly magazines, such as *Time, Redbook,* and *Sports Illustrated.* There's nothing wrong with these publications. In fact, you may end up using some in your paper. But as you dig more deeply into your subject, you'll find that the information in popular magazines will often begin to tell you what you already know.

Fortunately, there are alternatives to the *Reader's Guide* that may prove even more useful in locating articles for your paper. One alternative is the *Magazine Index,* which catalogs over four hundred popular periodicals. Begun in 1976, the *Magazine Index* is available on microfilm or CD. Perhaps the most common and most helpful periodical index is a computerized index called *InfoTrac,* which includes over nine hundred periodicals in a variety of disciplines. InfoTrac includes some scholarly journals that contain articles written by experts in their fields. It also indexes the *Wall Street Journal* (the last six months) and the *New York Times* (the last sixty issues). InfoTrac listings are updated monthly and cover the current year and the three years before that. If you're looking for periodical sources from earlier than three years ago, use the *Reader's Guide,* which began indexing general periodicals in 1890.

Using InfoTrac is easy. You can search by subject, author, title, or keyword and in most cases even get a printout of the sources you find. One of the nice things about using a computerized index such as this is that it will often help you narrow your search with the "see also" prompt.

Step Six: If your library has InfoTrac, give it a spin. Review the commands, and begin a search for articles on your topic. Of course, ask for help if you need it. Find a useful citation, and record the following information about it. (You might also want to attach the printout you received and hand it in with this exercise.)

Subject heading: _____

Author: _____

Title: _____

Title of periodical in full: _____

_____

Volume or issue number and date: _____

Pages covered by the article: _____

If your library doesn't feature a computer index to periodicals, check the *Magazine Index* or *Reader's Guide* for sources, starting with the most recent issue (unless coverage of your topic is limited to a specific time).

If using InfoTrac didn't produce many sources for you, try different subject headings. Also consider if perhaps articles on your topic were published more than three years ago. Check the printed version of the *Reader's Guide* for older articles, but remember that one measure of the value of a source in an academic paper is its currency (depending on the subject, of course). Finally, it's possible, though unlikely, that your topic just doesn't lend itself to treatment in periodicals. If so, try another topic that interests you to get some practice with periodical indexes.

You may discover, much to your delight, that InfoTrac provides you with a long list of periodicals that seem helpful. But there may be a hitch: Your library may not have all of them. You may be able to find that out quickly by consulting a catalog produced by your library that lists its periodical subscriptions and where each is located. The catalog is often a bound computer printout, frequently located near the periodical indexes. Ask the reference staff where this list is.

Does the library have the periodical you listed above? ___*yes* ___*no*

If so, where is it located: _____

For the moment, don't bother hunting down any periodicals. You'll have time for that later. Generally, periodicals published more than a year ago are bound together and shelved alphabetically on a floor in the main library or in one of the satellite libraries on campus. Current issues, published within the last year, are often shelved separately, unbound.

Indexes to Specialized Periodicals

Although *Time* and *Sports Illustrated* were great sources for that paper on steroid use by high school athletes you wrote for English your senior year, you will soon find that as you research this college paper, popular periodicals will quickly stop telling you much that's new to you. Popular periodicals can be good sources for memorable quotes, anecdotes, or case studies, but often, the articles are written by nonexperts whose treatments of topics are fairly superficial, at least for academic papers. You need to dig deeper.

If you used InfoTrac for Step Six, you may have discovered a few periodicals appearing on your printout—such as *Science, Foreign Affairs,* or *Psychology Today*—that are somewhat more authoritative than everyday magazines, partly because they are written for a less general audience. They are still popular periodicals, however, and of limited use.

The college researcher should make a practice of consulting scholarly publications, whenever possible. Simply put, these periodicals are written for and by people in their respective fields. For example, the *American Journal of Political Science* is one of a handful of professional periodicals read by political scientists. English instructors might read *College English*, and psychologists, *Psychology Review*.

Getting through articles in scholarly journals like these may sometimes be difficult—the terminology may be unfamiliar to you, and the prose pretty dense. But often, the task is well worth the effort because you'll uncover information on your topic you won't find anywhere else. With a little practice, you'll learn to skim journal articles for useful information.

Sometimes journal articles are reports of new studies, which makes them *primary sources,* or feature analyses by people who are leaders in their fields. (See "Primary Over Secondary Sources" in Chapter 2 for further explanation.) Skillful use of scholarly sources in your paper can be a big boost. They not only enhance the authority of your paper; you'll discover that through your familiarity with some of the important thinkers on your topic, you will become something of an expert yourself.

But how do you find scholarly sources? Not surprisingly, there are computer databases (many now on CD–ROM) and bound indexes to choose from. If your library has compact disc technology, use it; it has enormous advantages in searching for journal articles. But you should be familiar with the key bound indexes, too. They're listed below. All are published by the same company that produces the *Reader's Guide,* so they're similarly organized and used.

FIVE KEY JOURNAL INDEXES

Humanities Index (1974–date)*
Covers roughly 260 journals in archaeology, classical studies, language and literature, area studies, folklore, history, performing arts, philosophy, religion, and theology.

Social Science Index (1974–date)*
Covers 263 journals in anthropology, economics, environmental science, geography, law and criminology, medical science, political science, psychology, and sociology.

General Science Index (1978–date)
Covers about 115 journals in astronomy, atmospheric science, biology, botany, chemistry, environment and conservation, food and nutrition, genetics, mathematics, medicine and health, microbiology, oceanography, physics, physiology, and zoology.

*If you want to search for sources prior to 1974, check the predecessors to this index: the *International Index* (1907–1965) and the *Social Science and Humanities Index* (1965–1974).

Education Index (1929–date)
Indexes well over 300 journals in the arts, audiovisual education, comparative and international education, computers in education, English language arts, health and physical education, language and linguistics, library and information science, multicultural/-ethnic education, psychology and mental health, religious education, science and mathematics, social studies, special education and rehabilitation, and education research.

Business Periodicals Index (1958–date)
Covers journals in the following subjects: accounting, advertising and marketing, agriculture, banking, building, chemical industry, communications, computer technology and applications, drug and cosmetic industries, economics, electronics, finance and investments, industrial relations insurance, international business, management, personnel administration, occupational health and safety, paper and pulp industries, petroleum and gas industries, printing and publishing, public relations, public utilities, real estate regulation of industry, retailing, taxation, and transportation.

If your library has computer workstations set up to use compact discs, then you may rarely have to consult printed indexes to find journal articles on your topic. The books *are* worth checking when the database you consult doesn't cover the years you need or you want to look for articles published in the last few months. Though CDs are usually updated several times a year, they frequently don't contain the most recent issues of the journals they cover.

The indexes listed above are also *general indexes* of academic journals. There are a multitude of printed *specialized indexes* you might want to check that aren't on CD. For example, if you're writing a paper on deforestation in the Pacific Northwest, it might be worth checking the *Environmental Index* as well as the *General Science Index* on CD.

But in most college libraries, the new CDs are the easiest, most efficient way to search for academic articles. Between fifteen hundred and three thousand databases are available to libraries on CD, and more appear everyday. Many of the general indexes listed above are also on CD. The following is a list of additional databases that are popular with college researchers:

ABI/Inform covers business, economic and management topics, as well as the health care industry. It indexes about nine hundred journals in those fields, a third of which include not just citations but the full texts of the articles.

ERIC indexes education-related periodicals. It's the electronic equivalent of the *Current Index to Journals in Education* and *Resources in Education*. ERIC is an enormously useful database for a variety of subjects, even those that are not exclusively education related.

MLA Bibliography is the key index for literature, linguistics, languages, and folklore, covering about three thousand journals in those fields. The CD version covers nine years on one disc.

Medline is the computerized version of *Index Medicus,* a widely used reference in the fields of medicine, pharmacy, pharmacology, and nursing.

PAIS (or the Public Affairs Information Service) covers politics, government, economics, and international and consumer affairs. It is also available in a bound version.

Psyclit is the computerized version of *Psychological Abstracts*. It indexes about fourteen hundred journals and is one of the most widely used databases in the field of psychology.

Sociofile indexes over fifteen hundred journals in sociology, anthropology, and social work and also covers some areas of education, health, and psychology.

Step Seven: Search one or more of the indexes above for scholarly articles on your topic. Use either the bound indexes or, if your library has them, the appropriate databases on CD. Try several subject headings.

For *one* citation that seems promising, take down the following:

Subject heading: _____

Author(s): _____

Title of article: _____

Title of periodical: _____

Volume, date, page numbers: _____

Does the library have it? ___yes ___no

If you came up empty handed, you may have to find a more specialized index in the field you're working. You'll have the chance to do that in the third week (see "Second-Level Searching" in Chapter 3). It's also possible that your topic simply hasn't been of scholarly

TIPS FOR SEARCHING ON A CD

Despite the explosion of databases on CD in a broad range of fields, they are often quite similar to use. Here are a few general points that should help you search successfully on most CDs:

1. *Computers take your mistakes seriously.* If you misspell a word, the computer will take you literally and search for it, as is. Ask the computer to search a database for articles on "Acholoics Anonymous," and you'll come up empty handed. Check your spelling, and you'll save time.

2. *Search topics need not be described in full sentences.* Actually, it's better to break your topic down into several headings that seem useful. If you're looking for information on the effects of medication on hyperactive children, break the topic down into three concepts—hyperactivity, medication, and children—and then search for articles about each. Most CD databases come with books of indexing terms, or subject headings—a sort of *Library of Congress Subject Headings* equivalent for computers. These manuals are very useful for finding search terms on your topic.

3. *Understand the difference between* and *and* or. These are not words the computer will search for, but they offer it key instructions about what to do. The word *or* tells the computer to look for synonyms, broadening your search. For example, if you ask it to search for "food *or* nutrition *or* diet," the system will retrieve records with any of these terms. In this case, it would produce a downpour of articles. The word *and* narrows the search, telling the computer to locate only those records that contain the words you specify. For example, telling the computer to find "hyperactivity *and* medication *and* children" will only produce records containing all those terms.

concern. That doesn't necessarily mean you should abandon your idea. You may be able to find plenty of good sources other than journal articles. But for practice, use one of the indexes and look up something else that interests you, such as alcohol abuse patterns among college students.

If you did come up with some promising journal citations, don't bother hunting them down now.

Newspaper Articles

If your tentative research topic is local, current, or controversial, then newspapers can be useful sources. You'll rarely get much in-depth information or analysis from newspapers, but they can often provide good quotes, anecdotes, and case studies as well as the most current printed information available on your topic. Newspapers are also sometimes considered primary sources because they provide firsthand accounts of things that have happened.

Some newspapers are indexed. Generally, only those publications considered *national newspapers* are catalogued and saved, usually on microfilm but sometimes on CD. Among the national publications are the *New York Times*, the *Los Angeles Times*, the *Christian Science Monitor*, the *Washington Post*, and the *Wall Street Journal*. The index for each national newspaper is a separate bound volume or may be included on a computer database, such as Newsbank, or a microfilm index, such as the Newspaper Index.

Your college library probably subscribes to a variety of local or state papers, as well, which are often not indexed. Some may be on microfilm going back many years. If your topic involves an event that occurred at a specific time—say November 22, 1963—then you can simply scan the unindexed newspapers for coverage on and around that date.

Step Eight: Check the index for the *New York Times* (or any of the other bound volumes), a computer database like Newsbank, or the *Newspaper Index* for articles on your topic. Try several subject headings, and note the "see also" prompts. If your topic doesn't lend itself to coverage in newspapers, find microfilm of the *New York Times* edition that was published on the day of your birth. If your library has a machine for photocopying from microfilm, make a copy of an article on your topic or the front page of the *Times* published on your birthday. Attach the photocopy to this exercise when you hand it in. If there is no copying machine, take down the following information:

Subject heading: _____

Title of article: _____

Newspaper: _____

Date and page number: _____

Government Documents

The United States Government is the largest publisher in the world, and if your college library is a *depository* for government documents, it may receive almost everything the federal government publishes. Usually, there's one depository library in each state. Nondepository libraries may still receive government documents, though, and most college libraries do have a selective collection that is sometimes catalogued separately.

The great thing about government documents is that they cover a broad range of subjects. The bad news is that you may go nuts trying to find what you're looking for. Because government publications often arrive daily at your campus library, in one big pile, the staff has its hands full, cataloguing and shelving the material. Government document librarians sometimes live on the edge of chaos.

Subject title

Indians of North America — Census, 1990.
American Indians and Alaska Natives—
the Census counts for you! (C 3.272:D-
3207 (I/AK)),   90-9318

Indians of North America — Child welfare.
Foster care : use of funds for youths
placed in the Rite of Pasage program :
briefing report to the Honorable
George Miller, House of Representa-
tives / (GA 1.13:HRD-87-23 BR),   90-
8009

Title of document; —————— Regulating Indian child protection and
brief description of preventing child abuse on Indian reser-
type (report, study, vations : report (to accompany S.
hearing documents, 1783). United States. Congress. Senate.
etc.) Select Committee on Indian Affairs. (Y
1.1/5:101-203),   90-5566 ——————— *Entry number*
begins with year
of publication;
Indians of North America — Children — *keyed to separate*
Crimes against. *volume with fuller*
Federal government's relationship with *description of*
American Indians : hearings before the *document*

FIGURE 1-3 Using the *Monthly Catalog of Government Publications* is usually a two-step process. Check the subject/title/keyword index for pertinent headings. Then write down the *entry number* for a promising document, and look for the number in the separate volumes of entry numbers, which are listed sequentially. In this figure, the researcher is looking for a document on child abuse on American Indian reservations.

Entry number

SuDoc number (call number to help locate document in stacks)

90-5566

Y 1.1/5:101-203

United States. Congress. Senate. Select Committee on Indian Affairs.

Physical description of document; black dot indicates routinely sent to depository libraries

Regulating Indian child protection and preventing child abuse on Indian reservations : report (to accompany S. 1783). — [Washington, D.C.? : U.S. G.P.O., 1989]

12 p. ; 24 cm. — (Report / 101st Congress, 1st session, Senate ; 101-203) Caption title. Distributed to some depository libraries in microfiche. Shipping list no.: 89-803-P. "November 13 ... 1989." ●Item 1008-C, 1008-D (MF)

1. Child abuse — Law and legislation — United States. 2. Indians of North America — Child welfare. 3. Indians of North America — Children — Legal status, laws, etc. I. Title. II. Series: United States. Congress. Senate. Report ; 101-203. OCLC 20777673

FIGURE 1-4 Here's what the researcher discovered using the entry number for the document on American Indian child abuse.

As always, there are printed and computer indexes to government documents. The most important index, the *Monthly Catalog of United States Government Publications*, is available in both forms (see Figures 1-3 and 1-4). You can search a document in the *Monthly Catalog* by author, title, subject, series, stock number, and title keyword. Your library may have the *Government Publications Index*, which is drawn from the *Monthly Catalog*, available on CD.

Step Nine: Check one of the indexes mentioned to locate any government documents on your topic that may be useful. Try a few possible subject headings, and go back a few years if you need to. If you find something interesting, take down the bibliographic information below.

Subject heading: _____

Full name of government branch that published document: _____

_____

Title: _____

Date: _____

Place and publisher*: _____

*Usually "Washington, D.C.: Government Printing Office."

If you got nowhere looking in a government publications index, it's possible that your topic just doesn't lend itself to this type of source. The best bets, obviously, are topics that have to do with law, government, public policy, and the like. If you don't find anything on your topic, just for practice, try a topic that will be indexed—say, student loans.

If you did uncover something promising and your library doesn't have it, you can often send for the material by writing to:

Superintendent of Documents
Government Printing Office
Washington, D.C. 20402

It usually doesn't cost anything to get materials, and they should arrive in a few weeks, which is just enough time to be useful for your paper.

Don't bother locating the document in your library. You can do that later. For now, reward yourself with an Almond Joy. You've finished the library exercise and are familiar with the most important reference sources used by college researchers. You also may be well on your way through the initial stage of research on your tentative topic. In the second week, you'll refine your research strategy and learn about a few more reference sources that are specialized. These can be especially useful if you're having trouble finding information.

□ ■ □

Considering Nonlibrary Sources: Interviews and Surveys

Before you prepare to begin library research in earnest next week, consider two alternative sources of information that may be extremely valuable: interviews and informal surveys. When I was writing my book on lobsters, I did lots of library research, particularly on the biology of the animal. I read studies on how female lobsters choose mates (they like those with the most appealing urine smell), examined charts on how fast lobsters grow and how old they are when they end up on my plate (about seven years), and consulted research by fisheries experts on rates of exploitation by the lobster industry.

I was especially interested in that last topic because one of the questions that triggered my search was wondering whether lobsters were being overfished. I learned about recruitment failure and fishing effort and the relationship between carapace length and maturity. Based on what I read, I concluded that almost all legal-sized lobsters are caught by fishermen every year and that at that size, they haven't had a chance to reproduce. But it wasn't until I stopped reading and interviewed a man named Guy Marchessault, a government biologist, that the meaning of all this became clear. "It's almost as if you drafted all thirteen-year-old, prepubescent kids and shot them all," he said. "How will you maintain a population of people if you don't let them reproduce? That's the conundrum with respect to lobsters."

Not only did talking to Guy clear up my own confusion; he provided me with a memorable quote that would do the same for my readers, too.

You can find people who are experts in almost every conceivable field right on your own campus. And you'll probably find more experts who can be reached by phone with just a little digging. (See "Finding Experts" in Chapter 2 for information on arranging interviews.) You may also know people who may not be authorities in the field you're researching but who have relevant experience to share. For example, André was researching a paper on banning fraternities and interviewed a fraternity president whose house was threatened with closure. Another student, Taylor, explored the impact of divorce on father-daughter relationships by interviewing her father.

When interviewing is expanded to include a group of people, usually by asking each person a standard set of questions, you are conducting an informal survey. Your results will not be statistically valid, but you may get a sense of what people think about some aspect of your research topic. The range of responses you receive may be illuminating, as well.

Very few topics don't lend themselves to interviews or surveys. However, you must determine whom to talk to about your topic. Who might be an expert and have useful information, or who has experience that is relevant? Jot down some tentative ideas in your research journal, and discuss them with your instructor next week.

2

□ ■ □

The Second Week

NARROWING THE SUBJECT

It never occurred to me that photography and writing had anything in common until I found myself wandering around a lonely beach one March afternoon with a camera around my neck. I had a fresh roll of film, and full of ambition, I set out to take beautiful pictures. Three hours later, I had taken only three shots, and I was definitely not having fun. Before quitting in disgust, I spent twenty minutes trying to take a single picture of a lighthouse. I stood there, feet planted in the sand, repeatedly bringing the camera to my face, but each time I looked through the viewfinder, I saw a picture I was sure I'd seen before, immortalized on a postcard in the gift shop down the road. Suddenly, photography lost its appeal.

A few months later, a student sat in my office, complaining that he didn't have anything to write about. "I thought about writing an essay on what it was like going home for the first time last weekend," he said, "but I thought that everyone probably writes about that in Freshman English." I looked at him and thought about lighthouse pictures.

Circling the Lighthouse

Most every subject you will choose to write about for this class and for this research paper has been written about before. The challenge is not to find a unique topic (save that for your doctoral dissertation) but to find an angle on a familiar topic that helps readers to see what they probably haven't noticed before. In "Why God Created

Flies," Richard Conniff took the most common of subjects—the housefly—and made it seem new by giving us a close look at its unusual habits and the surprising things he had to say about how the fly may be punishment for our own arrogance.

I now know that I was mistaken to give up on the lighthouse. The problem with my lighthouse picture, as well as with my student's proposed essay on going home, was not the subject. It was that neither of us had yet found our own angle. I needed to keep looking, walking around the lighthouse, taking lots of shots until I found one that surprised me, that helped me to see the lighthouse in a new way, in *my* way. Instead, I stayed put, stuck on the long shot and the belief that I couldn't do better than a postcard photograph.

It is generally true that when we first look at something, we mostly see its obvious features. That became apparent when I asked my Freshman English class one year to go out and take pictures of anything they wanted. Several students came back with single photographs of Thompson Hall, a beautiful brick building on our campus. Coincidentally, all were taken from the same angle and distance— straight on and across the street—which is the same shot that appears in the college recruiting catalog. For the next assignment, I asked my students to take multiple shots of a single subject, varying angle and distance. Several students went back to Thompson Hall and discovered a building they'd never seen before, though they walk by it everyday. Students took abstract shots of the pattern of brickwork, unsettling shots of the clock tower looming above, and arresting shots of wrought iron fire escapes, clinging in a tangle to the wall.

The closer students got to their subjects, the more they began to see what they had never noticed before. The same is true in writing. As you move in for a closer look at some aspect of a larger subject, you will begin to uncover information that you—and ultimately your readers—are likely to find less familiar and more interesting. One writing term for this is *focusing*. (The photographic equivalent would be *distance from the subject*.)

From Landscape Shots to Close-Ups

When you wrote research reports in high school, you were a landscape photographer, trying to cram into one picture as much information as you could. A research report is a long shot. The college research paper is much more of a close-up, which means narrowing the boundaries of your topic as much as you can, always working for a more detailed look at some smaller part of the landscape.

Of course, you are not a photographer, and finding a narrow focus and fresh angle on your research topic is not nearly as simple as it might be if this were a photography exercise. But the idea is the same. You need to see your topic in as many ways as you can, hunting for the angle that most interests you; then go in for a closer look. One way to find your *focus* is to find your *questions*.

□ *EXERCISE 2-1*
Finding the Questions

Though you can do this exercise on your own, your instructor will likely ask that it be done in class this week. That way, students can all help each other. (If you do try this on your own, only do Steps 3 and 4 in your research notebook.)

Step 1: Take a piece of paper or a large piece of newsprint, and post it on the wall. At the very top of the paper, write the title of your tentative topic (e.g., "Legalization of Marijuana").

Step 2: Take a few minutes and briefly describe why you chose the topic.

Step 3: Spend five minutes or so and briefly list what you know about your topic already (e.g., any surprising facts or statistics, the extent of the problem, important people or institutions involved, key schools of thought, common misconceptions, observations you've made, important trends, major controversies, etc.).

Step 4: Now spend fifteen or twenty minutes brainstorming a list of questions *about your topic* that you'd like to answer through your research. Make this list as long as you can; try to see your topic in as many ways as possible. Push yourself on this; it's the most important step.

Step Five: As you look around the room, you'll see a gallery of topics and questions on the walls. At this point in the research process, almost everyone will be struggling to find her focus. You can help each other. Move around the room, reviewing the topics and questions other students have generated. For each topic posted on the wall, do two things: Add a question *you* would like answered about that topic that's not on the list, and check the *one* question on the list you find most interesting. (It may or may not be the one you added.)

□ ■ □

If you do this exercise in class, when you return to your newsprint, note the question about your topic that garnered the most interest. This may not be the one that interests you the most, and you may choose to ignore it altogether. But it is helpful to get some idea of what typical readers might most want to know about your topic.

You also might be surprised by the rich variety of topics other students have tentatively chosen for their research projects. The last time I did this exercise, I had students propose papers on controversial issues like the use of dolphins in warfare, homelessness, the controversy over abolishment of fraternities, the legalization of marijuana, and the censorship of music. Other students proposed somewhat more personal issues, such as growing up with an alcoholic father, date rape, women in abusive relationships, and the effects of divorce on children. Still other students wanted to learn about more historical subjects, including the role of Emperor Hirohito in World War II, the student movement in the 1960s, and the Lizzie Borden murder case. A few students chose topics that were local. For example, one student whose great uncle was a union organizer wanted to investigate a strike that occurred seventy years ago at the old woolen mill in his hometown. Another student investigated a murder that took place on the Isle of Shoals, an island off the New Hampshire coast, a hundred years ago.

If the topic you've tentatively chosen is broad—such as abortion, whales, or child abuse—then Exercise 2-1 may help you discover the questions needed to narrow your topic into something more manageable. For example, if you're considering a paper on abortion, you'll quickly see how many angles there are on such a complicated subject: What is the history of abortion rights in the United States? How will the new conservative majority on the Supreme Court influence *Roe* v. *Wade?* What is the impact of the abortion issue on local election campaigns? Each one of these questions could easily be answered in a ten-page paper, and most of these topics could likely be narrowed further.

Knowing the many questions your research project *could* answer is a start. But you obviously need to limit how many questions to ask, too. Once you've unleashed the many possibilities, you must harness a few in the service of your paper. If you need some help with that, try the next exercise.

☐ *EXERCISE 2-2*
Finding the Focusing Question

Review the questions you or the rest of the class generated in Exercise 2-1, Steps 4 and 5, and ask yourself, Which questions on the list am I most interested in that could be the focus of my paper? Remember, you're not committing yourself yet.

FOCUSING: A CASE STUDY

Al, a student working on the topic children of alcoholics, came up with the following questions from Exercise 2-2:

Which family members are most affected by the drinker?

What can they realistically do to encourage the drinker to stop?

How likely is it that I will drink because my father did?

How effective is AA? Al-Anon? ACOA?

What's the relationship between these organizations?

What do they mean by "tough love?"

Do teenage children of alcoholics have any special problems?

How do the reactions of children differ?

Does a family share any of the responsibility for the alcoholic's disease?

Does it matter whether the father or mother is the drinker, or are the problems for the family the same in both cases?

What do they mean by "adult child?"

Al, the son of an alcoholic, had plenty of good questions. He had already done some reading on the subject, which helped, but he wasn't quite sure what he wanted to focus on. One question intrigued him the most—Do teenage children of alcoholics have any special problems?—but he was afraid the focus was too narrow. Would he be able to find enough information? Al was also interested in the last question, the meaning of the term *adult child*. But was that subject too broad? He was aware that scores of books had been published on adult children of alcoholics in recent years and thought he might be swamped by information.

If you can, start with the narrower focus. As you immerse yourself in research, you can broaden it a bit if you're having difficulty finding information, or you may encounter some interesting material that encourages you to change the focus altogether. If you start with a closer look at some aspect of your subject, your research efforts will be more efficient and the information you unearth will more likely surprise you.

(continued)

Al tentatively chose the narrower focusing question: Do teenage children of alcoholics have any special problems? Working from that main question, he generated an additional list of questions that he may need to explore:

> Does anything about being a teenager make alcoholism harder?
>
> What do I remember from my own experience with my father at that age?
>
> Do groups like Al-Anon and ACOA have special meetings for teens?
>
> How do teenagers with alcoholic parents deal with the pressures to drink themselves?

Armed with this focus and some ideas about what to look for, Al was ready to begin his library work in earnest.

Step 1: Write the *one* question that you think would be the most interesting focus for your paper on the top of a fresh piece of newsprint or paper. This is your *focusing question.*

Step 2: Now build a new list of questions under the first one. What else do you need to know to answer your focusing question? For example, suppose your focusing question is, Why do some colleges use unethical means to recruit athletes? To explore that focus, you might need to find out:

> Which colleges or universities have the worst records of unethical activities in recruiting?
>
> In which sports do these recruiting practices occur most often? Why?
>
> What are the NCAA rules about recruiting?
>
> What is considered an *unethical practice?*
>
> What efforts have been undertaken to curb bad practices?

Many of these questions may already appear on the lists you and the class generated, so keep them close at hand and mine them for ideas. Examine your tentative focusing question carefully for clues about what you might need to know.

□ ■ □

Choosing a Trailhead

The importance of finding a narrow focus early can't be overestimated. I asked a reference librarian recently what she thought was the most common problem with student research papers. "That's easy," she said. "Students haven't narrowed their topics sufficiently. They come to us and ask where to begin looking for information on air pollution, and I could send them to any one of a hundred places."

Your research will be much more efficient if you have a limited focus, allowing you to concentrate on perhaps five relevant articles rather than wading through fifty about the broader topic. And by taking a closer look at a smaller part of your subject, you're much more likely to encounter information that will surprise you and your readers.

Settling on *one* central question that your research paper will attempt to answer is key. I call this a *trailhead question,* or the one that provides a path into your subject. It is just one of many paths, but it's the one that—at least for now—you're most interested in following. As you "follow it" into the library this week, you may encounter other questions and other trails that take you off in new directions. That's fine. But at least have an initial direction.

What's Your Purpose?

Sometimes with high school research reports, it didn't seem to matter what you thought about the subject you were writing about. It seemed that what really mattered was whether you followed the proper format, cited sources correctly, or had a long bibliography. Though following the technical conventions is important in the college research paper, what matters even more is what you do with the information you find. Your paper must have a *purpose*.

Do You Have a Thesis?

In a broad sense, the purpose of your paper might be *to persuade, to analyze,* or *to explain* some aspect of your subject. Your purpose even might be a combination of all three. More specifically, your purpose in writing this paper is to find out *what you want to say* about your topic—in other words, finding your *thesis,* or your main idea—and then using persuasion, analysis, or exposition to make that idea convincing to someone else. You may have learned that you need to define your thesis before you begin the research. That might be appropriate if you already know what you think. Last semester, I had a student, Kate, who believed strongly in the legalization of marijuana; she wanted to write a persuasive paper arguing that limited legalization was workable. Kate started with a thesis and went from there.

You might have a more tentative notion of what your paper's point will be, based on your current understanding of the topic. For example, the student investigating children of alcoholics, Al, believed that the answer to his focusing question—Do teenage children of alcoholics have an especially difficult time?—might be that they do. That's what his own experience seemed to tell him. It's possible that the research will convince Al otherwise, or finding new information may help him make his thesis more specific. Perhaps the controlling idea of Al's paper might later become the assertion that teenage children of alcoholics have particular difficulty maintaining relationships later in life.

You may have chosen your topic precisely because *you don't know what you think*. So how do you know what you want to say until you've learned what others have said and had the chance to explore your topic? What I love about research is that it is a process of discovery. That demands an openness to what you'll find and a willingness to change your mind.

If, at this point, you can state your thesis, it would be useful to do so. But don't be inflexible. As with my students and their pictures of Thompson Hall, the more you look, the more you'll see. Be open to surprise.

If you can't state your thesis yet, don't worry. You can nail that down later, after you've done some digging. (See Exercise 4-1, "Reclaiming Your Topic," in Chapter 4.) But as you begin to mine your topic for information this week, always keep two questions in mind: What do I think? and What do I want to say?

☐ *EXERCISE 2-3*
Charting Your Course

You're now standing at the trailhead, ready to begin the journey into researching your topic. Before you do, in your research notebook, jot down the answers to the following questions. They'll help you get your bearings. Your instructor may ask you to bring this information to class or conference this week.

- What is my tentative focusing question?
- What other questions might help me explore that focus?
- What is my tentative thesis?

☐ ■ ☐

DEVELOPING A
RESEARCH STRATEGY

Library Research

If you're finding questions about your topic that light small fires under you, then you may feel ready to plunge headlong into research this week. Before you do, plan your attack. At this point, you will likely return to the library with a stronger sense of what you want to know than you had last week, when you worked through the library exercise. But keep in mind that you still have many trails to follow and a formidable mass of information to consider. Where should you begin? How do you know where to go from there?

Moving from General to Specific

Often, researchers move from general sources to those that give topics more specific treatment. Look at it this way: You're not likely much of an authority on your topic yet, but by the time you write the final draft of your paper, you will be. What you have going for you at this point is your own curiosity. You're going to teach yourself about child abuse or the effects of caffeine, starting with the general knowledge you can find in the *New York Times* or *Redbook* and moving toward more specialized sources, such as the *Journal of Counseling Psychology* and the *Journal of New England Medicine*. Plan to begin with the general sources, as you did in Week 1 when you surveyed the landscape of your subject with the general encyclopedia and the *Reader's Guide*. Then move to progressively more specialized indexes and materials, digging more deeply as you become more and more of an expert in your own right.

Visualize books and articles—and the indexes that will help you find them—as occupying some spot on an inverted pyramid. Those sources toward the top are often written by nonexperts for a general audience. Those sources toward the bottom are more likely written by experts in the field for a more knowledgeable audience. An inverted pyramid of sources is shown in Figure 2-1.

Consider beginning with these generalized references, which will lead you to sources intended for a popular audience:

- General encyclopedias, almanacs, and dictionaries (e.g., *Encyclopaedia Britannica, Webster's Dictionary*)
- Indexes to popular periodicals and newspapers (e.g., *Reader's Guide,* InfoTrac, Newsbank)
- Card catalog (for popular books)

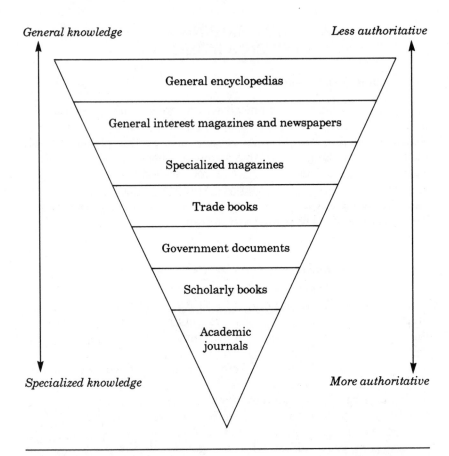

General knowledge   *Less authoritative*

General encyclopedias

General interest magazines and newspapers

Specialized magazines

Trade books

Government documents

Scholarly books

Academic journals

Specialized knowledge   *More authoritative*

FIGURE 2-1   Pyramid of sources

After consulting these sources, move to more specialized references, which will often lead you to books and articles written by experts on your topic for a more knowledgeable audience:

- Specialized encyclopedias and dictionaries (e.g., *Encyclopedia of Religion and Ethics, Dictionary of Philosophy and Psychology*—see "Second-Level Searching," Chapter 3)
- Specialized fact books (e.g., *Statistical Abstracts of the United States, Facts on File*—see "Finding 'Quick Facts," Chapter 5)
- Academic indexes (e.g., the *Humanities* and *Social Science Indexes,* ERIC, Psyclit, or other CD databases).

- Card catalog (for more authoritative books on your topic)
- Government documents
- Biographical indexes
- Bibliographic indexes (see "Third-Level Searching," Chapter 3)
- Dissertation abstracts (see "Third-Level Searching," Chapter 3)

You may find as you work that this progression from the more general to the more specialized treatment of your topic occurs quite naturally. You'll quickly find that articles in popular magazines, newspapers, and books tell you what you already know. Your hunger to unearth new information will inevitably lead you to more specialized indexes, and you'll be able to read the articles they lead you to with more understanding as you become more of an authority on your topic.

Evaluating Sources

The aim of your research strategy is not only to find interesting information on your topic but to find it in *authoritative* sources. What are authoritative sources? In most cases, they are the most current sources. (The exception may be sources on historical subjects.) Authoritative sources are also those types found on the bottom of the pyramid (see Figure 2-1).

In part, the kinds of sources you rely on in preparing your paper depend on your topic. Sandra has chosen as her tentative focusing question, What impact will the 1992 presidential election have on campaign finance reforms? Because Sandra's topic addresses recent public policy, she'll likely find a wealth of information in newspapers and magazines but not much in books. She certainly should check the academic indexes on this topic—a CD database called PAIS, or Public Affairs Information System, would be a good bet—because it's likely that political scientists have something to say on the subject.

Why Journal Articles
Are Better Than Magazine Articles

If your topic has been covered by academic journal articles, rely heavily on these sources. I've already mentioned that an article on, say, suicide among college students in a magazine like *Time* is less valuable than one in the *American Journal of Psychology*. Granted, the latter may be harder to read. But you're much more likely to learn something from a journal article because it's written by an expert and is usually narrowly focused. Also, because academic articles are carefully documented, you may be able to mine bibliographies for additional sources. And finally, scholarly work, such as that published in academic journals and books (usually published by university presses), is especially authoritative because it's subject to peer review. That means that every manuscript submitted for publication is reviewed by other authorities in the field, who scrutinize the author's evidence, methods, and arguments. Those articles that end up being published have truly passed muster.

Look for Often-Cited Authors

As you make your way through information on your topic, pay attention to names of authors whose work you often encounter or who are frequently mentioned in bibliographies. These individuals are often the best scholars in the field, and it will be useful to become familiar with their work and use it, if possible, in your paper. If an author's name keeps turning up, use it as another term for searching the card catalog and the indexes. Doing so might yield new sources you wouldn't necessarily encounter using subject headings. A specialized index—such as the *Social Science* and *Humanities Indexes*—will help you search for articles both by a particular author and by other authors who cite a particular author in their articles. (For more information on how to use the citation indexes, see "Using Citation Indexes" in Chapter 3.)

Primary Over Secondary Sources

Another way of looking at information is to determine whether it's a *primary* or a *secondary* source. A primary source presents the original words of a writer—her speech, poem, eyewitness account, letter, interview, autobiography. A *secondary* source presents somebody else's work. Whenever possible, choose a primary source over a secondary one, since the primary source is likely to be more accurate and authoritative.

The subject you research will determine the kind of primary source you encounter. For example, if you're writing a paper on a novelist, then his novels, stories, letters, and interviews are primary sources. My topic on the engineering of the Chicago River in 1900, a partly historical subject, might lead me to a government report on the project or a firsthand account of its construction in a Chicago newspaper. Primary sources for a paper in the sciences might be findings from an experiment or observations and for a paper in business, marketing information or technical studies.

Not All Books Are Alike

When writing my high school research reports, I thought that a book was always the best source because, well, books are thick, and anyone who could write that much on any one subject probably knows what she's talking about. Naive, I know.

One of the things college teaches is *critical thinking*—the instinct to pause and consider before rushing to judgment. I've learned not to automatically believe in the validity of what an author is saying (as you shouldn't for this author), even if he did write a thick book about it.

If your topic lends itself to using primarily books as sources, then evaluate the authority of each before deciding to use it in your paper. This is especially important if your paper relies heavily on one particular book. Consider the following:

- Is the book written for a general audience or more knowledgeable readers?
- Is the author an acknowledged expert in the field?
- Is there a bibliography? Is the information carefully documented?
- How was the book received by critics? To find out, consider checking the following indexes, which may feature summaries of reviews or refer you to articles reviewing the book in magazines and journals. Entries are usually listed by author, title, or reviewer.

   Book Review Digest. New York: Wilson, 1905–date. *Provides summaries and quotations from reviews.*

   Current Book Review Citations. New York: Wilson. *Indexes reviews in over one thousand periodicals.*

Arranging Interviews

A few years ago, I researched a local turn-of-the-century writer named Sarah Orne Jewett for a magazine article. I dutifully read much of her work, studied critical articles and books on her writing, and visited her childhood home, which is open to the public in South Berwick, Maine. My research was going fairly well, but when I sat down to begin writing the draft, the material seemed flat and lifeless. A few days later, the curator of the Jewett house mentioned that there was an eighty-eight-year-old local woman, Elizabeth Goodwin, who had known the writer when she was alive. "As far as I know, she's the last living person who knew Sarah Orne Jewett," the curator told me. "And she lives just down the street."

The next week, I spent three hours with Elizabeth Goodwin, who told me of coming for breakfast with the famous author and eating strawberry jam and muffins. Elizabeth told me that many years after Jewett's death, the house seemed haunted by her friendly presence. One time, when Elizabeth lived in the Jewett house as a curator, some unseen hands pulled her back as she teetered at the top of the steep stairs in the back of the house. She likes to believe it was the author's ghost.

This interview transformed the piece by bringing the subject to life—first, for me as the writer, and then later, for my readers. Ultimately, what makes almost any topic compelling is discovering why it matters to *people*—how it affects their lives. Doing interviews with people close to the subject, both experts and nonexperts, is often the best way to find that out.

Last week, I urged you to consider whether interviews could be a part of your research, perhaps an integral part. If you have doubts, reconsider, because material from interviews may transform your paper in the way it did mine.

If you'd like to do some interviews, now is the time to begin arranging them.

Finding Experts

You may be hesitant to consider finding authorities on your topic to talk to because, after all, you're just a lowly student who knows next to nothing. How could you possibly impose on that sociology professor who published the book on anti-Semitism you found in the library? If that's how you feel, keep this in mind: *Most people, no matter who they are, love the attention of an interviewer, no matter who she is, particularly if what's being discussed fascinates them both.* Time and again, I've found my own shyness creep up on me when I pick up the telephone to arrange an interview. But almost invariably, when I get there and start talking with my interview subject, the experience is great for us both.

How do you find experts to interview?

■ *Check your sources.* As you begin to collect books and articles, note the authors and their affiliations. I get calls from time to time from writers who came across my book on lobsters in the course of their research and discovered that I was at the University of New Hampshire. Sometimes the caller will arrange a phone interview or, if he lives within driving distance, a personal interview.

■ *Check the phone book.* The familiar Yellow Pages can be a gold mine. Carin, who was writing a paper on solar energy, merely looked under that heading and found a local dealer who sold solar systems to homeowners. Mark, who was investigating the effects of sexual abuse on children, found a counselor who specialized in treating abuse victims.

■ *Ask your friends and your instructors.* Your roommate's boyfriend's father may be a criminal attorney who has lots to say about the insanity defense for your paper on that topic. Your best friend may be taking a photography course with a professor who would be a great interview for your paper on the work of Edward Weston. One of your instructors may know other faculty working in your subject area who would do an interview.

■ *Check the faculty directory.* Many universities publish an annual directory of faculty and their research interests. On my campus, it's called the *Directory of Research and Scholarly Activities.* From it, I know, for example, that two professors at my university have expertise in eating disorders, a popular topic with student researchers.

■ *Check the* Encyclopedia of Associations. This is a wonderful reference book that lists organizations with interests ranging from promoting tofu to preventing acid rain. Each listing includes the name of the group, its address and phone number, a list of its publications, and a short description of its purpose. Sometimes, these organizations can direct you to experts in your area who are available for live interviews or to spokespeople who are happy to provide phone interviews.

Finding Nonexperts
Affected by Your Topic

The distinction between *expert* and *nonexpert* is tricky. For example, someone who lived through twelve months of combat in Vietnam certainly has direct knowledge of the subject, though probably he hasn't published an article about the war in *Foreign Affairs.* Similarly, a friend who experienced an abusive relationship with her boyfriend or overcame a drug addiction is, at least in a sense, an authority on abuse or addiction. Both individuals would likely be invaluable interviews for papers on those topics. The voices and the stories of people who are affected by the topic you're writing about can do more than anything else to make the information come to life, even if they don't have Ph.D.'s.

You may already know people you can interview about your topic. Last semester, Amanda researched how mother-daughter relationships change when a daughter goes to college. She had no problem finding other women anxious to talk about how they get along with their mothers. A few years ago, Dan researched steroid use by student athletes. He discreetly asked his friends if they knew anyone who had taken the drugs. It turned out that an acquaintance of Dan's had used the drugs regularly and was happy to talk about his experience.

If you don't know people to interview, try posting notices on campus kiosks or bulletin boards. For example, "I'm doing a research project and interested in talking to people who grew up in single-parent households. Please call 868-9000." Also poll other students in your class for ideas about people you might interview for your paper. Help each other out.

Making Contact

By the end of this week, you should have some people to contact for interviews. First, consider whether to ask for a personal or telephone interview or perhaps, as a last resort, to simply correspond by mail. The personal interview is almost always preferable; you cannot only listen but watch, observing your subject's gestures and the setting, both of which can be revealing. When I'm interviewing someone in her office or home, for example, one of the first things I may jot down are the titles of books on the bookshelf. Sometimes, details about gestures and settings can be worked into your paper. Most of all, the personal interview is preferable because it's more natural, more like a conversation.

Be prepared. You may have no choice in the type of interview. If your subject is off campus or out of state, your only options may be the telephone or the mail.

When contacting a subject for an interview, first state your name and then briefly explain your research project. If you were referred to the subject by someone she may know, mention that. A comment like, "I think you could be extremely helpful to me" or "I'm familiar with your work, and I'm anxious to talk to you about it" works well. That's called *flattery,* and as long as it isn't excessive or insincere, we're all vulnerable to it.

It is gracious to ask your prospective subject what time and place for an interview may be convenient for her. Nonetheless, be prepared to suggest some specific times and places to meet or talk. When thinking about when to propose the interview with an expert on your topic, consider arranging it *after* you've done some research. You will not only be more well informed; you will have a clearer sense of what you want to know and what questions to ask. (For information on preparing for and conducting an interview, see "Conducting Interviews" in Chapter 3.)

Planning Informal Surveys

Christine was interested in dream interpretation, especially exploring the significance of symbols or images that recur in many people's dreams. She could have simply examined her own dreams, but she thought it might be more interesting to survey a group of fellow students, asking how often they dream and what they remember about it. An informal survey, in which she would ask each person several standard questions, seemed worth trying.

You might consider it, too, if the responses of a group of people to some aspect of your topic would reveal a pattern of behavior, attitudes, or experiences worth analyzing. Informal surveys are decidedly unscientific. You probably won't get a large enough sample size, nor do you likely have the skills to design a poll that would produce statistically reliable results. But you probably won't actually base your paper on the survey results, anyway. Rather, you'll present specific, concrete information that *suggests* some patterns in your survey group or, at the very least, some of your own findings will help support your assertions.

Defining Goals and Audience

Begin planning your informal survey by defining what you want to know and whom you want to know it from. Christine suspected that many students have dreams related to stress. She wondered if there were any similarities among students' dreams. She was also curious about how many people remember their dreams, and how often, and if that might be related to gender. Finally, Christine wanted to find out whether people have recurring dreams and if so, what those were about. There were other things she wanted to know, too. But she knew she had to keep the survey short, probably no more than seven questions.

If you're considering a survey, in your research notebook, make a list of things you might want to find out and specify what group of people you plan to talk to. College students? Female college students? Attorneys? Guidance counselors? Be as specific as you can about your target group.

What Types of Questions?

Next, consider what approach you will take. Will you ask *open-ended questions,* which give respondents plenty of room to invent their own answers? For example, Christine might ask, Have you ever had any dreams that seem related to stress? The payoff for an open-ended question is that sometimes you get surprising answers. The danger, which seems real with Christine's question, is that you'll get no answer at all. A more *directed question* might be, Have you ever dreamed that you showed up for class and didn't know that there was a major exam that day? Christine will get an answer to this question—yes or no—but it doesn't promise much information. A third possibility is the *multiple-choice question.* It ensures an answer and is likely to produce useful information. For example:

Have you ever had any dreams similar to these?
- a. You showed up for a class and didn't know there was a major exam.
- b. You registered for a class but forgot to attend.
- c. You're late for a class or an exam but can't seem to move fast enough to get there on time.
- d. You were to give a presentation but forgot all about it.
- e. None of the above.*

Ultimately, Christine decided to combine the open-ended question about stress and the multiple-choice approach, hoping that if one didn't produce interesting information, the other would (see Figure 2-2). She also wisely decided to avoid asking more than seven questions, allowing her subjects to respond to her survey in minutes.

Survey Design

A survey shouldn't be too long (probably no more than six or seven questions), it shouldn't be biased (asking questions that will skew the answers), it should be easy to score and tabulate results (especially if you hope to survey a relatively large number of people), it should ask clear questions, and it should give clear instructions for how to answer.

As a rule, informal surveys should begin as polls often do: by getting vital information about the respondent. Christine's survey began with questions about the gender, age, and major of each respondent (see Figure 2-2). Depending on the purpose of your survey,

*Reprinted with permission of Christine Berquist.

The following survey contains questions about dreaming and dream content. The findings gathered from this survey will be incorporated into a research paper on the function of dreaming and what, if anything, we can learn from it. I'd appreciate your honest answers to the questions. Thank you for your time!

General Subject Information

Gender: ☐ Male   ☐ Female

Age: _____

Major: _____

Survey Questions
(circle all letters that apply)

1. How often do you remember your dreams?
   A. Almost every night
   B. About once a week
   C. Every few weeks
   D. Practically never

2. Have you ever dreamt that you were:
   A. Falling?
   B. Flying?

3. Have you ever dreamt of:
   A. Your death?
   B. The death of someone close to you?

4. Have you ever had a recurring dream?
   A. Yes
   B. No

   If yes,   How often? _____
           What period of your life? _____
           Do you still have it? _____

5. Have you ever had any dreams similar to these?
   A. You showed up for a class and didn't know there was a major exam.
   B. You're late for a class or an exam but can't seem to move fast enough to get there.
   C. You were to give a presentation but forgot all about it.

6. Do you feel your dreams:
   A. Hold some deep, hidden meanings about yourself or your life?
   B. Are meaningless?

7. Please briefly describe the dream you best remember or one that sticks out in your mind. (Use the back of this survey.)

FIGURE 2-2 Sample informal survey

Source: Reprinted with permission of Christine Berquist.

you might also want to know things such as whether respondents are registered to vote, whether they have political affiliations, what year of school they're in, or any number of other factors. Ask for information that provides different ways of breaking down your target group.

Avoid Loaded Questions.   Question design is tricky business. An obviously biased question—Do you think it's morally wrong to kill unborn babies through abortion?—is easy to alter by removing the charged and presumptuous language. (It is unlikely that all respondents believe that abortion is "killing.") One revision might be, Do you support or oppose providing women the option to abort a pregnancy during the first twenty weeks? This is a direct and specific question, neutrally stated, that calls for a yes or no answer. The question would be better if it were even more specific.

Controversial topics, like abortion, are most vulnerable to biased survey questions. If your topic is controversial, take great care to eliminate bias by avoiding charged language, especially if you have strong feelings yourself.

Avoid Vague Questions.   Another trap is vague questions: Do you support or oppose the university's alcohol policy? In this case, don't assume that respondents know what the policy is unless you explain it. Since the campus alcohol policy has many elements, this question might be redesigned to ask about one of them: The university recently established a policy that states that underage students caught drinking in campus dormitories are subject to eviction. Do you support or oppose this policy? Other, equally specific questions, might ask about other parts of the policy.

Drawbacks of Open-Ended Questions.   Open-ended questions often produce fascinating answers, but they can be difficult to tabulate. Christine's survey asked, Please briefly describe the one dream you best remember or one that sticks out in your mind. She got a wide range of answers—or sometimes no answer at all—but it was hard to quantify the results. Most everyone had different dreams, which made it difficult to discern much of a pattern. She was still able to use some of the material as anecdotes in her paper, so it turned out to be a question worth asking.

Designing Multiple-Choice Questions.   The multiple-choice question is an alternative to the open-ended question, leaving room for a number of *limited* responses, which are easier to quantify. Christine's survey had a number of multiple-choice questions.

The challenge in designing multiple-choice questions is to provide choices that will likely produce results. From her reading and talking to friends, Christine came up with what she thought were three stress-related dreams college students often experience (see question 5, Figure 2-2). The results were interesting (45 percent circled "B") but unreliable, since respondents did not have a "None of the above" option. How many respondents felt forced to choose one of the dreams listed because there was no other choice? Design choices you think your audience will respond to, but give them room to say your choices weren't theirs.

Continuum Questions. Question 6 (see Figure 2-2) has a similar choice problem in that it asks a direct either/or question: Do you feel your dreams: (a) Hold some deep, hidden meanings about yourself or your life? or (b) Are meaningless? Phrased this way, the question forces the respondent into one of two extreme positions. People are more likely to place themselves somewhere in between.

A variation on the multiple-choice question is the *continuum,* where respondents indicate how they feel by marking the appropriate place along a scale. Christine's question 6 could be presented as a continuum:

How do you evaluate the significance of your dreams? Place an "X" on the continuum in the place that most closely reflects your view.

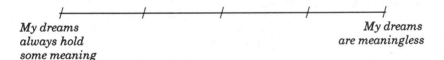

*My dreams
always hold
some meaning*

*My dreams
are meaningless*

Though it is a bit more difficult to tabulate results of a continuum, this method often produces reliable answers if the instructions are clear.

Planning for Distribution

Surveys can be administered in person or by phone, with the surveyor asking each respondent the questions and recording the answers, or by letting respondents fill out the surveys themselves. Although there are some real advantages to administering the survey yourself (or lining up friends to help you do it), reflect on how much time you want to devote to gathering the information. How important will the survey be to your paper? Are the results crucial to your argument? If not, consider doing what Christine did: Print up several hundred survey forms that are easy for respondents to fill out themselves, and distribute them with some help from your instructor or friends.

The next question is, How can you make sure you get back as many of the survey forms as possible? That topic is more fully discussed in the third week. (See "Conducting Surveys," Chapter 3.) For now, draft a survey, and line up some people to review it for you, including your instructor.

LOOKING BACK
BEFORE MOVING ON

With a tentative focus decided and a strategy planned, you're well prepared to immerse yourself in research. It might seem odd to do all this planning before you ever crack a card catalog, but it pays off in a much more efficient search.

Be prepared for surprises along the way. If the research and the writing process suddenly leads you down trails you didn't expect, it doesn't mean you've done something wrong. If the thesis you declare this week is shot full of holes next week, it doesn't mean that you're stupid. Through research, you discover what you didn't know and what you didn't know you knew. Research is supposed to rattle your cage, particularly if you've chosen a topic about which you have some passion. Get ready for an adventure.

3

□ ■ □

The Third Week

NOTETAKING
AS PREWRITING

I was never crazy about taking notes for a research paper. Note-taking seemed so tedious. Instead, I developed a love affair with the photocopier and walked around sounding like a slot machine, my pockets full of change, ready to bolt to the nearest copier whenever I encountered a promising article. I collected these articles to read later. I also checked out scores of books that seemed useful, rather than taking the time to skim them in the library and jot down notes on what seemed important. I was quite a sight at the end of the day, walking back to my dormitory or apartment, reeling under the weight of a mound of books and articles, all precariously balanced, defying natural laws.

When the time came to begin writing my paper, the work seemed agonizingly slow. I would consult my meager notes, thumb through two or three books from the stack, reread a dog-eared copy of an article, stop and think, write a line or two, stop and go back to a book, and then maybe write another line or two. I was always a slow writer, but I now realize that one major reason I got bogged down writing my research paper drafts was my inattention to note-taking. I paid the price for doing so little writing before I had to do the writing.

Becoming an
Activist Notetaker

Notetaking can and probably should begin the process of writing your paper. Notetaking is not simply a mechanical process of vacuuming up as much information as you can and depositing it on notecards or in a notebook with little thought. Your notes from sources are your first chance to *make sense* of the information you encounter, to make it your own. You do need more time to take thoughtful notes, but doing so pays off in writing a draft more quickly and in producing a paper that reflects your point of view much more strongly.

I'll show you what I mean. Here is a short passage from a book on soccer, *The Simplest Game,* by Paul Gardner:

> For American soccer the problem is two-fold. First the majority of people coaching youth soccer did not play the sport themselves, or played it only at a rather crude level. In other words, they are not in a position to coach by example. Second, even if the coaches were themselves skilled players, it is not at all clear to what extent ball skills can be coached.*

Jason, who was writing a paper that focused on the failings of American soccer, took the following notes on the passage. Notice how he used the source as a launching place for his own thinking. In this case, Jason didn't even quote Gardner but took several of the author's ideas and explored how they fit in his own experience.

So many times when I was young and playing soccer
the emphasis was placed simply on winning when it
should have been placed on teaching the skills
necessary to play. I remember being in the pack of
kids chasing the ball around just kicking it. The
coach I had never emphasized ball control, we
kicked and ran. That's it. The fastest players and
hardest kickers were the best. More time needs to

*Paul Gardner, *The Simplest Game* (Boston: Little, Brown, 1976), 193.

```
be spent on handling the ball and knowing what to
do with it in certain situations.*
```

Here is the passage in Jason's research paper that incorporated the earlier notes. Notice the similarity?

```
So many times when I was young and playing soccer
like Joey, the emphasis was on winning rather than
the skills necessary to play. I remember being in
the same pack of kids as Joey, chasing the ball
around. The coach that I had never emphasized ball
control. I can still hear him yell, "Dump and
chase!" Although it is unclear to what extent ball
skills can be coached, the coach should at least
spend time with players showing them technique
(Gardner 193).*
```

Because Jason was committed to thoughtful notetaking *as* he read, he got a jumpstart on his draft. But even more important, he took command of the material, using the original source purposefully, helping him convince readers that American soccer will never be competitive without major reforms.

Jason's complaint about the way young American soccer players are trained to "dump and chase" is actually a good metaphor for the way most students approach notetaking: Simply shovel as much information (mostly quotes) on notecards as you can and chase after more. But notetaking, like soccer, is a skill, and a remarkably undervalued one at that. Test your notetaking skills with the following exercise.

❑ *EXERCISE 3-1*
Creative Translations

The following passage is from Andrew Merton's article "Return to Brotherhood."

*Jason Pulsifer, University of New Hampshire, 1991. Used with permission.

For many adolescent males just out of high school, the transition to college represents a first step in a struggle for a kind of "manhood" from which women are viewed as objects of conquest—worthy, but decidedly inferior, adversaries. The idea of women as equals is strange and inconvenient at best, terrifying at worst. Unfortunately, most colleges and universities provide refuges ideally suited to reinforce these prejudices: fraternities.*

In your notebook, rewrite the passage in your own words in roughly the same length. This is called *paraphrasing*. You'll find it's easier to do if you first focus on understanding what Merton is trying to say and then write without looking much at the passage, if possible. If this is an in-class exercise, exchange your rewrite with a partner. Then read the following section on plagiarism.

□ ■ □

Recognizing Plagiarism

Simply put, *plagiarism* is using others' ideas *or* words as if they were your own. The most egregious case is handing in someone else's work with your name on it. Some schools also consider using one paper to meet the requirements of two classes to be a grave offense. But most plagiarism is unintentional. I remember being guilty of plagiarism when writing a philosophy paper my freshman year in college. I committed the offense largely because I didn't know what plagiarism was and I hadn't been adequately schooled in good scholarship (which is no excuse).

The best antidote to plagiarism is good notetaking. Examine the following two student paraphrases of the Merton passage. If each appeared in a final paper as you see it below, which student do you think would be guilty of plagiarism?

STUDENT A

According to Merton, for a lot of adolescent males
just out of high school, going to college is,
among other things, a journey into "manhood."
Women may become the respected enemy, seen as
things to conquer. The notion that women might be

*Andrew Merton, "Return to Brotherhood," *Ms.*, September 1985, 61+.

equals is not a comfortable one for these men, who often find fraternities a refuge ideally suited to promoting this stereotype.

STUDENT B

Many young men graduating from high school come to the university on the threshold of "manhood." As they come to terms with this, women become "worthy, but decidedly inferior, adversaries," an attitude that makes the notion of equality between the genders "inconvenient" or even "terrifying." The college fraternity becomes a safe haven for these men (Merton 192).

Both students' versions follow the organization of the original material fairly closely. Although doing so is not necessarily a fault, it does increase the risk of plagiarism. Student A most clearly crossed that line. You may not have thought so at first. After all, the writer did mention Merton in the beginning, whereas the second student did not.

But a closer look will reveal a problem with version A: Merton's words have become the writer's. Notice the phrase "for a lot of adolescent males" in version A. Merton used nearly the same language. In the last line of the paraphrase, "ideally suited" and "refuge" have been borrowed directly from Merton, without giving him credit using quotation marks (even though the word order has been altered somewhat). There's another more serious problem with Student A's paraphrase: Though Merton was mentioned in the text of the paraphrase, he must still be cited as the source. Using the Modern Language Association (MLA) citation system (which you'll learn more about in Chapter 4), a parenthetical reference should have been provided, listing the author and page number from which the material came.

Tactics for Avoiding Plagiarism

The use of quotation marks around the borrowed language would have helped Student A. Student B was careful about that; in her version, distinctive phrases from the original were all flagged by enclosing them in quotation marks. Though Student B didn't mention Merton, she did include a parenthetical citation of the source. But there's still a problem: Because the citation appears at the end of the paraphrase, it's unclear what part has been borrowed. Just the last line? Both paraphrases are poor, but it wouldn't take much to redeem Student B's version. She could simply clear up the confusion by mentioning Merton in the text. For example, she could begin as Student A did: "According to Andrew Merton, many young men . . ."

To avoid plagiarism, you must do two things: Let readers know (1) exactly what material is not your own and (2) exactly where that borrowed material came from. One notable exception to this is when you include what may be considered *common knowledge* in your paper. (See Chapter 4 for a fuller discussion of the common knowledge exception.) For example, you wouldn't need to cite the fact that John F. Kennedy was assassinated in Dallas in November 1963. That fairly well known piece of information doesn't belong to anyone, and it could be used without citation.

You'll learn more about how to cite material in the fourth week (Chapter 4), when you begin to write your paper. For now, keep the following in mind:

1. When you borrow language from an original source, always signal you've done so by using quotation marks.
2. Whenever possible, attribute the borrowed words, ideas, or information to its author *in your text* (e.g., "According to Andrew Merton" or "Merton argues" or "Merton observes," etc.).
3. Whether you attribute the borrowed material in your text or not, *you must cite* the original source. (For more information on how to use parenthetical citations, see "The Basics of Using Parenthetical Citation" in Chapter 4.)

☐ *EXERCISE 3-2*
Checking for Plagiarism

Look over your partner's paraphrase (or your own if you're not in class) of the Merton passage from Exercise 3-1, and ask your partner to examine yours. Do either of you see anything that could be considered plagiarism? Pay particular attention to language. Are the word choices of the paraphrase distinct from those of the original passage? Are quotes used to signal borrowed language? Discuss ways to remedy any potential problems.

Don't be alarmed if you were guilty of plagiarism here. Your error was unintentional. You were also doing an exercise. If your paraphrase did have problems, think back on how you wrote it. Did you spend a lot of time rereading the original as you were writing? Unintentional plagiarism often occurs because you just can't free yourself from the author's words. That freedom comes, in part, by finding your own writing voice as you begin to take notes. Your voice will likely be quite different from those of your sources and will naturally lead you away from their language and toward your own.

□ ■ □

How to Be a Purposeful Notetaker

Paraphrasing

You've already had practice with the paraphrase (a restatement of a source in roughly equal length) in Exercise 3-2. You may have discovered that writing a good paraphrase is harder than you thought, especially when being cautious to avoid plagiarism. Paraphrasing requires that you take possession of the information, make sense of it for yourself, and then remake it sensibly in your own words. But paraphrasing gets easier with practice. And when you begin to master the art of the paraphrase, you will also begin to take charge of your topic, *using* information deliberately, according to your own purpose.

In the last exercise, you were asked to paraphrase a passage on how fraternities promote sexist attitudes among young men. Some of you might be young men, who also happen to be fraternity brothers. You may not have thought much of the author's point of view. Suppose you were writing a paper whose purpose was to argue *against* a movement to abolish fraternities. Would that alter how you paraphrased the passage? Would you recombine or emphasize different elements of it?

Melding Paraphrase and Purpose.　Paraphrasing shouldn't be divorced from your purpose in writing the paper. Let me show you what I mean. The following line is from Paulo Friere's essay "The 'Banking' Concept of Education":

> In the banking concept of education, knowledge is a gift bestowed by those who consider themselves knowledgeable upon those whom they consider to know nothing.*

---

*Paulo Friere, "The 'Banking' Concept of Education," trans. Myra Bergman Ramos, in *Pedagogy of the Oppressed* (New York: Continuum, 1970).

A fairly neutral paraphrase of the Friere passage might be something like this:

```
One approach to education is to view students

as empty banks and teachers as depositors of

knowledge.
```

But suppose you're taking notes for a paper that focuses on educational reform, and you really agree with Friere's view that the "banking concept" is suspect, seeing it as strong evidence that something is wrong with the system. Your paraphrase will likely be quite different, perhaps this:

```
According to Paulo Friere, a noted critic of

current teaching methods, all too often teachers

see students as simply empty bank accounts into

which they must deposit knowledge.
```

See the difference? In this paraphrase, the writer emphasizes who is making the claim—"a noted critic"—and also stresses the banking metaphor, which implies that teachers disparage students by considering them intellectually bankrupt. The writer not only captures Friere's theme but deliberately picks up on the tone of his passage. And why not? Friere's critical tone nicely serves the writer's purpose: arguing for educational reforms.

Let's take this one step further. If good notes reflect a writer who actively responds to what a source is saying, then a paraphrase (or a summary or quote) can be a launching place for the writer's own thinking, a tool for her own analysis. This is when notetaking becomes most useful. Look what the same writer might do with the Friere passage:

```
Friere's "banking concept of education"--which

suggests that students are things into which

knowledge must be deposited--only further

alienates them from learning, reinforcing the idea

that knowledge isn't meant to be used but simply

absorbed like a sponge.
```

Technically, this is still a paraphrase, but it's so much more than a parroting of information. The writer is taking Friere's idea and using it to make a point of her own, extending her own analysis. Friere steps in and out, while the writer takes over.

As you're taking notes, *look for these opportunities to actively use sources to push your own thinking.* Though such notetaking requires a little more thought, the notes you produce will later become the meat of your research paper. You are, in effect, writing the paper as you research, saving time later. Just one note of caution: In your enthusiasm, be careful not to misrepresent the original author's ideas.

You may think it will take forever to take notes like these, but, with practice, you will find notetaking goes more quickly than you thought. Again, the key is to find some distance from the source so you can reflect on what the author's saying and how it relates to what you think. Two things will help you get that distance, especially when paraphrasing: Write your notes in your own voice, and don't feel obligated to mimic the original author's organization and emphasis. Select, recombine, and use only what you think is important. A technique discussed later in this chapter, "The Double-Entry Journal," also encourages this kind of notetaking. Give it a try.

Summarizing

I heard recently that, in order to sell a movie to Hollywood, a screenwriter should be able to summarize what it's about in a sentence. *"The Big Chill* is a film about six friends from the sixties who reunite some years later and are suddenly confronted with reconciling past and present." That statement hardly does justice to the film—which is about so much more than that—but I think it basically captures the story and its central theme.

Obviously, that's what a *summary* is: a reduction of longer material into some brief statement that captures a basic idea, argument, or theme from the original. As does paraphrasing, summarizing often requires careful thought, since you're the one doing the distilling, especially if you're trying to capture the essence of a whole movie, article, or chapter that's fairly complex.

But many times, summarizing involves simply boiling down a passage—not the entire work—to its basic idea. Mark, who researched drinking patterns among college students, found an article from the *Journal of Studies on Alcoholism* that surveyed students on how much they drink. Much of the article discussed methodology, which wasn't very useful to his paper, but one passage had some interesting facts:

Among respondents, 74% of the men and 85% of the women reported they did some drinking. A disproportionate share of the
moderate only drinkers are women (87%), whereas a disproportionate share of the heaviest drinkers are men (79%). With the
exception of the differences in the proportion of abstainers,
these findings are consistent with those of previous studies.
Studies have found the sex difference in abstinence (i.e., women
greater than men) to have decreased substantially (Hanson,
1977) or to have disappeared altogether (Glassco, 1985). On the
other hand, studies continue to find that heavy drinking is more
frequent among men than among women (Beck 1983; Egns,
1977; Strauss and Bacon 1953; Weschseler and McFadden,
1979; Wecshler and Rohiman, 1981).

Male and female respondents were compared in terms of
all the variables found related to drinking. Only two variables
distinguished the sexes—the encouragement by best male
friends to drink frequently and in heavy amounts. Men received
such encouragement more frequently than did women.

There's nothing particularly distinctive about how this information is said—in fact, it's pretty dry—so there's nothing particularly
quotable. And paraphrasing the whole passage seems unnecessary,
since some of the prose repeats itself, offering support from other
studies for assertions already made. But embedded in this passage is
some pretty interesting stuff, especially given Mark's purpose in
writing the research paper: to explain drinking patterns among college students and to discover why they seem to drink so much.

A simple summary might be something like this:

```
According to the Wiggins article, college men

drank more heavily than women, but men were more

likely than women to be encouraged to drink by

their best friends.
```

This summary captures what was most important in the longer
passage, especially given the purpose of the student's paper. Mark
now has some evidence of why some of his male college friends drink
heavily: They are encouraged by their buddies. And taking the time to
simply summarize the salient parts of the article now will save Mark
a lot of time later. He won't need to mess around with a photocopy of
the journal article, rereading the whole thing to rediscover what was
important. He will already know. And he may even be able to trans-

fer this summary directly to the appropriate part of his paper (with the proper citation, of course).

A summary such as this one, where you distill only part of a larger source, is selective. You choose to emphasize some key part of a source because it fits your paper's purpose. But the same warning applies to selective summarizing as was given earlier about paraphrasing: Don't misrepresent the general thrust of the author's ideas. Ask yourself, Does my selective use of this source seem to give it a spin the author didn't intend? Most of the time, I think you will discover the answer is no.

A summary, similar to a paraphrase, can prompt your own thinking. Remember Jason's notes on American soccer at the beginning of this chapter? His summary of a section of Gardner's book, which claimed that American soccer players are not taught necessary ball-handling skills, provided Jason with an opportunity to reflect on his own experience as a player and how that seemed to confirm Gardner's point.

As with paraphrase, your most useful summaries will be those that provide an opportunity for your own analysis, that get you thinking. As you take notes, look for the chance to let your summaries take off. Explore connections and contradictions with other sources as well as with your own experiences and observations. For example, here's what Taylor, who is critical of fraternities, did in her notes with a summary of the Merton passage on fraternities, discussed earlier:

```
Andrew Merton argues that fraternities are a "safe
refuge" for maturing young men who are threatened
by women. What makes them safe is what someone
else called "a conspiracy of silence" between
brothers about sexist behavior. It violates the
code to confront a brother. An exclusively male
culture will always treat women as outsiders.
```

Here, the writer's summary is the starting place for a brief discussion about Merton's premise, including a connection with something else Taylor had heard or read. Once again, you can see the writer taking over here, taking command of the original material, not just reciting its main point.

These kinds of notes, into which you inject your own thinking, may be new to you. This type of notetaking is a far cry from simply jotting down facts from the encyclopedia. But if you chose your topic because it's interesting to you, you may discover that it's quite natural to be an activist notetaker. You want to make sense of things because you want to learn.

Quoting

What will *not* seem new to you, most likely, is the habit of quoting sources in your notes and your paper. The quotation mark may be the student researcher's best friend, at least as demonstrated by how often papers are peppered by long quotes!

As a general rule, the college research paper should contain no more than 10 or 20 percent quoted material, but it's an easy rule to ignore. For one thing, quoting sources at the notetaking and drafting stages is quicker than restating material in your own words. When you quote, you don't have to think much about what you're reading; you just jot it down the way you see it, and if you have to, think about it later. That's the real problem with verbatim copying of source material: There isn't much thinking involved. As a result, the writer doesn't take possession of the information, shape it, and be shaped by it.

That's not to say that you should completely avoid quoting sources directly as a method of notetaking. If you're writing on a literary topic, for example, you may quote fairly extensively from the novel or poem you're examining. Or if your paper relies heavily on interviews, you'll want to bring in the voices of your subjects, verbatim.

When to Quote. As a rule, jot down a quote when someone says or writes something that is distinctive in a certain way and when restating it in your own words wouldn't possibly do the thought justice. I'll never forget a scene from the documentary *Shoah,* an eleven-hour film about the Holocaust, which presented an interview with the Polish engineer of one of the trains that took thousands of Jews to their deaths. Now an old man and still operating the same train, he was asked how he felt now about his role in World War II. He said quietly, "If you could lick my heart, it would poison you."

It would be difficult to restate the Polish engineer's comment in your own words. But more important, it would be stupid even to try. Some of the pain and regret and horror of that time in history is embedded in that one man's words. You may not come across such a distinctive quote as you read your sources this week, but be alert to *how* authors (and those quoted by authors) say things. Is the prose unusual, surprising, or memorable? Does the writer make a point in an interesting way? If so, jot it down.

Heidi, in her paper on the children's TV program "Sesame Street," began by quoting a eulogy for Muppets creator Jim Henson (see Appendix B). The quote is both memorable and touching. Heidi made an appropriate choice, establishing a tone that is consistent with her purpose: to respond to certain critics of the program. The fact that a quote sounds good isn't reason enough to use it. Like anything else, quotes should be used deliberately, with purpose.

There are several other reasons to quote a source as you're notetaking. Sometimes, it's desirable to quote an expert on your topic who is widely recognized in the field. Used to support or develop your own assertions, the voice of an authority can lend credit to your argument and demonstrate your effort to bring recognized voices into the discussion.

Another reason to quote a source is when his explanation of a process or idea is especially clear. Such quotes often feature metaphors. Robert Bly's *Iron John,* a book that looks at American men and their difficult journey into manhood, is filled with clear and compelling explanations of that process. As a son of an alcoholic father, I found Bly's discussion often hit home. Here, using a metaphor, he explains in a simple but compelling way how children in troubled homes become emotionally unprotected, something that often haunts them the rest of their lives:

> When a boy grows up in a "dysfunctional" family (perhaps there is no other kind of family), his interior warriors will be killed off early. Warriors, mythologically, lift their swords to defend the king. The King in a child stands for and stands up for the child's mood. But when we are children our mood gets easily overrun and swept over in the messed-up family by the more powerful, more dominant, more terrifying mood of the parent. We can say that when the warriors inside cannot protect our mood from being disintegrated, or defend our body from invasion, the warriors collapse, go into a trance, or die.*

I'm sure there's a more technical explanation for the ways parents in dysfunctional families can dominate the emotional lives of their children. But the warrior metaphor is so simple, and that is, partly, its power. As you read or take notes during an interview, be alert to sources or subjects who say something that gets right to the heart of an important idea. Listen for it.

---

*Robert Bly, *Iron John: A Book About Men* (Reading, MA: Addison-Wesley, 1990), 147.

If your paper is a literary topic—involving novels, stories, poems, and other works—then purposeful and selective quoting is especially important and appropriate. The texts and the actual language the writers use in them are often central to the argument you're making. If you're writing about the misfit hero in J. D. Salinger's novels, asserting that he embodies the author's own character, then you'll have to dip freely into his books, quoting passages that illustrate that idea.

Quoting Fairly. If you do choose to quote from a source, be careful to do three things: (1) Quote accurately, (2) make sure it's clear in your notes that what you're jotting down is quoted material, and (3) beware of distorting a quote by using it out of context. The first two guidelines protect you from plagiarism, and the last ensures that you're fair to your sources.

To guarantee the accuracy of a quote, you may want to photocopy the page or article with the borrowed material. A tape recorder can help in an interview, and so can asking your subject to repeat something that seems especially important. To alert yourself to which part of your notes is a quote of the source's words, try using oversized quotation marks around the passage so that it can't be missed.

Guarding against out-of-context quotations can be a little more difficult. After all, an isolated quote has already been removed from the context of the many other things a subject has said. That shouldn't be a problem if you have represented her ideas accurately. However, sometimes a quote can misrepresent a source by what is omitted. Simply be fair to the author by noting any important qualifications she may make to something said or written, and render her ideas as completely as possible in your paper.

☐ *EXERCISE 3-3*
Good Notes on Bad Writing

Get some practice with purposeful notetaking with the article "The Importance of Writing Badly," which follows. First, read it carefully, paying attention to what you agree or disagree with in the essay. Then, in your research notebook:

1. Summarize the article in a sentence or two.
2. Select at least two passages that seem quotable to you, and carefully jot them down.
3. Below your summary, do a five-minute fastwrite in which you explore your reaction to the article. What did it make you think or remember about the way you learned to write? What asser-

tions did you really agree with or disagree with? Why? What is the author missing in his argument? How might you go further?
4. Now take ten minutes and compose a paragraph that brings in summary, quote, and perhaps paraphrase to support your own reactions to the ideas in the article. Obviously, take care to avoid any plagiarism by using your own voice, by attributing the source, and by using quotations marks to signal borrowed language. Use the article, but make it your own.

□ ■ □

The Importance of Writing Badly
by Bruce Ballenger

I WAS grading papers in the waiting room of my doctor's office the other day, and he said, "It must be pretty eye-opening reading that stuff. Can you believe those student's had four years of high school and still can't write?"

I've heard that before. I hear it almost every time I tell a stranger that I teach writing at a university.

I also hear it from colleagues brandishing red pens who hover over their students' papers like Huey helicopters waiting to flush the enemy from the tall grass, waiting for a comma splice or a vague pronoun reference or a misspelled word to break cover.

And I heard it this morning from the commentator on my public radio station who publishes snickering books about how students' abuse the sacred language.

I have another problem: getting students to write badly.

Most of us have lurking in our past some high priest of good grammar whose angry scribbling occupied the margins of our papers. Mine was Mrs. O'Neill, an eighth grade teacher with a good heart but no patience for the bad sentence. Her favorite comment on my writing was "awk," which now sounds to me like the grunt of a large bird, but back then meant "awkward." She didn't think much of my sentences.

I find some people who reminisce fondly about their own Mrs. O'Neill, usually an English teacher who terrorized them into worshipping the error-free sentence. In some cases that terror paid off when it was finally transformed into an appreciation for the music a well-made sentence can make.

But it didn't work that way with me. I was driven into silence, losing faith that I could ever pick up the pen without breaking the rules or drawing another "awk" from a doubting reader. For years I wrote only when forced to, and when I did it was never good enough.

Many of my students come to me similarly voiceless, dreading the first writing assignment because they mistakenly believe that how they say it matters more than discovering what they have to say.

The night before the essay is due they pace their rooms like expectant fathers, waiting to deliver that perfect beginning. They wait and they wait and they wait. It's no wonder the waiting often turns to hating what they have written when they finally get it down. Many pledge to steer clear of my English classes, or any class that demands much writing.

My doctor would say my students' failure to make words march down the page with military precision is another example of a failed educational system. The criticism sometimes takes on political overtones. On my campus, for example, the right-wing student newspaper demanded an entire semester of Freshman English be devoted to teaching students the rules of punctuation.

There is, I think, a hint of elitism among those who are so quick to decry the sorry state of the sentence in the hands of student writers. A colleague of mine, an Ivy League graduate, is among the self-appointed grammar police, complaining often about the dumb mistakes his students make in their papers. I don't remember him ever talking about what his students are trying to say in those papers. I have a feeling he's really not all that interested.

Concise, clear writing matters, of course, and I have a responsibility to demand it from my students. But first I am far more interested in encouraging thinking than error-free sentences. That's where bad writing comes in.

When I give my students permission to write badly, to suspend their compulsive need to find the "perfect way of saying it," often something miraculous happens: Words that used to trickle forth come gushing to the page. The students quickly find their voices again, and even more important, they are surprised by what they have to say. They can worry later about fixing awkward sentences. First they need to make a mess.

It's harder to write badly than you might think. Haunted by their own Mrs. O'Neill, some students can't overlook the sloppiness of their sentences or their lack of eloquence, and quickly stall out and stop writing. When the writing stops, so does the thinking.

The greatest reward in allowing students to write badly is that they learn that language can lead them to meaning, that words can be a means for finding out what they didn't know they knew. It usually happens when the words rush to the page, however awkwardly.

I don't mean to excuse bad grammar. But I cringe at conservative educational reformers who believe writing instruction should return to primarily teaching how to punctuate a sentence and use Roget's Thesaurus. If policing student papers for mistakes means alienating young writers from the language we expect them to master, then the exercise is self-defeating.

It is more important to allow students to first experience how language can be a vehicle for discovering how they see the world. And what matters in this journey—at least initially—is not what kind of car you're driving, but where you end up.

Three Notetaking Tips That Will Save You a Headache Later On

1. *Before you take any notes, write down the complete bibliographic information on the source (author, title, publication information).* Why? Because you'll save yourself a late-night trip back to the library to get the bibliographic information on that one source you forgot to write down. In the first week, the library exercise (Exercise 1-4) gave you some practice in getting what you need to cite a source. You'll need to cite slightly different information for a journal article than for, say, a book. Get all of the information for every source. (See "Preparing the 'Works Cited' Page" in Chapter 5 for exactly what bibliographic information you'll need to list different kinds of sources in your paper.)

2. *When you do take notes, make sure you get the page the material was taken from.* It's so easy to forget. But as you'll see later, you need to show exactly where you borrowed from a source when you cite the material in the text of your paper. If you go to the next page of a source in the middle of your notes on it, use the symbol "/" to remind yourself of that fact. If you skip more than one page, use "//" in your notes as a reminder. Or use a system like the double-entry journal (see later in this chapter) that encourages you to note page numbers in the margins as you go along.

3. *Be accurate.* Sure, you think. That's obvious. But there are so many ways to mess up. The most common mistake is to quote a

source inaccurately—inadvertently leaving out a word, using the wrong word, misspelling a word, or leaving out a chunk of the original passage without signaling to your readers that you've done so. Remember to use an *ellipsis* (three dots, ". . .") to indicate where you've left out a portion of the author's text that you decided wasn't important to your point. Also keep track of when you're quoting in your notes by using oversized quotation marks that cannot be missed. Most important, make sure you've summarized the author's ideas fairly and accurately and that he meant to say what you've represented as such.

NOTETAKING TECHNIQUES

I must confess to an irrational dislike of notecards—too many bad memories of running around my public library at home, clutching a stack of 3" × 5" index cards bound by a fat rubber band, each containing some fragment of knowledge I had to figure out what to do with. Those notecards are the most tangible relics of my research failures.

But many of us were initially taught to use notecards for good reason: Researchers *do* often deal with fragments of information as they research their papers, and it is challenging to organize that material. Notecards—systematically used—can help solve those problems. I still don't like them, but a lot of people do.

A few years from now, by the time you've written a score of research papers for college courses, you'll probably also have strong opinions about which notetaking method works for you. Following are reviews of two notetaking methods for you to consider as you begin to fashion your own way of doing things. Use the method that makes the most sense to you, adapting it to your needs.

The Notecard System

You've probably used notecards before, but I'll review some of the ways researchers make them work. The 3" × 5" card is the traditional size. It is easy to handle, and its small size challenges you to be selective about what you write down. Other people swear by the 4" × 6" size. Try them both and see what you think.

Generally, you develop two separate stacks of cards as you work: bibliography cards and actual notes cards.

Bibliography cards (see Figure 3-1) each list complete bibliographic information (author, title, publication information) for a

Bly, Robert. <u>Iron John: A Book</u>
<u>About Men.</u> Boston: Addison-Wesley
Publishing Co, Inc., 1990.

A

Larson, Richard L. "The 'Research
Paper' in the Writing Course:
A Non-Form of Writing." College
English 44 (1982); 811.

B

Diamonti, Nancy.
    Personal interview.
    Dover, 5 Nov. 1990.

C

FIGURE 3-1 Sample bibliography notecards: (A) a book; (B) a periodical;
(C) an interview

source, one source per card. Note that a bibliography card for a book may also include the library call number. Prepare the bibliography card for each source as soon as you begin working from it. Don't put this off, or you may forget.

This bundle of cards is your working bibliography. As you collect cards, keep them in alphabetical order to simplify writing your "Works Cited" page when you draft your paper.

Index cards containing notes are each keyed to a bibliography card. A lot of people use a coding system—usually, numbering each bibliography card and the notes that correspond to that source—but it's too easy to mess up the numbers and end up citing the wrong source. Though it takes a little more time, list the last name of each source and the page number of the material at the top of each note-card (see Figure 3-2).

Developing a System

The notecard method pays off if you develop a system for orga-nizing the information *before* you start. You can alter the system as you go along, but you have to put some thought into it before you plunge headlong into notetaking.

Keying to Your Outline.   Think about how you can break your topic down into different categories of information that then can be described by a corresponding keyword on each notecard. For example, if you can tentatively outline your paper at this point, you can key each card to part of the outline. Christine's rough outline for her paper on the function of dreams had the following parts: History of Dreams, Dream Research, Theories and Interpretations of Dream Functions, and Dreaming Trends. All of these are convenient key-words for her cards (see Figure 3-2). A single source may provide cards in one or more of the categories, even if only a note or two.

Keying to Your Questions.   Another approach is to key cards to the questions that will help you answer your central focusing ques-tion. You developed a tentative list of those in your research notebook last week. For example, the paper that asks Why do college students drink so much? raises these subsidiary questions: Does it have to do with the availability of alcohol? Is there statistical evidence that stu-dents drink a lot? Do college men drink more than women? Does the existence of fraternities and sororities have anything to do with drinking patterns? What is the "drink of choice" among college stu-

Long 787-821   <u>Theories of Dreams</u>

Basically 3 theories that explain purpose and
meaning of dreams.
   1   reveal our hidden thoughts and tensions
   2   manifest the random firings of neurons
   3   clear our brains of useless material

Dreams provide "the royal road" to the
unconscious.

---

*Always cite
last name
of source
and page
numbers*

*Quotation marks darkened to
emphasize what is quoted*

*Categories of
information,
keyed to
outline*

Boxer 50   <u>Interpretation</u>

According to Hobson, dreams can be emotional
because the brainstem activitates to emotional
center - the limbic center - and because the
'startle network' (part of brain that speeds
the heart) is turned on-

Hobson: dreams have no hidden meaning. The
brain "makes the best of a bad job . . . its
like a Rorschach test: the brain stem throws
up some inkblot and the cerebral cortex tries
to figure out what it might be"

FIGURE 3-2   Sample notes on notecards

dents? Each of these questions offers a keyword for use in organizing separate categories of cards (e.g., Availability, Statistical Evidence, Gender, etc.).

Keying to Your Categories. You might also key notecards to useful categories of information that could apply to any paper: Anecdotes, Case Studies, Statistics, Research Findings, Survey Results, and Quotes. Though these keywords are somewhat less precise than those identified earlier, they may prove useful in the early stage of notetaking.

Coming up with a system for organizing the information you collect on index cards does take a little time, and it may even seem a little compulsive. But when you're done taking notes, you'll be able to lay all your cards on the table and see at a glance how the pieces fit together, rather than frantically flipping the pages in your notebook, trying to find what you need.

What distinguishes the notecard method from most others is the ability to organize information by *topic*. When it works, the index card system really makes writing the paper easier. On the other hand, when you use a notebook or a journal for notetaking, you're much more likely to organize the information by *source*. The principle advantage of the notebook is that you don't get as confused about what came from where. One notebook system—the double-entry journal—has a really appealing feature: It actively encourages you to think about your sources and what they have to say.

The Double-Entry Journal

The double-entry approach is basically this: Divide each page of your research notebook into two columns (or use opposing pages). On each left side, compile your notes from a source—paraphrases, summaries, quotes—and on each right side, comment on them. Your commentary can be pretty open ended: What strikes you? What was confusing? What was surprising? How does the information stand up to your own experiences and observations? Does it support or contradict your thesis (if you have one at this point)? How might you use the information in your paper? What purpose might it serve? What do you think of the source? What further questions does the information raise that might be worth investigating? How does the information connect to other sources you've read?

There are a variety of ways to approach the double-entry journal. The method I favor is first, to take notes in the left column as I read through the source. Then I put the source aside and fastwrite my response in the right column, referring to my notes in the left whenever it seems helpful to push my thinking along. Figure 3-3 presents two pages from my journal, in which I took notes on an article on teaching the research paper.

Notice that the bibliographic information on the source—in this case, an article by Richard Larson—is listed at the top of the first page and then abbreviated at the top of subsequent pages in my notebook. I also listed the page number from which the material was taken in the far-lefthand margin. That way, I never lose track of what came from where.

My notes in the left columns of these pages are a combination of paraphrases, summaries, and quotes. I flagged the quotes with oversized quotation marks to avoid confusion. You may notice my analysis in the right column is not necessarily correlated to the notes in the left. I just pick up on an idea and run with it until it stalls, and then I consult my notes to get me going again. The writing in this column isn't particularly polished. That doesn't bother me. I can fix it up if I use this material in a paper.

Jason used a slightly different approach in researching a paper on the failings of American soccer. Figure 3-4 shows several pages of his double-entry notes on Gardner's *The Simplest Game.* Jason used the left column exclusively for quoting and the right for summaries, paraphrases, and analyses of those passages.

What I like about the double-entry journal system is that it turns me into a really active reader as I'm taking notes for my essay. That blank column on the right, like the whirring of my word processor right now, impatiently urges me to figure out what I think through writing. All along, I've said the key to writing a strong research paper is *making the information your own.* Developing your own thinking about the information you collect, as you go along, is one way to do that. Thoughtful notes are so easy to neglect in your mad rush to simply take down a lot of information. The double-entry journal won't let you neglect your own thinking, or at least, it will remind you when you do.

The double-entry system does have a drawback. Unlike index card systems, double-entry journals don't organize your information particularly well. A lot of page flipping is involved to find pieces of information as you draft your paper. But I find I often remember which sources have what information, partly because I thought about what might be important as I read and took notes on each source.

Larson, Richard L. "The Research Paper in the Writing Course: A Non-form of Writing." College English 44 (1982)

1590

5-29

812

"The 'generic research' paper as a concept" is unworkable, and gives students mistaken notions of what research is.

Range of research activities besides library research are often, by implication, omitted. (e.g. interviews, experiments, observations, lectures, etc).

813

Research is an "activity" not a kind of writing. Larson argues that suggesting that a research paper is recognizably distinct is mistaken "If almost any paper is potentially a paper incorporating the fruits of research, the term "research paper" has virtually no value as an identification of a kind of substance in a paper."

"research, by Larson's def: ...any process by which data outside the immediate and purely personal experiences of the writer are gathered." That broad definition is not implied by the way research paper

Larson's is a cogent analysis of how we teach research papers as these kind of "generic" creatures that are readily identifiable as a distinct genre. It's crucial that students see research as a source of information that can inform all writing, even the personal essay. To teach it, as Larson observes, as a "separately defined activity" is to defeat that purpose. (See quote on next page). He also makes a strong point about the emphasis on library research as the only acceptable kind of research. That's a "disservice" to our students and also simply wrong. Research should not be so narrowly defined. Larson supports my belief that there should be an emphasis on non-library sources — especially interviews — in The Curious Researcher. Expand the notion of research, though undoubtedly the library will be a key source always.

FIGURE 3-3 Sample double-entry journal: Basic style

Larson, Richard L. ②
"Research Paper in Writing Course"

1591

is currently taught. Almost always meant to suggest library research.

814 No accepted modes of discourse in composition provides readily identifiable home for the research paper. (See Kinneavy, A Theory of Discourse).

→ "But much is lost by teaching the research paper in writing courses as a separately defined activity. For by teaching the generic 'research paper' as a separate activity, instructors in writing signal to their students that there is a kind of writing that incorporates the results of research, and there are (by implication) many kinds of writing that do not and need not do so."

815 Larson observes that we often presume to prepare students for writing research papers in other disciplines, but how can we presume to do so? Are we equipped to teach students how to evaluate data from an anthropological investigation or a scientific experiment, or design an psychological study → cont'd next page

Discussion here is impt., but I was unfamiliar w/ works Larson cited— check Kinneavy, D'Angelo A Conceptual Theory of Rhetoric. Larson's observation that research paper is not identifiable form, though many suggest it is, is crucial evidence supporting contention that all forms are subservient to purpose. The real struggle for a writer is not to first pick an appropriate form off the shelf, but to discover her purpose and that find a form that serves it. (Murray). So many writer teachers traditionally teach students to master-form before they learn to take command of the inquiry. Especially true of the research paper.

FIGURE 3-3 Continued

Jason Pulsifer

Gardner, Paul   The Simplest Game
Boston: Little, Brown; c 1976

p. 101   England:

The number of games played will be 42 in league, 6 in English Cup, plus anything from 2 to 13 games in European competition — a total of 54 games.

The players in the US would never play such a lengthy schedule. In the USL now they play 20 games max. and games are only played 1 or 2 times a week at the most.

For a top player, the weekly basic wage would be between £150 and £200 ($5,600–$20,300/year), for an average player around £70 ($8,320/yr); bonuses will average £60 for a tie, £120 for a win, perhaps adding £3500 a year.

If a player is selected to play for the national team, he will be paid (by the Football Association) a fee of £200 for each game, plus £200 for a win, or £100 for a tie. If it's a WC game fees and bonuses are considerably higher. The English players who won the WC

In the 1990 WC US players received ~~about~~ ~~3500 4000~~ hardly anything except the memory of a lifetime. To prove the meager earnings of US players, Eric Wynalda got a red card (ejection) which means a $7,000 fine, he couldn't even pay it because his yearly earnings were about

---

FIGURE 3-4 Sample double-entry journal: Alternate style
Source: Jason Pulsifer, University of New Hampshire, 1991. Used with permission.

Gardner, Simplest Game

in 1966, for instance, received $3,500 $4000. Americans $5000 each, which was thought to be a staggering figure at the time, but which now looks utterly puny when compared to the $150,000 that each WC player received as a bonus in 1974.

don't want to spend big money on soccer. Partly because there are no players worth it.

p.102 At the center of all this money-making and money spending is the soccer player himself. He may be Dutch or Brazilian or English or Italian or Mexican or, indeed, from almost anywhere in the

103 world. To try & paint the picture of a "typical" professional soccer player is like chasing a will-o'-the-wisp, because the game is played by too many countries, cultures and races for a meaningful average to be arrived at. Nevertheless, there are 2 characteristics likely to hold good for any randomly selected player. He will be from a working-class background and he will have finished his formal education in his early teens.

So wrong in the U.S. Everywhere else in the world soccer is a blue collar sport (working class) but in the U.S. it's mostly played by upper-middle class children whose families are well-off and previously come from white collar background.

Children in other countries mostly Underdeveloped Countries play soccer all day long. They don't have much schooling so it leaves more time for them to do other things like play soccer. A rough estimate would be that a Brazilian child plays everyday for at least 5-8 hours while U.S. children have soccer practice 2 days a week and 1 game on Sat. Practices run about 90 minutes - 2 hours.

Another discrepancy between soccer players in the U.S.

FIGURE 3-4 Continued

DIGGING DEEPER
FOR INFORMATION

At the end of the third week of the research assignment last semester, Laura showed up at my office, looking pale.

"I spent all night at the library, and I couldn't find much on my topic," she said. "What I *could* find, the library didn't have—it was missing, or checked out, or wasn't even part of the collection. I may have to change my topic."

"I hate libraries!" she said, the color returning to her face.

Laura's complaint is one that I hear often at this point in the research process, especially from students who have dutifully tried to find a narrow focus for their papers, only to realize—they think—that there isn't enough information to make the topic work. They have tried the card catalog, and InfoTrac, and the newspaper indexes. They have even tried the *Social Science Index* or *Humanities Index* or several CD databases for journal articles. The students found a few articles but not enough for a ten-page paper. Like Laura, they may decide to broaden their focus or bail out on their topic altogether, even though they're still interested in it.

I always give these frustrated students the same advice: Don't despair yet. And don't give up on your narrow focus or your topic until you've dug more deeply for information. There are still some more specialized indexes to try and some nonlibrary sources to consider. You are, in a sense, like the archaeologist who carefully removes the dirt from each layer of a dig site, looking to see what it might reveal. If little turns up, the next layer is systematically explored and then the next, until the archaeologist is convinced she's digging in the wrong place. Student researchers too often give up the dig before they've removed enough dirt, believing too quickly there's nothing there.

If you're still curious about your topic and your tentative focus but you're not finding much information, work through the following three levels of the search before you decide to explore different ground. It might also be productive to expand the site of your search; you might basically be looking in the right place but not ranging far enough, perhaps limiting yourself to looking at books and articles when the real riches are in less conventional sources, possibly outside the library.

To help keep track of the ground you cover as you dig more deeply into your topic, check off the sources you've consulted at the end of each section in "Mapping Your Search," listing the names of the sources you used in the blanks. Your instructor may ask you to show her the trails you've followed as you discuss where else to look.

First-Level Searching

The library exercise completed in the first week (Exercise 1-4) asked you to search basic reference sources: general encyclopedias, books, periodicals, newspapers, and government documents. Consider these sources the first level of the dig. Make sure that you check *all* of them before you move to the next level. Here are a few sources that students commonly neglect:

■ *Bibliographies in the backs of articles and books.* These can provide a wealth of possibilities. Look for additional sources cited by the author that seem promising.

■ Social Science, Humanities, *or* General Science Indexes *(books or computer).* Remember, these are general indexes to journal articles published every year. Go back a few years if you haven't done so already. Because these are less familiar indexes, students often neglect to use them. It's crucial to at least check these for articles on your topic.

■ *Government documents.* This is a much neglected source of information from the largest publisher in the world. Make sure you check the *Monthly Catalog of U.S. Government Publications.*

■ *Alternative subject headings.* Maybe you've been too wedded to a particular subject heading in doing your initial search. Try some variations. Go back to the *LC Subject Headings* for some other possibilities, or pay attention to the "see also" prompts in the indexes you're looking at.

MAPPING YOUR SEARCH:
THE FIRST LEVEL

Check off the sources you've consulted, and list the names of indexes you've reviewed in the spaces provided.

☐ General encyclopedias _____

_____

☐ Card catalog

☐ Popular periodical indexes _____

_____

☐ Academic journal indexes _____

_____

☐ Newspaper indexes _____

_____

☐ Government document indexes _____

_____

Second-Level Searching

By the time you reach this level in your dig, you will have at least consulted the major general indexes on your topic. If you're swamped with information at this point, it means one of two things: You're a thorough researcher, or your focus is too broad. You decide which it is, though I strongly encourage you to consider tightening your focus and resuming the dig. You're likely to find even more interesting stuff that will contribute to a paper that will probably surprise both you and your readers.

If you're still coming up empty handed and not finding much information after completing the first-level search, obviously, proceed with the second level.

For all of the searches suggested in the following sections (except those of computer databases), Sheehy's *Guide to Reference Books* is invaluable.* It's like a mall—you can do all your shopping there. All you need to know is where to look, and to determine that, place your topic in one or more general fields: humanities, social and behavioral sciences, history and area studies, or science, technology, and medicine. Under each general topic, find several more specific areas of study that might include your topic. Look for the specialized reference sources in that field that seem promising.

Guide to Reference Books is my favorite general reference work of its type, but if your library doesn't have it, try these alternatives:

Hillard, James. *Where to Find What: A Handbook to Reference Service.* Metuchen, NJ: Scarecrow, 1984.
McCormick, Mona. *The New York Times Guide to Reference Materials.* New York: Times Books, 1985.

*Eugene P. Sheehy, ed., *Guide to Reference Books,* 10th ed. (Chicago: ALA, 1986).

Specialized Indexes to Journals

You're familiar with the *Social Science* and *Humanities Indexes,* which are general indexes to journal articles in various fields. What you may not know is that each discipline has its own more specialized indexes. For example, in psychology, *Psychological Abstracts* provides brief summaries of research published in the field every year in all the key journals. (The CD version is called Psyclit.) In political science, there's the Public Affairs Information Service (PAIS), often available as a computer database. Philosopher's have the *Philosopher's Index,* and biologists have *Biological Abstracts* (also on CD). Often, these specialized indexes include material that you won't find in the more general indexes because specialized indexes cover more journals in a given field. That's why they're worth checking, even if you've been through the *Social Science, General Science,* or *Humanities Indexes.*

Following is a list of one key index in each field. There are more. For a more complete list, check the *Guide to Reference Books.* You can find the indexes listed most often as bound volumes in your campus library, but many are also available as databases on CD. Ask your reference librarian in which forms they are available.

ART
Art Index. New York: Bowker, 1929–date.

BIOLOGICAL SCIENCES
Biological Abstracts. Philadelphia: Biological Abstracts, 1926–date.

BUSINESS
Business Periodicals Index. New York: Wilson, 1958–date.

CHEMISTRY
Chemical Abstracts: Key to the World's Chemical Literature. Columbus, OH: American Chemical Society, 1907–date (weekly).

COMMUNICATIONS
Communications Abstracts. Beverly Hills, CA: Sage, 1978–date.

COMPUTER SCIENCE
Applied Science and Technology Index. New York: Wilson, 1958–date.

ENVIRONMENT
Biological Abstracts. Philadelphia: Biological Abstracts, 1926–date.

ECONOMICS
Journal of Economic Literature. Nashville, TN: American Economic Association, 1964–date.

EDUCATION
Education Index. New York: Wilson, 1929–date.

ENGLISH AND LITERATURE
MLA International Bibliography of Books and Articles on the Modern Language and Literatures. New York: Modern Language Association, 1921–date.

FILM
Film Literature Index. Albany, NY: Film and Television Documentation Center, 1973–date.

GEOGRAPHY
Social Sciences Index. New York: Wilson, 1974–date.

GEOLOGY
Bibliography and Index of Geology. Boulder, CO: AGA, 1933–date.

HEALTH AND PHYSICAL EDUCATION
Education Index. New York: Wilson, 1929–date.

HISTORY
America: History and Life. Santa Barbara, CA: ABC-Clio, 1964–date.

JOURNALISM
Humanities Index. New York: Wilson, 1974–date.

MATHEMATICS
General Science Index. New York: Wilson, 1978–date.

MEDICINE
Cumulated Index Medicus. Bethesda, MD: U.S. Department of Health and Human Services, 1959–date.

MUSIC
Music Index. Warren, MI: Information Coordinations, 1949–date.

PHILOSOPHY
Philosopher's Index. Bowling Green, KY: Bowling Green University, 1967–date.

PHYSICS
Applied Science and Technology Index. New York: Wilson, 1958–date.

POLITICAL SCIENCE
Social Science Index. New York: Wilson, 1974–date.

PSYCHOLOGY
Psychological Abstracts. Lancaster, PA: APA, 1974–date.

RELIGION
Religion and Theological Abstracts. Chicago: ATLA, 1949–date.

SOCIOLOGY
Sociological Abstracts. New York: Sociological Abstracts, 1952–date.

WOMEN'S STUDIES
Women's Studies Abstracts. Rush, NY: Rush, 1972–date.

Specialized Dictionaries and Encyclopedias

Every discipline also has its own specialized dictionaries and encyclopedias. Such encyclopedias, especially, can provide useful articles. For example, if you were researching steroid use by athletes, you could check the *Encyclopedia of Sports*.* If you were researching the work of American photographer Ansel Adams, you might consult the *Encyclopedia of American Art*.** Specialized dictionaries can also be handy to help translate difficult technical terms encountered as you

---

Encyclopedia of Sports (New York: Barnes and Noble, 1978) (supplements).
**Encyclopedia of American Art* (New York: Dutton, 1981).

read journal articles in the field. For a complete list of specialized dictionaries and encyclopedias in your subject area, consult the *Guide to Reference Books.*

Bibliographies

Another kind of specialized reference book available in most disciplines is the bibliographic index. Don't confuse this type of source with the bibliographic citations at the end of a book or article. That's a bibliography, too—a list of materials used by the author. A bibliographic index also lists books and articles but for a particular field of study, broken down according to various areas of interest. For example, the student working on the paper mentioned earlier about special problems faced by teenage children of alcoholics could look in the index at the back of the *Guide to Reference Books* under "Alcoholism" and find the page number for bibliographies on the subject. There's quite a list, including a bibliography of books and articles on alcohol and reproduction, another on alcohol education materials published in the United States, and many other lists of sources on areas of interest in the study of alcoholism. One bibliography seems particularly promising: *Alcoholism and Youth: A Comprehensive Bibliography,* by Grace Barnes.*

A good bibliography can save you a lot of work. Someone else has gone to the trouble of surveying the literature for you, and you can pick and choose what seems useful. One disadvantage is that often bibliographies do not include recent material. Obviously, check when the reference was published, and decide how far back you want to go.

Specialized Computer Databases

The bound reference book is quickly being replaced by the computer terminal, and in many ways, that's good. For instance, once you get past any lingering "computerphobia," you'll find searching databases is easy and efficient. Many of the specialized indexes mentioned above are available both as bound books and on computer. There are also a number of additional specialized databases in each field to which your library may subscribe. For example, ABI/INFORM is a database in the business field that's available at a computer terminal in my campus library. ERIC is another database commonly available for researchers in education.

---

*Grace Barnes, *Alcoholism and Youth: A Comprehensive Bibliography* (Westport, CT: Greenwood, 1982).

Ask your reference librarian what's available. A useful directory to computer databases, organized by subject or name, is:

> *Computer-Readable Databases: A Directory and Data Source-book*. Edited by Martha E. Williams. Chicago: American Library Association, 1985–date (2 vol).

MAPPING YOUR SEARCH:
THE SECOND LEVEL

Document your dig into second-level sources here. Check the types of sources you consulted, and list the specific titles.

☐ Specialized encyclopedias and dictionaries _____

_____

☐ Specialized journal indexes _____

_____

☐ Bibliographies _____

_____

☐ Computer databases _____

_____

Third-Level Searching

By now, you're already way past the superficial searching for information you used to do for high school research papers. The *Reader's Guide* may already seem almost elementary. By the time you've completed first- and second-level searches for information, you've been pretty thorough. You've worked through general indexes as well as specialized indexes and encyclopedias and databases. If you're still not comfortable with how much information you've collected, move on to a third-level search or try expanding the search (see later in this chapter).

You may feel as if you have plenty of information to work with at this point. If so, it may be time to think about writing your paper. However, as you begin your draft next week or revise it later, you may discover that you had less material than you thought and need to do some more digging. A third-level search may be the place to start.

Search by Author

Typically, most searching is done by subject, but you may suddenly open up new doors if you begin using particular authors' names as keywords. Look for authors' names that repeatedly appear in bibliographies from articles and books you've found on your topic. These people are likely important authorities in the field and may have much more to say about your topic. Also note the names of authors whose work you particularly like or who seem influential. Use the card catalog and periodical indexes to see what else these authors have written. Is any of this information relevant?

Using Citation Indexes.   Three citation indexes may also prove valuable when you have some authors' names to work with:

> *Arts and Humanities Citation Index.* Philadelphia: Institute for Scientific Information, 1977–date.
> *Science Citation Index.* Philadelphia: Institute for Scientific Information, 1961–date.
> *Social Science Citation Index.* Philadelphia: Institute for Scientific Information, 1966–date.

Each of these indexes has three separate but related volumes: the *Source Index,* the *Citation Index,* and the *Permuterm Subject Index.*

Among other things, these indexes identify when the authors were cited *by other writers* in their own work, which may be relevant to your work. For example, when researching the purpose of dreaming, Christine came across an influential theory and book, *The Dreaming Brain* by J. Allan Hobson,* that she wanted to discuss in her paper. The *Social Science Citation Index* helped her find other authors who mentioned Hobson in their articles, including a review of *The Dreaming Brain* (see Figure 3-5). By looking under "Hobson" in the *Source Index,* Christine was also able to find articles Hobson had written in a given year and a complete bibliography for each (see Figure 3-6).

The *Permuterm Subject Index* is the place to check if you don't have a specific author in mind. It will refer you to authors in the *Source Index.* The citation indexes take a little getting used to, but they're often full of helpful leads.

---

*J. Allan Hobson, *The Dreaming Brain* (New York: Basic Books, 1988).

Author

Reference year (* means undated); title of Hobson's book

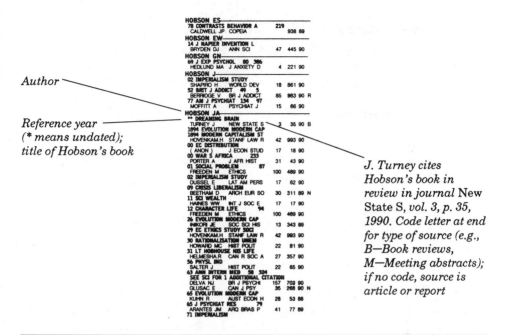

J. Turney cites Hobson's book in review in journal New State S, *vol. 3, p. 35, 1990. Code letter at end for type of source (e.g., B—Book reviews, M—Meeting abstracts); if no code, source is article or report*

FIGURE 3-5   Entry in the *Social Science Citation Index* for author J. A. Hobson, listing works that cited him in 1990

Source: From Social Science Citation Index®. Copied with the permission of the Institute for Scientific Information®, 1992.

Author of source in citation index

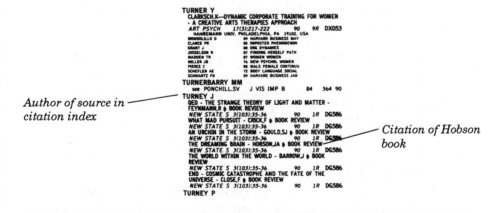

Citation of Hobson book

FIGURE 3-6   The *Source Index* will provide a fuller description of a source mentioned in the citation index, including the bibliography (if any) of the article. (Turney's book review had no bibliography.)

Bibliographies in Books and Articles

By now, you know that a bibliography in a published book or article can be a great help in your hunt for more information. A quick scan of the bibliography, even in a book that isn't exactly on your topic, can often suggest promising titles that are. Some books and articles have bibliographies, and others don't. Fortunately, there's a quick way to find out:

> *Bibliographic Index: A Cumulative Bibliography of Bibliographies.* New York: Wilson, 1938–date.

This index, published annually, is organized by subject and lists books and journals published on that subject that feature bibliographies, including the pages where they can be found.

Unpublished Scholarly Papers

A vast amount of scholarly research is generated each year by graduate students working on advanced degrees. Much of this material is unpublished and therefore uncataloged in the usual indexes. But alas, there's an index to these sources, too:

> *Dissertation Abstracts International.* Ann Arbor, MI: University Microfilms, 1970–date (from 1938–51, titled *Microfilm Abstracts,* and from 1952–69, *Dissertation Abstracts*).

This index is worth checking. When I was writing my book on lobsters, I found a wonderful doctoral dissertation on a Maine island lobstering community that proved fascinating and useful.

First look for the subject/author index in a given year, which will then direct you to the *abstract,* or summary, of the paper in which you're interested. The abstract may be enough. If you want the entire paper, you can order it by mail through University Microfilms, Inc., Ann Arbor, MI 48106. (Copies, however, are costly—about $34.)

Essays and Articles Buried in Books

Somewhere, there may be an article or essay that's perfect for your paper, but you'll never find it because it's buried in a book about a related subject or the book's title doesn't sound promising when you come across it in the card catalog. How do you dig out this hidden gem? Check the following index:

Essay and General Literature Index. New York: Wilson, 1900–
33, supplements 1934–date.

This index covers the humanities and the social sciences and
is easy to use. Search by subject or author. See the example in Figure
3-7.

Hurston, Zora Neale, 1907-1960

About

Bell, B. W. The Harlem Renaissance and
the search for new modes of narrative. (*In*
Bell, B. W. The Afro-American novel and
its tradition p93-149)

Cooke, M. G. Solitude: the beginnings
of self-realization in Zora Neale Hurston,
Richard Wright, and Ralph Ellison. (*In*
Cooke, M. G. Afro-American literature in
the twentieth century p71-109)

Fox-Genovese, E. My statue, my self: auto-
biographical writings of Afro-American wom-
en. (*In* The Private self; ed. by S. Benstock
p63-89)

Johnson, B. Thresholds of difference: structures of address in Zora Neale Hurston.
(*In* Johnson, B. A world of difference p172-
83)

Neal, L. Eatonville's Zora Neale Hurston:
a profile. (*In* Neal, L. Visions of a liberated
future p81-96)

Pryse, M. Introduction: Zora Neale Hurston, Alice Walker, and the "ancient power"
of black women. (*In* Conjuring; ed. by M.
Pryse and H. J. Spillers p1-24)

About individual works

Their eyes were watching God

Awkward, M. "The inaudible voice of it
all": silence, voice, and action in Their eyes
were watching God. (*In* Awkward, M.
Inspiriting influences p15-56)

Callahan, J. F. "Mah tongue is in mah
friend's mouf": the rhetoric of intimacy and
immensity in Their eyes were watching God.
(*In* Callahan, J. F. In the African-American
grain p115-49)

Dixon, M. Keep me from sinking down:
Zora Neale Hurston, Alice Walker, and Gayl
Jones. (*In* Dixon, M. Ride out the wilderness
p83-120)

Gates, H. L. Color me Zora: Alice Walker's
(re) writing of the speakerly text. (*In* Gates,
H. L. The Signifying Monkey p239-58)

Gates, H. L. Color me Zora: Alice Walker's
(re)writing of the speakerly text. (*In* Intertex-
tuality and contemporary American fiction;
ed. by P. O'Donnell and R. C. Davis p144-
67)

Gates, H. L. Zora Neale Hurston and
the speakerly text. (*In* Gates, H. L. The
Signifying Monkey p170-216)

Johnson, B. Metaphor, metonymy, and
voice in: Their eyes were watching God.
(*In* Johnson, B. A world of difference p155-
71)

Meese, E. A. Orality and textuality in
Zora Neale Hurston's Their eyes were watching God. (*In* Meese, E. A. Crossing the
double-cross p39-53)

Spillers, H. J. A hateful passion, a lost
love. (*In* Feminist issues in literary scholarship; ed. by S. Benstock p181-207)

Wainwright, M. K. The aesthetics of community: the insular black community as
theme and focus in Hurston's Their eyes
were watching God. (*In* Harlem Renaissance:
revaluations; ed. by A. Singh, W. S. Shiver,
and S. Brodwin p233-43)

FIGURE 3-7 A student researching African-American author Zora Neale
Hurston in the *Essay and General Literature Index* would find a listing of
essays and articles about her and her work. Information such as this is often
hard to find because the essays and articles are buried in collections.

Source: From *Essay and General Literature Index*, 1985–1989, Cumulative, Volume
11, pages 776–777. Copyright © by The H. W. Wilson Company. Material reproduced
with permission of the publisher.

MAPPING YOUR SEARCH:
THE THIRD LEVEL

After you complete a third-level search, check the types of sources you consulted, and list the specific titles.

☐ Citation indexes _____

_____

☐ Dissertation indexes _____

_____

☐ Bibliographic indexes _____

_____

☐ *Essay and General Literature Index* _____

_____

Expanding the Site of the Search

Library Sources

Sometimes, you're digging in the right place, but the site needs to be expanded. Students rarely take advantage of the enormous resources of their campus libraries. Most stick to the card catalog or the periodical indexes. But libraries contain some unusual sources of information, such as special collections and media departments, that can produce useful material on your topic.

Special Collections. Many university libraries are home to unusual collections of material—historical documents, personal papers of prominent people, and the like—and may even be designated archives for significant works. Often, this material is catalogued separately. If your library has a special collection, consult the staff there about whether it may contain any useful material on your topic.

Audiovisual Departments. Audiovisual materials (films, records, tapes, slides, videocasettes, etc.) are available in separate departments in many libraries. These materials are often catalogued separately. You may find some surprisingly useful sources on your topic in this catalog, such as a taped lecture by an authority who spoke on your campus or a film that offers some useful case studies.

Pamphlets. Pamphlet collections vary widely from library to library. Large libraries sometimes have extensive collections; small libraries, very few. If you have the time, you can send to various agencies for pamphlets relevant to your topic. Use the following index to find out what's available and who can provide it:

> *Vertical File Index: A Subject and Title Index to Selected Pamphlet Material.* New York: Wilson, 1932/35–date.

Other Libraries. Your hometown library will likely not have a good collection of scholarly journals and books, but it may contain some useful sources that were perhaps missing or checked out from your university library's collection. Other public libraries in the area might be worth checking, too. Also remember that you can probably make use of interlibrary loan to get materials from other libraries without running all over the place to collect them yourself, though you'll need some lead time. (See Chapter 1, "Interlibrary Loan.")

Also consider other specialized libraries. Most museums have their own collections, which they often make available to college researchers. Historical societies and many large corporations have libraries, as well.

Nonlibrary Sources

It's so easy to forget that research doesn't begin and end at the library's front door. Be creative about other places to look!

Bookstores. Your campus library may not have recently published books on your topic (titles published in the last year), but your campus or local bookstore might. First, to find out what books seem promising that may not be listed in your library's card catalog, check one or more of the bibliographies of these trade books:

> *Subject Guide to Books in Print.* New York: Bowker, 1957–date. *As the title implies, organized by subject.*
> *Books in Print.* New York: Bowker, 1948–date. *Lists books by title and author.*
> *Paperbound Books in Print.* New York: Bowker, 1955–date. *Lists only paperbacks.*

If you find a promising title, check the local bookstores to find out if the book is in stock. If a book is not available and you have a week or ten days, you can also ask to order the book. Most bookstores will do this for you. The obvious drawback to this approach is that you have to buy the book you want. It may very well be worth it for a book that seems especially useful.

Writing Letters.   There are people and organizations out there with exactly what you need. If you have enough lead time, you can write or call and have them send along some information. How do you find out who these people and organizations are and how you can contact them?

First, ask people you know for information: your instructor, your friends, the people you interview for your paper. Also pay attention to the names of groups that crop up in your reading as well as the names of experts and the institutions they're associated with. Several reference sources can also help:

> *Encyclopedia of Associations.* Edited by Deborah M. Burek. Detroit, MI: Gale Research, 1992. *Three parts; the last is a name and keyword index.*
>
> *Research Centers Directory.* Edited by Karen Hill. Detroit, MI: Gale Research, 1992. *Two volumes; covers 12,000 nonprofit and university-related research organizations.*

Both books will give you addresses and phone numbers of a variety of institutions and groups and, in many cases, names and phone numbers of key contact people (see Figure 3-8).

Lectures.   Every week on my campus, there are ten or more public lectures on a variety of subjects, ranging from the biodynamics of the rain forest to the dangers of date rape. A lecture on your topic— or a closely related one—could be a boon to your research, providing not only fresh material that often has a local angle but also a live person to quote and interview. Going to lectures on the hope of finding useful information is a hit-or-miss approach. Nonetheless, keep your eye on the listings of public lectures in your campus newspaper.

TV and Radio.   Most people in the United States get most of their information about public issues from television. That doesn't mean TV is the best source of information, but it is certainly an influential one. Television and radio news, public affairs programs, and even talk shows can be useful sources of information. *TV Guide* can be a useful reference, and so can the local newspaper, which may list the topics discussed on various television talk shows that day.

★11863★   NARANON **(Substance Abuse)**
World Service Office
PO Box 2562
Palo Verdes, CA 90274   Phone: (213) 547-5800
Nonmembership. Provides assistance to drug-dependent individuals and their families. Organizes discussion groups. **Telecommunications Services:** Telephone referral service. Group is distinct from Narcotics Anonymous (see separate entry) located in Van Nuys, CA.

★11863★   NARCOTIC EDUCATIONAL FOUNDATION OF AMERICA
(Substance Abuse) (NEFA)
5055 Sunset Blvd.   Phone: (213) 663-5171
Los Angeles, CA 90027   Henry B. Hall, Exec. Dir.
Founded: 1924. To provide education about narcotics and other drugs in order to warn youth and adults about the dangers of drug abuse. Has produced films and maintains film library. Operates speakers' bureau, counseling and referral service, library, and reading room. Conducts research. Helps produce television and radio programs.

Publications: *Get the Answers - An Open Letter to Youth, Some Things You Should Know About Prescription Drugs, Drugs and the Automotive Age,* and other *Student Reference Sheets* outlining the dangers associated with the use of various substances.

FIGURE 3-8 The *Encyclopedia of Associations* will provide a researcher writing about drug abuse treatment, for example, the names of several organizations to write to or call for information.

Source: From *Encyclopedia of Associations,* 26th Edition, Volume 1, edited by Deborah M. Burek. Copyright © 1991 by Gale Research Inc. Reproduced by permission of the publisher.

MAPPING YOUR SEARCH:
EXPANDING THE SEARCH

Document the ground you covered when you expanded your search here.

☐ Special collections

☐ A-V department

☐ Pamphlets

☐ Other libraries _____

_____

_____

☐ Bookstores

☐ Lectures

☐ TV and radio

Conducting Interviews

You've already thought about whether interviews might contribute to your paper. Last week, you began to build a list of possible interview subjects and probably contacted several of them. By the end of this week, you should begin interviewing.

I know. You wouldn't mind putting it off. But once you start, it will get easier and easier. I should know. I used to dread interviewing strangers, but after making the first phone call, I got some momentum going, and I began to enjoy it. It's decidedly easier to interview friends, family, or acquaintances, but that's the wrong reason to limit yourself to people you know.

Whom to Interview? Interview people who can provide you with what you want to know. And that may have changed after your research this week. In your reading, you might have encountered the names of experts you'd like to contact, or you may have decided that what you really need is some anecdotal material from someone with experience in your topic. It's still not too late to contact interview subjects who didn't occur to you last week. But do so immediately.

What Questions to Ask? The first step in preparing for an interview is to ask yourself, What's the purpose of this interview? In your research notebook, make a list of *specific questions* for each person you're going to interview. Often, these questions have been raised by your reading or other interviews. What theories or ideas encountered in your reading would you like to ask your subject about? What specific facts have you been unable to uncover that your interview subject may provide? What don't you understand that he or she could explain? Would you like to test one of your own impressions or ideas on your subject? What about the subject's work or experience would you like to learn? Interviews are wonderful tools for clearing up your own confusion and getting specific information that is unavailable anywhere else.

Now make a list of more *open-ended questions* you might ask each or all the people you're going to talk to. Frankly, these questions are a lot more fun to ask because you're more likely to be surprised by the answers. For example:

- In all your experience with _____ , what has most surprised you?
- What has been the most difficult aspect of your work?
- If you had the chance to change something about how you approached _____ , what would it be?

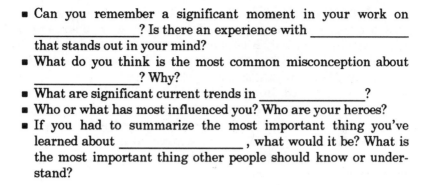

- Can you remember a significant moment in your work on _____? Is there an experience with _____ that stands out in your mind?
- What do you think is the most common misconception about _____? Why?
- What are significant current trends in _____?
- Who or what has most influenced you? Who are your heroes?
- If you had to summarize the most important thing you've learned about _____ , what would it be? What is the most important thing other people should know or understand?

As you develop both specific and open-ended questions, keep in mind what you know about each person—his or her work in the field and personal experience with your topic. You may end up asking a lot of the same questions of everybody you interview, but try to familiarize yourself with any special qualifications a subject may have or experiences he or she may have had. That knowledge might come from your reading, from what other people tell you about your subject, or from your initial telephone call to set up the interview.

Also keep in mind the *kinds* of information an interview can provide better than other sources: anecdotes, strong quotes, and sometimes descriptive material. If you ask the right questions, a live subject can paint a picture of his experience with your topic, and you can capture that picture in your paper.

During the Interview. Once you've built a list of questions, be prepared to ignore it. Interviews are conversations, not surveys. They are about human interaction between two people who are both interested in the same thing.

I remember interviewing a lobsterman, Edward Heaphy, on his boat. I had a long list of questions in my notebook, which I dutifully asked, one after the other. My questions were mechanical, and so were his answers. I finally stopped, put my notebook down, and talked informally with Edward for a few minutes. Offhandedly, I asked, "Would you want your sons or daughter to get in the business?" It was a totally unplanned question. Edward was silent for a moment, staring at his hands. I knew he was about to say something important because, for the first time, I was attentive to him, not my notepad. "Too much work for what they get out of it," he said quietly. It was a surprising remark after hearing for the last hour how much Edward loved lobstering. What's more, I felt I had broken through. The rest of the interview went much better.

Much of how to conduct an interview is common sense. At the outset, clarify the nature of your project—what your paper is on and where you're at with it. Briefly explain again why you thought this individual would be the perfect person to talk to about it. I find it often helps to begin with a specific question that I'm pretty sure my subject can help with. But there's no formula. Simply be a good conversationalist: listen attentively, ask questions that your subject seems to find provocative, and enjoy with your subject sharing an interest in the same thing. Also don't be afraid to ask what you fear are obvious questions. Demonstrate to the subject that you *really* want to understand.

Always end an interview by making sure you have accurate background information on your subject: name (spelled correctly), position, affiliation, age (if applicable), phone number. Ask if you can call him with follow-up questions, should you have any. And always ask your subject if he can recommend any additional reading or other people you should talk to. Of course, mention that you're appreciative of the time he has spent with you.

Notetaking.   There are basically three ways to take notes during an interview: use a tape recorder, a notepad, or both. I adhere to the third method, but it's a very individual choice. I like tape recorders because I don't panic during an interview that I'm losing information or quoting inaccurately, but I don't want to spend hours transcribing the tapes. So I also take notes on the information I think I want to use, and if I miss anything, I consult the recording later. It's a backup. Sometimes, I find that there is no recording—the machine decided not to participate in the interview—and at least I have my notes. Again, a backup.

Get some practice developing your own notetaking technique by interviewing your roommate or taking notes on the television news. Devise ways to shorten often-used words (e.g., *t* for *the, imp* for *important,* and *w/o* for *without*).

Conducting Surveys

Last week, you considered whether your topic lends itself to an informal survey. If so, you generated three types of questions you might ask: *open ended, multiple choice,* and *directed* (see "Survey Design" in Chapter 2). After all the reading you did this week, you likely have some fresh ideas of questions you might ask. Finalize the questions, and begin distributing the survey to the target group you defined earlier.

Distribution. Surveys administered by telephone have some advantages. People are more likely to be direct and honest over the phone, since they are relatively anonymous. Surveys are also more likely to be completed correctly, since the answers are recorded by the survey giver. However, making multiple phone calls can be tedious and expensive, if your target group goes beyond the toll-free calling area. But you may have no choice, especially if the target group for your survey isn't exclusively on campus.

The alternative to conducting a telephone survey is to distribute the survey yourself. The university community, where large numbers of people are available in a confined area, lends itself to administering surveys this way, if there's a university audience you're interested in polling. A survey can be distributed in dormitories, dining halls, classes, or anywhere else the people you want to talk to gather. You can stand outside the student union and stop people as they come and go, or you can hand out your survey to groups of people and collect them when the participants have finished. Your instructor may be able to help distribute your survey to classes. I asked a number of my colleagues to distribute Christine's survey (see Figure 2-2) in their Freshman English classes, a required course representing a relatively random sample of freshmen. Since the survey only took five minutes to fill out, other instructors were glad to help, and in one day, Christine was able to sample more than ninety students.

The campus and its activities often self-select the group you want to survey. Anna, writing a paper on date rape, surveyed exclusively women on campus, many of whom she found in women's dormitories. For his paper on the future of the fraternity system, David surveyed local "Greeks" at their annual awards banquet.

How large a sample should you shoot for? Since yours won't be a scientific survey, don't bother worrying about statistical reliability; just try to survey as many people as you can. Certainly, a large (say, more than one hundred) and representative sample will lend more credence to your claims about any patterns observed in the results.

LOOKING BACK
BEFORE MOVING ON

You've just completed a crucial week in your research project. If you've been thorough in your hunt for information and thoughtful about taking notes on what you find, your paper is more than half completed. But remember, the research process—like the writing process—is *recursive.* That is, you may find yourself circling back to previous steps, especially those in the section "Digging Deeper for Information."

Before you move on, it may help to quickly trace where you've been searching and what you've found this week. Any steps you've missed or had trouble with may be the place to start next week. You may also want to show your instructor the trail you've followed. He might suggest some other places to look.

4

□ ■ □

The Fourth Week

GETTING TO THE DRAFT

It is *not* 2 A.M. Your paper is *not* due in twelve hours but in one or two weeks. For some students, beginning to write a research paper this early—weeks before it's due—will be a totally new experience. An early start may also, for the first time, make the experience a positive one. I know that starting early will help ensure writing a better paper.

Still, there are those students who say they thrive on a looming deadline, who love working in its shadow, flirting with failure. "I work best that way," they say, and they wait until the last minute and race to the deadline in a burst of writing, often sustained by cigarettes and strong doses of caffeine. It works for some students. Panic is a pretty strong motivator. But I think most who defend this habit confuse their relief at successfully pulling off the assignment once again with a belief that the paper itself is successful.

Papers done under such pressure often aren't successful, and that is particularly true of the last-minute research paper, where procrastination is especially deadly. Research writing is recursive. You often have to circle back to where you've already been, discovering holes in your research or looking at your subject from new angles. It's hard to fit in a trip back to the library the night before the paper is due, when you've just started the draft and need to check some information. This book is designed to defeat procrastination, and if, in the past few weeks, you've done the exercises, taken thoughtful notes, and attempted a thorough search for information, you probably have the urge to begin writing.

On the other hand, you may feel as if you don't know enough yet about your topic to have anything to say. Or you may be swamped with information, and your head may be spinning. What do you do with it all?

When Christy came to my office last semester, she was three weeks into her research on a paper that asked, Why do diets fail? She really wanted to know, since she was having such a hard time with her own diet. Though she'd really done a good job collecting information, she was exasperated.

"I found a whole bunch of articles on how heredity affects obesity," she said, "and all this stuff on how people's upbringing determines how they eat. I also found some articles that said our bodies *want* to be a certain weight."

It sounded pretty interesting to me.

"I've got all this information, but I'm worried that I'll lose my focus," she said. *"And so much of it seems contradictory.* I don't know what to think."

When the Experts Disagree

Christy was pretty sure she was in trouble because her sources sometimes didn't agree on the same things. I thought she was right where she should be: standing on the curb at a busy intersection, watching the experts on her topic collide and then go off in different directions. Knowledge in any field—nutrition, literature, or entomology—is not static. It is contested—pushed, pulled, probed, and even sometimes turned over completely to see what is underneath. Scholars and experts devote their lifetimes to disagreeing with each other, not because they enjoy being disagreeable but because when knowledge is contested, it is advanced.

When I researched lobsters, I discovered a fascinating scientific mystery: More than 90 percent of the lobsters that grow to the minimum legal size every year end up on someone's dinner table. At that size, most lobsters haven't even had a chance to breed. How is it possible, asked the scientists, that there are any lobsters left at that rate of exploitation? I discovered several explanations. Some people argued that the millions of lobster traps—each of which is designed to allow undersize lobsters to escape—serve as a kind of giant soup kitchen, providing extra food to lobsters. That, some experts said, accounted for lobster's resilience. Other experts believed that laws protecting females carrying eggs have worked remarkably well. Still others believed that lobsters migrate into areas depleted by overfishing. Recently, another idea won favor with scientists. They suggested that large lobsters at the edge of the continental shelf are the "parental stock" for coastal lobsters, sending their larval offspring inshore on tides and currents.

Evaluating Conflicting Claims

As a writer—and in this case, a nonexpert—I had to sort through these conflicting opinions and decide which I thought were most convincing. I had to claim my point of view and later make it convincing to my own readers.

That was Christy's challenge, and it's your challenge, too. When you're thorough in your research, you're bound to find sources that square off against each other or come at your subject from different directions. What do you make of these competing claims and differing perspectives?

The easiest thing to do is simply suppress the views that you don't agree with. You can do that if the views lack credibility, but even incredible ideas can *become* credible. Some years ago, the idea that the continents were essentially floating plates, which through the millennia had drifted apart, was viewed with great skepticism. Now plate tectonics is a chapter in all standard geology texts. Other ideas—like the assertion by neo-Nazi groups that the Holocaust didn't happen—are clearly outrageous. But a discussion of those ideas sometimes can be instructive, as well.

Before you dismiss or suppress any idea that seems at odds with what you think, consider the source and the strength of the argument. Here are some suggestions that may help you evaluate both:

1. Who is making the claim? Is it someone who is a respected authority in the field?
2. How convincing is the evidence he provides to support the assertions?
3. Do other credible sources lend support to the claim?
4. What do your own experiences and observations (if any) suggest about what a source is saying? What makes sense to you?
5. How many people believe the assertion? Even if a claim seems wrong, is it influential?
6. What does the advocacy of a clearly wacky idea say about the nature of the problem you're researching?

☐ *EXERCISE 4-1*
Reclaiming Your Topic

More than two weeks ago, you began researching a topic that you may have known little about. But you were curious enough to dive in and immerse yourself in the research, listening to the voices of people who know more than you. You may feel, as Christy did, that your paper is beginning to slip away from you; there is just too much information, or the contradictions can't possibly be sorted out. It might seem presumptuous to think that your ideas matter. You may feel as if you're in over your head. After all, you're not an expert.

If you're not at all confused at this stage in the research process, that's great. Now is the time, through writing, to tighten your grasp on the material. But if you're feeling overwhelmed, writing now can help you get a grip. Try this exercise, another "loop write" similar to the one you did earlier in the book. This exercise will take about forty minutes.

Step 1: Spend ten or fifteen minutes reviewing all of the notes you've taken so far and skimming key articles or passages from books. Glance at your most important sources. Let your head swim with information.

Step 2: Now clear your desk of everything but your research notebook. Remove all your notes and all your sources. You won't use them while doing the rest of this exercise. Trust that you'll remember what's important.

Step 3: Now fastwrite about your topic for eight minutes. Tell the story of how your own thinking about your topic has evolved. When you began the project, what did you think? Then what happened, and what happened after that? What were your preconceptions about your topic? How have they changed? This is an open-ended fastwrite. Don't let the writing stall out. If you run out of things to say, talk to yourself through writing about your research, thinking about other trails you might follow. Time yourself.

Step 4: Skip a few lines in your notebook. Write "Moments, Stories, People, and Scenes." Now fastwrite for another ten minutes, this time, focusing on more specific case studies, situations, people, experiences, observations, and so on that stand out in your mind from the research done so far or perhaps from your own experience with the topic. Keep your pen moving for a full ten minutes. Time yourself.

Step 5: Skip a few more lines. For ten minutes, quickly write a dialogue between you and someone else about your topic. You choose who to converse with—a friend, your instructor. Don't plan the dialogue. Just begin with the question most commonly asked about your topic, and take the conversation from there, writing both parts of the dialogue.

Step 6: Finally, skip a few more lines and write these two words in your notebook: "So What?" Now spend a few minutes trying to summarize the most important thing *you* think people should understand about your topic based on what you've learned so far. Distill these comments down to a sentence or two. This may be hard, but it's important. Remember, you can change your mind later.

What did doing this exercise accomplish, besides giving you a cramp in your writing hand? If the exercise worked, you probably already know. By freeing yourself from the chorus of expert voices in your sources and thinking to yourself about what the ideas you've collected mean, you've taken possession of the information again. You may have reaffirmed your purpose in writing the paper.

It may help you grasp the meaning of this exercise—and what completing it can do for you—by looking at how another student, Candy,* found her purpose in writing. After reviewing her notes and materials (Step 1) and then putting them away in preparation to write (Step 2), Candy was ready for Step 3, the first fastwrite. She told the story of finding her focus—how child abuse affects language development—by noting things that struck her as she went along:

STEP 3

> Well, lets see, in the beginning. I was going to do the effects in general of child abuse. As I was researching this, I discovered that I would have to narrow it down because there was so much information on the general effects of child abuse. Initially, when I came across the idea that child abuse creates an impairment in speech and language development, I almost just threw it out. But, I went ahead and read the

*The following excerpts are reprinted with permission of Candyce C. Collins.

article. It was very interesting and I
was able to relate to it. I have taken a
course in Linguistics so, I was able to
relate to how this could be possible.
So, I looked further into the topic of
the effects that child abuse has on
the language development of children
and found quite a bit of information.
It became more and more interesting
to me as I read the information and
all the tests that have been run to
prove this idea. Before I began research,
I never thought that this could
be a possible effect of child abuse.
But, after researching and thinking
more and more about it, I find
it quite logical.

By focusing on specifics in Step 4, the second fastwrite, you should discover some ways to anchor your ideas about the topic to particular people, situations, and case studies you discovered in your reading or from your own experience. Making these connections will not only strengthen your own thinking; case studies and personal accounts often make compelling examples, important to your paper.

In doing Step 4, Candy recalled the story of Genie, a girl who was confined to a closet by an abusive parent until she was thirteen. Genie later became a case used at the beginning and ending of Candy's paper. Here's Candy's second fastwrite:

STEP 4

One case study that stands out is
a story about Genie. This, little girl
had an extreme case of child abuse
and neglect when she was a child up
until she was 13 when she was found.

At 13, she spoke nothing. Now, this is a severe case of language deficiency as a result of child abuse but it goes on to show that it happens. She was locked away in her room, tied to her crib. Her father would beat her when ever she made a noise, so as she got older, she feared to say or utter a sound, so she didn't. As a result, she was unable to talk. She was never brought out in the world, never watched TV or heard the radio.

Other studies have been done on groups of abused, neglected, and both abused and neglected children. The tests prove that all three groups showed signs of slower language development when compared to non abused children. The highest results were found in the neglected only children, then the both neglected and abused and lastly the abused only children. This is due to the fact that the two groups of children that were abused, had some stimulation in their lives even though it might not have been pleasant.

Step 5, the dialogue writing activity, invites someone else to the discussion of your topic, challenging you to consider an audience. What might most people want to know about your topic? How might you explain the answers? These questions may later shape how you organize your paper.

Candy's dialogue started with the question that began her research—What are some of the effects of child abuse?—and then went from there, getting more and more specific. Can you visualize the inverted pyramid progression of her questions and answers? Candy later used this form in part of her paper.

It actually might be more productive to construct a more free-wheeling dialogue than Candy's. Have a real conversation with an imagined reader. Push yourself with questions that really get you thinking about your topic and that might help you see it in a fresh way.

Here's Candy's dialogue:

STEP 5

what are some of the effects that children suffer from as a result of child abuse?

Well, there's lots of them. One in particular that most don't think of is that child abuse can cause language development problems in children.

What kind of language problems do they have?

Primarily, they lack the ability to communicate as well with others than do the nonabused children. Studies show that they have a distinct style of communication. One that is more aggressive and hostile and they try to avoid any true contact through conversations. In extreme cases, like one girl named Genie whose dad beat here when ever she made a sound, couldn't speak at all by the age of 13.

What causes this development problem with language?

When it comes down to it, the main reason is that these children are lacking the normal stimulation that they should receive. They're not exposed to the experiences that would be necessary to learn new words. Also, they are deprived of the parent-child relationship that is an important part of the language aquisition process.

What types of abuse are you talking of? Is it all kinds?

No, its not all kinds of abuse that cause this. It is limited to those children who were either neglected, physically abused or both. Primarily, those that were solely neglected suffer the most. It has been proven that sexual abuse doesn't have an adverse effect on language but in fact these children seem more mature as far as language goes. But, I didn't research far into that.

Finally, asking "So What?" in Step 6 should help you redefine your thesis, or the controlling idea of your paper. In fact, your thesis may change. But for now, you need some brief statement—a sentence or two—that summarizes the most important thing you want your readers to understand.

Candy's answer to the "So What?" question later became the main point of her paper:

STEP 6

> "So What?"
> Child abuse has a negative effect on the language development of a child. This is a result of the childs lack of stimulation, interaction, experiences and parent-child relationships which, are all essential to the ₍proper₎ development of language.

If you're not happy with your answer to "So What?" spend some more time thinking about it. Don't proceed too much further with writing until you have some kind of tentative thesis statement to keep in mind. Put your thesis on an index card or piece of paper, and post it over your desk as a reminder. Pull it down and revise it, if necessary, as you continue with research and writing. But keep that thesis up there on the wall, at least while you're writing the first draft.

□ ■ □

If Exercise 4-1 didn't work for you, you may need to collect more information. Consider circling back to some of the suggestions made in the third week in "Digging Deeper for Information" (see Chapter 3). But if you feel ready to begin writing a draft, read on.

Beginning at the Beginning

John McPhee, a staff writer for *New Yorker* magazine and one of the masters of writing the research-based essay, gave a talk some years back about beginnings, which vex many writers.

> The first part—the lead, the beginning—is the hardest part of all to write. I've often heard writers say that if you have written your lead you have written 90 percent of the story. You have tens of thousands of words to choose from, after all, and only one can start the story, then one after that, and so forth. And your material, at this point, is all fresh and unused, so you don't have the advantage of being in the middle of things. You could start in any of many places. What will you choose?

Leads must be sound. They should never promise what does not follow. Leads, like titles, are flashlights that shine down into the story.*

Flashlights or Floodlights?

I love this: *"Leads . . . are flashlights that shine down into the story."* An introduction, at least the kind I was taught to write in high school, is more like a sodium vapor lamp that lights up the whole neighborhood. I remember writing introductions to research papers that sounded like this:

```
There are many critical problems that face society
today. One of these critical problems is environ-
mental protection, and especially the conservation
of marine resources. This paper will explore one
of these resources--the whale--and the myriad ways
in which the whale-watching industry now poses a
new threat to this species' survival. It will look
at what is happening today and what some people
concerned with the problem hope will happen
tomorrow. It will argue that new regulations need
to be put into affect to reduce boat traffic
around our remaining whales, a national treasure
that needs protection.
```

This introduction isn't that bad. It does offer a statement of purpose, and it explains the thesis. But the window it opens on the paper is so broad—listing everything the paper will try to do—that readers see a bland, general landscape. What's to discover? The old writing formula for structuring some papers—"Say what you're going to say, say it, and then say what you said"—breeds this kind of introduction. It also gets the writer started on a paper that often turns out as bland as the beginning.

*John McPhee, University of New Hampshire, 1977.

Consider this alternative opening for the same paper:

Scott Mercer, owner of the whale-watching vessel
Cetecea, tells the story of a man and his son who
decide that watching the whales from inside their
small motorboat isn't close enough. They want to
swim with them. As Mercer and his passengers
watch, the man sends his son overboard with
snorkel and fins, and the boy promptly swims
towards a "bubble cloud," a mass of air exhaled by
a feeding humpback whale below the surface. What
the swimmer didn't know was that, directly below
that bubble cloud, the creature was on its way up,
mouth gaping. They were both in for a surprise. "I
got on the P.A. system and told my passengers, just
loud enough for the guy in the boat to hear me,
that either that swimmer was going to end up as
whale food or he was going to get slapped with a
$10,000 fine. He got out of the water pretty fast."

I think this lead accomplishes nearly as much as the bland version but in a more compelling way. It suggests the purpose of the paper—to explore conflicts between whale lovers and whales—and even implies the thesis—that human activity around whales needs more regulation. This lead is more like McPhee's "flashlight," pointing to the direction of the paper without attempting to illuminate the entire subject in a paragraph. An interesting beginning will also help launch the writer into a more interesting paper, for both reader and writer.

It's probably obvious that your opening is your first chance to capture your reader's attention. But how you begin your research paper will also have a subtle yet significant impact on the rest of it. The lead starts the paper going in a particular direction; it also establishes the *tone*, or writing voice, and the writer's relationships to the subject and the reader. Most writers at least intuitively know this, which is why beginnings are so hard to write.

Writing Multiple Leads

One thing that will make it easier to get started is to write three leads to your paper, instead of agonizing over one that must be perfect. Each different opening you write should point the "flashlight" in a different direction, suggesting different trails the draft might follow. After composing several leads, you can choose the one that you—and ultimately, your readers—find most promising.

Writing multiple openings to your paper might sound hard, but consider all the ways to begin:

■ *Anecdote.* Think of a little story that nicely frames what your paper is about, as does the lead about the man and his son who almost became whale food.

■ *Scene.* Begin by giving your readers a look at some revealing aspect of your topic. A paper on the destruction of tropical rain forests might begin with a description of what the land looks like after loggers have left it.

■ *Profile.* Try a lead that introduces someone who is important to your topic. Candy's lead, using a case study on Genie, the abused thirteen-year-old, is a good example.

■ *Background.* Maybe you could begin by providing important and possibly surprising background information on your topic. A paper on steroid use might start by citing the explosive growth in use by high school athletes in the last ten years. A paper on a novel or an author might begin with a review of what critics have had to say.

■ *Quotation.* Sometimes, you encounter a great quote that beautifully captures the question your paper will explore or the direction it will take. Heidi's paper on whether "Sesame Street" provides children with a good education began by quoting a tribute from *U.S. News and World Report* to Jim Henson after his sudden death (see Appendix B).

■ *Dialogue.* Open with dialogue between people involved in your topic. Dan's paper on the connection between spouse abuse and alcoholism began with a conversation between himself and a woman who had been abused by her husband (see Appendix C).

■ *Question.* Pointedly ask your readers the questions you asked that launched your research or the questions your readers might raise about your topic. Here's how Kim began her paper on adoption: Could you imagine going through life not knowing your true identity?

■ *Contrast.* Try a lead that compares two apparently unlike things that highlight the problem or dilemma the paper will explore. Dusty's paper "Myth of the Superwoman" began with a comparison between her friend Susan, who married at 21 and grew up believing in Snow White and Cinderella, and herself, who never believed in princes or white horses and was advised by her mother that it was risky to depend on a man.

■ *Announcement.* Sometimes the most appropriate beginning *is* one like the first lead on whales and whale-watchers mentioned earlier, which announces what the paper is about. Though such openings are sometimes not particularly compelling, they are direct. A paper with a complex topic or focus may be well served by simply stating in the beginning the main idea you'll explore and what plan you'll follow.

☐ *EXERCISE 4-2*
Three Ways In

Step 1: Compose three different beginnings, or leads, to your research paper. Each should be one or two paragraphs (or perhaps more, depending on what type of lead you've chosen and on the length of your paper). Think about the many different ways to begin, as mentioned earlier, and experiment. Your instructor may ask you to write the three leads in your research notebook or type them on a separate piece of paper and bring them to class.

Step 2: Get some help deciding which opening is strongest. Circulate your leads in class, or show them to friends. Ask each person to check the one lead he likes best, that most makes him want to read on.

Step 3: Choose the lead you like (even if no one else does). To determine how well it prepares your readers for what follows, ask a friend or classmate to answer these questions: Based on reading only the opening of the paper: (a) What do you predict this paper is about? What might be its focus? (b) Can you guess what central question I'm trying to answer? (c) Can you predict what my thesis might be? (d) How would you characterize the tone of the paper?

It's easy to choose a opening that's catchy. But the beginning of your paper must also help establish your purpose in writing it, frame your focus, and perhaps even suggest your main point, or thesis. The lead will also establish the voice, or tone, the paper will adopt (see the following section). That's a big order for one or two paragraphs, and you may find that more than a couple of paragraphs are needed to do it. Tentatively select the one opening (or a combination of several) from this exercise that does those things best. I think you'll find that none of the leads you composed will be wasted; there will be a place for the ones you don't use somewhere else in the paper. Keep them handy.

□ ■ □

Deciding on a Voice

How you begin has another subtle influence on your draft: It establishes the tone, or writing voice, you will adopt in your paper. Though you may think *writing voice* is not something you've considered much before, you probably paid a lot of attention to it when writing the that essay accompanied your college applications. Does this *sound* right? you wondered, considering whether what you wrote would impress the admissions officer. Did you sound like college material? You also know how to *change* your writing voice. For example, next time you get a speeding ticket and write home to ask for money to pay for it, notice the voice you adopt. And then, when you write your best friend a letter about the same incident, notice how your voice changes.

Of all the writing assignments you've done over the years, the research paper is probably the one in which you paid the most attention to writing voice. Research papers are supposed to sound a certain way, right? They're supposed to be peppered with words such as *myriad* and *thus* and *facilitate.* They're supposed to sound like, well, nobody you know—detached, mechanical, and ponderous.

These are understandable assumptions. So many of the sources you've read in the past weeks have sounded that way. It's also difficult to avoid sounding detached when you're writing about a topic that holds little interest for you. But the writing voice you choose for this or any other paper you write *is* a choice. Don't assume that all research papers are supposed to sound a certain way and that you must mindlessly conform to that voice.

Considering Purpose, Audience, Subject, and Who You Are

How do you choose a writing voice for a research paper? Follow the same approach you would use when writing a letter to your parents, asking for money. Consider your *purpose,* your *audience,* and your *subject*. Most importantly, though, remember that, fundamentally, your writing voice is a reflection of *who you are*. Your natural writing voice is different from mine, just as your spoken voice is. You can change your spoken voice, something you're probably pretty experienced at already. But you may need to learn to know and appreciate your written voice—the voice that sounds like you. It might even be appropriate for this paper.

I faced a difficult decision about voice in writing this text. My purpose was to instruct students in research skills as well as to motivate them to find some enthusiasm for the assignment. In order to motivate my readers, I wanted to present the research paper in a new way. That purpose would not be served, I thought, by writing in the detached, impersonal voice most people associate with textbooks (and research papers). I chose to sound like *me,* hoping that, when explained in my voice, the subject would seem more accessible and my own enthusiasm for research would come through.

The Differing Voices of Research. The voice in a piece of writing often comes through in the very first line. In case you still think all research papers sound alike, listen to these first lines from student papers:

Ernst Pawel has said that "The Metamorphosis" by
Franz Kafka "transcends the standard categories of
literary criticism; it is a poisoned fairy tale
about the magic of hate and the power of hypocrisy
. . . charting the transmogrification of a lost
soul in a dead bug" (279).
—*From a paper on how Kafka writes the story to deal with his own childhood demons*

If the rising waters of the Renaissance lifted the
intellectual culture of Europe, it's fair to ask
whether women were in the boat.
—*From a paper on women artists in the Renaissance*

Even the sound of the word is vulgar.
—*From a paper on ticks*

```
Living during a period of war was something I had
never experienced until the escalation of the
recent Gulf crisis.
```
—*From a paper on Igor Stravinsky's "The Soldier's Tale"*

```
I have often worried in the past months if there
was either something wrong with or missing from
my brain.
```
—*From a paper on dream interpretation*

```
No more fat jokes.
```
—*From a paper on a daughter coming to terms with her mother's cancer*

These *are* different beginnings. But notice something all these beginnings share: They are concrete. None begins with a bland, broad stroke—some sweeping generalization or obvious statement (e.g., "War is an unhappy reality in today's society" or "Richard Wright's *Native Son* is about the African-American experience in America"). Rather, each gives the reader a specific handle on the topic. In some cases, the reader is given not only a concrete point of view but, through a distinctive voice, an individual writer, as well.

The voices in the previous examples could be considered along a continuum, beginning with the more formal and moving to the much less formal, ranging from the impersonal to the personal, from a less visible writer to one who steps forward immediately. Any one of these voices might be appropriate for your paper, depending on your subject, purpose, and audience and on who you are.

Generally, as the treatment of a topic becomes more technical and its audience, more knowledgeable, the individual voice of the writer becomes less important. The writing often has less life, but then, it's not meant to entertain.

If you're writing a research paper that's intended to report the results of an experiment, you may choose a more impersonal writing voice. In such a case, it doesn't matter who you are, so don't draw attention to it. What does matter is communicating the results, simply and clearly, in a style that doesn't draw attention to itself in any way. You will find that academic writing in some disciplines is expected to assume an impersonal tone and in fact has its own language (though you may not have to strictly conform to it in this research paper).

But it's likely that, at this stage, you're not writing a technical paper for an audience of experts. And though your primary purpose is not to entertain your readers, you *are* trying to make your material as interesting to others as it is to you. As suggested earlier in this book, ask your instructor if you have some latitude in choosing a voice for your paper. (See "Things to Ask Your Instructor" in the Introduction.) If so, review the lead you tentatively chose in Exercise 4-2. Does it establish a voice that's appropriate, given your topic, purpose, and audience? Do you like the way it sounds? Should you change it? Would another lead sound better? If so, write a new lead or choose another from the several leads you wrote earlier.

Writing for Reader Interest

You've tentatively chosen a lead for your paper. You've selected it based on how well you think it frames your tentative purpose, establishes an appropriate tone or voice, and captures your reader's attention. Before you begin writing your draft, consider these other strategies for writing a lively, interesting paper that will help keep readers turning pages.

Working the Common Ground

Here's how David Quammen, a nature writer, begins an essay on the sexual strategy of Canada geese:

> Listen: *uh-whongk, uh-whongk, uh-whongk, uh-whongk,* and then you are wide awake, and you smile up at the ceiling as the calls fade off to the north and already they are gone. Silence again, 3 A.M., the hiss of March winds. A thought crosses your mind before you roll over and, contentedly, resume sleeping. The thought is: "Thank God I live here, right here exactly, in their path. Thank God for those birds." The honk of wild Canada geese passing overhead in the night is a sound to freshen the human soul. The question is why.*

If you live in Puerto Rico or anywhere beyond the late-night call of geese flying overhead, this lead paragraph may not draw you into Quammen's article on the birds' sexual habits. But for the many of us who know the muttering of geese overhead, suddenly the writer's

---

*David Quammen, *The Flight of the Iguana* (New York: Delacorte, 1988), 233.

question—why this is a sound "to freshen the human soul"—becomes our question, too. *We want to know what he knows because he starts with what we both know already:* the haunting sound of geese in flight.

David Quammen, like Richard Conniff in his article "Why God Created Flies" (see Introduction), understands the importance of working the common ground between his topic and his readers. In "The Miracle of Geese," Quammen begins with an experience that many of us know, and once he establishes that common ground, he takes us into the less familiar territory he encountered while researching Canada geese. And we willingly go. Quammen gives us a foothold on his topic that comes from our own experience with it.

Conniff does much the same thing throughout "Why God Created Flies." He often reminds us of familiar moments, like trying desperately to kill a fly without a fly swatter, and then helps us understand what it is about the fly that makes it so elusive, using information from his research. Conniff explains the nature of the fly's wraparound eye, its nervous system, and the speed of its wingbeats. He works the common ground with his readers even more in his explanations, using comparisons that we can relate to:

> The fly's wings beat 165 to 200 times a second. Although this isn't all that fast for an insect, it's more than double the wing beat of the speediest hummingbird and about twenty times faster than any repetitious movement the human nervous system can manage.*

Information about insect anatomy that alone might be dry and uninteresting is brought to life because it's brought into the world that we know through our own observations and experiences and with surprising comparisons that make sense.

As you draft your research paper, look for ways to work the common ground between your topic and your readers: What typically is their relationship to what you're writing about? What might they know about the topic but not have noticed? How does it touch their world? What would they want to know from their own experiences with your topic?

Scott, writing a paper about the town fire department that services the university, began by describing a frequent event in his dormitory: a false alarm. He then went on to explore why many alarms

---

*Reprinted by permission of writer Richard Conniff, from *Audubon Magazine*, July, 1989 (p. 83).

are not really so false after all. He hooked his readers by drawing on their common experience with his topic.

Some topics, like flies and geese and divorce and alcoholism, may have very real connections to the lives of your readers. Many people have swatted flies, heard geese overhead, or watched parents or friends destroy themselves with booze. As you revise your paper, look for opportunities to encourage readers to take a closer look at something about your topic they may have seen before.

Topics Where Common Ground Is Hard to Find. Some topics don't yield common ground so directly. They may be outside the direct experiences of your readers. Though anabolic steroid use is widespread, when Joey talked to people about his paper on abuse of the drug by amateur athletes, he found they had only read about it. He decided to add some material about the most celebrated case of anabolic steroid abuse—Ben Johnson, the Canadian sprinter who in 1988 was stripped of his Olympic gold medal in the 100 meters—since most everyone had heard of the widely publicized case. Joey was able to work from that common ground into a discussion of why many athletes, like Johnson, are willing to risk everything to take the drugs.

Literary topics may also present a challenge in establishing common ground with readers, unless the author or work is familiar. But there are ways. When I was writing a paper on notions of manhood in Wallace Stegner's novels *The Big Rock Candy Mountain* and *Recapitulation,* I brought the idea of manhood home to my readers by describing my relationship with my own father and then comparing it to the relationship of two key characters in the books. (The beginning of that paper is presented as an example in Appendix D, "Tips for Researching and Writing Papers on Literary Topics.") Comparison to other more popular works that readers may know is often a way to establish some common ground.

Popular culture presented through the mass media—TV, radio, magazines, newspapers—may be the common ground you can mine between your readers and a topic removed from their world. None of your readers were likely in Iraq during the Gulf War, but for a paper on whether "smart bombs" are so smart, the story of the destroyed "air raid shelter" in Baghdad, where several hundred civilians perished, will be familiar to many.

In writing your paper, imagine the ways in which your topic intersects with the life of a typical reader, and in that way, bring the information to life.

Putting People on the Page

Essayist E. B. White once advised that, when you want to write about humankind, you should write about a human. The advice to look at the *small* to understand the *large* applies to most writing, not just the research paper.

Ideas come alive when we see how they operate in the world we live in. Beware, then, of long paragraphs with sentences that begin with phrases such as *in today's society,* where you wax on with generalization after generalization about your topic. Unless your ideas are anchored to specific cases, observations, experiences, statistics, and, especially, people, they will be reduced to abstractions and lose their power for your reader.

Using Case Studies. Strangely, research papers are often peopleless landscapes, which is one of the things that can make them so lifeless to read. Lisa wrote about theories of child development, citing studies and schools of thought about the topic yet never applying that information to a real child, her own daughter, two-year-old Rebecca. In his paper decrying the deforestation of the Amazon rain forest, Marty never gave his readers the chance to hear the voices of the Indians whose way of life is threatened.

Ultimately, what makes almost any topic matter to the writer or the reader is what difference it makes to people.

Candy's paper on child abuse and its effect on language development, for example, opened with the tragic story of Genie, who, for nearly thirteen years, was bound in her room by her father and beaten whenever she made a sound. When Genie was finally rescued, she could not speak at all. This sad story about a real girl makes the idea that child abuse affects how one speaks (the paper's thesis) anything but abstract. Candy gave her readers reason to care about what she learned about the problem by personalizing it.

Sometimes, the best personal experience to share is your own. Have you been touched by the topic? Kim's paper about the special problems of women alcoholics included anecdotes about several women gleaned from her reading, but the paper was most compelling when she talked about her own experiences with her mother's alcoholism.

Using Interviews. Interviews are another way to bring people to the page. In "Why God Created Flies," Richard Conniff brought in the voice of a bug expert, Vincent Dethier, who not only had interesting things to say about flies but who spoke with humor and enthusiasm. Heidi's paper on "Sesame Street" featured the voice of a school principal, a woman who echoes the point the paper makes about the value of the program (see Appendix B). Both research essays are filled not just with information about the topic but with people who are touched by it in some way.

As you write your paper, look for opportunities to bring people to the page. Hunt for case studies, anecdotes, and good quotes that will help your readers see how your topic affects how people think and live their lives.

Writing a Strong Ending

Readers remember beginnings and endings. We already explored what makes a strong beginning: It engages the reader's interest, it's more often specific than general, and it frames the purpose of the paper, defining for the reader where it is headed. A beginning for a research paper should also state or imply its thesis, or controlling idea.

We haven't said anything about endings yet, or "conclusions," as they are traditionally described. What's a strong ending? That depends. If you're writing a formal research paper (in some disciplines), the purpose of the conclusion is straightforward: It should summarize major findings. But if you're writing a less formal research essay, the nature of the conclusion is less prescribed. It could summarize major findings, but it could also suggest new directions worth exploring, highlight an especially important aspect of the topic, offer a rethinking of the thesis, or end the story of the search. The conclusion could be general, or it could be specific.

Endings to Avoid. The ending of your research paper could be a lot of things, and in a way, it's easier to say what it should *not* be:

■ Avoid conclusions that simply restate what you've already said. This is the "kick the dead horse" conclusion some of us were taught to write in school on the assumption that our readers probably aren't smart enough to get our point, so we'd better repeat it. This approach annoys most readers who *are* smart enough to know the horse is dead.

■ Avoid endings that begin with *in conclusion* or *thus*. Words such as these also signal to your reader what she already knows: that you're ending. Language such as this often begins a very general summary, which gets you into a conclusion such as the one mentioned above: dead.

■ Avoid endings that don't feel like endings—that trail off onto other topics, are abrupt, or don't seem connected to what came before them. Prompting your readers to think is one thing; leaving them hanging is quite another.

In some ways, the conclusion of your research paper is the last stop on your journey; the reader has traveled far with you to get there. The most important quality of a good ending is that it should add something to the paper. If it doesn't, cut it and write a new one.

What can the ending add? It can add a further elaboration of your thesis that grows from the evidence you've presented, a discussion of solutions to a problem that has arisen from the information you've uncovered, or perhaps a final illustration or piece of evidence that drives home your point. Heidi's conclusion for her paper on the value of "Sesame Street" added a final illustration:

I see enough evidence of the success of "Sesame Street" through watching my sister, as I've described, and other children I come in contact with. When Jim Henson died, the second-grade class at Nancy Diamonti's elementary school created watercolor portraits of their favorite "Sesame Street" characters, which were subsequently hung, along with a tribute the teacher composed on the same size paper, on the glass cases heading into the school courtyard. "It was touching because they felt so deeply about it," said Diamonti. . . . "[T]hey really talked a lot about how important 'Sesame Street' and its characters were to them." She reflected a moment and added, "Jim Henson was a part of it, but not all of it. Joan Ganz Cooney had a vision . . . an amazing vision" (Diamonti).

She certainly did.*

*Reprinted with permission of Heidi R. Dunham.

An ending, in many ways, can be approached similarly to a lead. You can conclude, as Heidi did, with an anecdote, a quotation, a description, a summary, or a profile. Go back to the discussion earlier in this chapter of types of leads for ideas about types of conclusions. The same basic guidelines apply.

Perhaps the strongest ending is one that somehow finds a way to circle back to the beginning. An example of this kind of conclusion—the "snake biting its tail" ending—is Conniff's last paragraph in "Why God Created Flies," where he returns to where he began his article: sitting in front of a beer, contemplating flies.

Using Surprise

The research process—like the writing process—can be filled with discovery for the writer if he approaches the topic with curiosity and openness. When I began researching the *Lobster Almanac,* I was constantly surprised by things I didn't know: lobsters are bugs; it takes eight years for a lobster in Maine to grow to the familiar one-pound size; the largest lobster ever caught weighed about forty pounds and lived in a tank at a restaurant for a year, developing a fondness for the owner's wife. I could go on and on. And I did in the book, sharing unusual information with my readers on the assumption that, if it surprised me, it would surprise them, too.

As you write your draft, reflect on the surprising things you discovered about your topic during your research and look for ways to weave that information into the rewrite. Later, after you have written your draft, share it with a reader and ask for her ideas about what is particularly interesting and should be further developed. For now, think about unusual specifics you may have left out.

However, don't include information, no matter how surprising or interesting, that doesn't serve your purpose. Christine's survey on the dreams of college freshmen had some fascinating findings, including some accounts of recurring dreams that really surprised her. She reluctantly decided not to say much about them, however, because they didn't really further the purpose of her paper, which was to discover what function dreams serve. On the other hand, Bob was surprised to find that some politically conservative politicians and judges actually supported decriminalization of marijuana. He decided to include more information about who they were and what they said in his revision, believing it would surprise his readers and strengthen his argument.

Considering Methods of Development

If you feel you have plenty of information and you're itching to get started writing the draft, maybe you should just follow your lead and see where it goes. Some of the best research papers I've read—and virtually all the research essays I've written—have grown organically from strong beginnings. When I write, I don't know what's going to happen until I see what I say.

Many people are not comfortable with such a free-fall approach to writing, including many professional writers. John McPhee is almost obsessed with the structure of his long research essays. He spends hours, positioning and repositioning index cards of information from his research on a corkboard, looking for the right way to organize his material. He does all this before he writes a word of the draft.

If you're more of a planner than a leaper, then one option is to develop an outline, a map that will guide you from the opening to the ending of your paper. (In fact, your instructor may require that an outline be submitted with the final paper.) I've always resisted outlines, largely because they seem to take the surprise out of writing the first draft for me. But many people are uncomfortable without having a sense of where they're going before they get there. And if the outline isn't rigid, it doesn't have to preclude productive surprises.

There are a variety of ways to approach an outline. It can be a short list of things you want to cover, each summarized in a few words or phrases. It can be a list of headings that neatly break down your topic. It can be a list of questions the paper will try to answer, in the order you suspect readers may ask them. Or it can be a list of topic sentences that may even begin paragraphs or sections in the draft. You decide how detailed the outline needs to be at this point.

But before you tackle an outline, it might be helpful first to decide on the basic design of the paper. The following sections review some very general methods of development that can be used alone or in combination, as they serve your purpose.

Narrative

Tell a story. It can be the story of someone who is affected by your topic, or it can be the story of what you've learned and how you learned it, a kind of "narrative of thought" that chronologically tells how your thinking about your topic evolved. Dan's research paper explored the connection between spouse abuse and alcoholism, beginning with the story of Louise, a woman who sought help from Dan while he was working at a counseling center. The paper continued using the narrative throughout, while Dan weaved in explanations gleaned from his research. Jessica began her research paper with a question about the meaning of a dream she had one night and then chronicled what she discovered about it and dream interpretation through her research and interviews.

Narratives often take a chronological structure (though not always), which makes them in some ways the easiest papers to organize. Can you build your paper around some story you can tell?

Problem-to-Solution

Begin by framing the problem the paper will explore, and then focus on one or more solutions that seem promising or intriguing. For example, Anne Marie's paper on acquaintance rape first set out to establish the severity of the problem and then focused on student education programs at several colleges that have met with some success in heightening student awareness of this kind of assault. Bob's paper posed the dilemma of widespread marijuana use and then developed legalization as a possible solution.

Papers that examine problems need not always provide solutions, however.

Cause-to-Effect or Effect-to-Cause

Causality, a primary interest of scientific researchers, can also be used to develop a research paper. Organize your paper around a cause of a problem, and then look at some effects, or vice versa. Consider beginning, for example, with a discussion of the dire effects of the removal of rain forests in Brazil, and then examine one cause— perhaps economic or political—that contributes to that problem. The key here is to avoid the temptation to examine *all* the causes and effects of a particular problem without ignoring its *complexity*. Things are seldom simple, and they are often interrelated. But pairing a cause and effect and building your paper around that can be illuminating. If your topic explores a problem, this may be a useful way to focus and organize your material.

Question-to-Answer

As mentioned earlier, all writing answers questions. You've been asked to identify the focusing question that your paper attempts to answer. Design the paper around that question and your exploration of the answers. Anne began her research paper with a question about the absence of nursery school in her education. Is preschool necessary, she asked, and does it contribute to later academic success? The rest of Anne's paper explored the answer, culled from both research and interviews. Question-to-answer is a quite natural method of development and can be combined with a narrative approach. How did you discover the answer to the question you pose? Be aware that this approach does not imply that you must find *the* answer. Again, things are rarely that simple or that neat. You may even note at the end of your paper that you asked the wrong question, a point that may be especially illuminating.

Known-to-Unknown or Unknown-to-Known

Chris investigated a mysterious murder that took place on the Isle of Shoals, a tiny cluster of islands off New Hampshire's coast, one hundred years ago. Based on documents he collected, he first examined what was known about the case, but the bulk of his paper discussed what remained a mystery.

You might also examine what is known and unknown about your topic, especially if it's the source of controversy. What do authorities on your topic seem to agree and disagree on? Where does controversy lie?

Simple-to-Complex

In a way, the simple-to-complex method of development is a variation of known-to-unknown. What is apparent about your topic? What is less obvious that reveals its complex nature? At first glance, Ken Kesey's book *One Flew Over the Cuckoo's Nest** is simply a powerful statement against institutional mistreatment of people who are mentally ill. But one student, Tim, found a more subtle, more disturbing misogynist theme. His paper first looked at the more obvious features of the novel but then focused on its less apparent antifeminist undercurrents.

General-to-Specific or Specific-to-General

Think of general-to-specific as the "funnel" approach, inverted or not. You start with a broad look at the topic, and then funnel down to some more specific aspect of it, or you begin with a narrow look and end up with some broader view. Jenny's paper on how children acquire language began with a specific anecdote about Kalinda, who

*Ken Kesey, *One Flew Over the Cuckoo's Nest* (New York: Signet, 1962).

is asked to read in front of her class and stumbles over a word. The paper then moved to a more general discussion of the forces that shape language acquisition. From there, it got specific again, discussing particular theorists and their ideas.

Good research writing sometimes has that quality: expansion and contraction, almost like breathing, moving in and out, again and again.

Comparison-and-Contrast

Comparison-and-contrast is a strategy for organization you're no doubt familiar with. Depending on your purpose, it can work very well. For example, Nick wanted to understand what lessons the United States learned from the Vietnam War. The more recent conflict with Iraq, an event that touched his life, seemed to be a useful comparison. How are the two wars different? he wondered. How are they similar? Another student, Linda, wrote a paper that compared and contrasted the creative processes involved in writing and photography. She discovered more similarities than she had expected.

Look for potentially revealing comparisons and contrasts, and organize your paper around them. You can deal with them separately—one and then the other—or you can alternate between the two, moving back and forth.

Combining Approaches

Remember that each of these methods of development can be used alone, but they will more likely be used in combination. Most papers move back and forth between the general and the specific, and many involve some kind of narrative. (After all, an anecdote or case study is a kind of story.) A paper on the destruction of the Brazilian rain forest may incorporate the cause-and-effect model mentioned above, but it may also find a place for comparison-and-contrast. For instance: What countries with rain forests have resisted economic pressures to cut trees? Would those approaches work in Brazil?

These strategies for organizing your paper are not meant to be formulas. Ignore them altogether if using them turns writing your first draft into a slow, mechanistic exercise. At best, these methods may give you a broad notion of how to organize an outline. Then you can fill in some of the detail—again, how much is up to you.

However you approach creating an outline at this stage, do so with your thesis in mind. Ask yourself, What do my readers need to know to understand my point, and *when* do they need to know it in my paper?

Writing with Sources

The need for *documentation*—that is, citing sources—distinguishes the research paper from most other kinds of writing. And let's face it: Worrying about sources can cramp your style. Many students have an understandable paranoia about plagiarism and tend, as mentioned earlier, to let the voices of their sources overwhelm their own. Students are also often distracted by technical details: Am I getting the right page number? Where exactly should this citation go? Do I need to cite this or not?

As you gain control of the material by choosing your own writing voice and clarifying your purpose in the paper, you should feel less constrained by the technical demands of documentation. The following suggestions may also help you weave reference sources into your own writing without the seams showing.

Blending Kinds of Writing and Sources

One of the wonderful things about the research essay is that it can draw on all four sources of information—reading, interviews, observation, and experience—as well as the four notetaking strategies discussed earlier—quotation, paraphrase, summary, and the writer's own analysis and commentary. Skillfully blended, these elements can make music.

Look at this paragraph from Heidi's paper on "Sesame Street":

```
There is more to this show than meets the eye,
certainly. It is definitely more than just a crowd
of furry animals all living together in the middle
of New York City. Originally intended as an effort
to educate poor, less privileged youth, "Sesame
Street" is set in the very middle of an urban
development on purpose (Hellman 52). As Jon Stone,
one of the show's founders and co-producers sees
it, the program couldn't be "just another escapist
show set in a tree house or a badger den" (52).
Instead, the recognizable environment gave
something to the kids they could relate to.
```

". . . It had a lot more real quality to it than,
say, 'Mister Rogers' . . . Kids say the reason
they don't like 'Mister Rogers' is that it's
unbelievable," says Nancy Diamonti.*

The writing is lively here, not simply because the topic is interesting to those of us who know the program. Heidi has nicely blended
her own commentary with summary, paraphrase, and quotation, all
in a single paragraph. She has also been able to draw on multiple
sources of information—an interview, some effective quotes from her
reading, and her own observations of "Sesame Street." We sense that
the writer is *using* the information, not being used by it.

Handling Quotes. Avoid the temptation, as Heidi did, to load
up your paragraphs with long or full quotes from your sources. I often
see what I call "hanging quotes" in research papers. Embedded in a
paragraph is a sentence or two within quotation marks. Though the
passage is cited, there's no indication of who said it. Usually, the
writer was too lazy to summarize or paraphrase or work *part* of the
quotation into his own prose.

Use quotations selectively. And if you can, blend them into your
own sentences, using a particularly striking or relevant part of the
original source. For example, consider how quotes are used in this
paragraph:

Black Elk often spoke of the importance of the
circle to American Indian culture. "You may have
noticed that everything an Indian does is in a
circle, and that is because the Power of the World
always works in circles, and everything tries to
be round . . . The sky is round, and I have heard
that the earth is round like a ball, and so are
all the stars." He couldn't understand why white
people lived in square houses. "It is a bad way to
live, for there is not power in a square."

*Used with permission of Heidi R. Dunham.

The quotes stand out, separate from the writer's own text. A
better use of quotes is to work the same material smoothly into your
own prose, doing something such as this:

Black Elk believed the "Power of the World always

works in circles," noting the roundness of the

sun, the earth, and the stars. He couldn't

understand why white people live in square houses:

"It is a bad way to live, for there is not power

in a square."

Occasionally, however, it may be useful to include a long quotation from one of your sources. A quotation that is longer than four
lines should be *blocked,* or set off from the rest of the text by indenting it ten spaces from the left margin. Like the rest of the paper, a
blocked quotation is also typed double-spaced. For example:

According to Robert Karen, shame is a particularly

modern phenomenon. He notes that in medieval

times, people pretty much let loose, and by our

modern tastes, it was not a pretty sight:

Their emotional life appears to have

been extraordinarily spontaneous and

unrestrained. From Joahn Huizinga's The

Waning of the Middle Ages we learn that

the average European town dweller was

wildly erratic and inconsistent,

murderously violent when enraged, easily

plunged into guilt, tears, and pleas for

forgiveness, and bursting with

psychological eccentricities. He ate

with his hands out of a common bowl,

blew his nose on his sleeve, defecated

> openly by the side of the road, made
> love, and mourned with great passion,
> and was relatively unconcerned about
> such notions as maladjustment or
> what others might think . . . In
> post-medieval centuries what I've
> called situational shame spread
> rapidly. . . . (61)

Note that the quotation marks are dropped around a blocked quotation. In this case, only part of a paragraph was borrowed, but if you quote one or more full paragraphs, indent the first line of each *three* spaces in addition to the ten the block is indented from the left margin.

We'll examine *parenthetical references* more fully in the next section, but notice how the citation in the blocked quotation above is placed *outside* the final period. That's a unique exception to the usual rule that a parenthetical citation is enclosed *within* the period of the borrowed material's final sentence.

Trusting Your Memory

One of the best ways to weave references seamlessly into your own writing is to avoid the compulsion to stop and study your sources as you're writing the draft. I remember that writing my research papers in college was typically done in stops and starts. I'd write a paragraph of the draft, then stop and reread a photocopy of an article, then write a few more sentences, and then stop again. Part of the problem was the meager notes I took as I collected information. I hadn't really taken possession of the material before I started writing the draft. But I also didn't trust that I'd remember what was important from my reading.

If, during the course of your research and writing so far, you've found a sense of purpose—for example, you're pretty sure your paper is going to argue for legalization of marijuana or analyze the symbolism on old gravestones on Cape Cod—then you've probably read purposefully, too. You *will* likely know what reference sources you need as you write the draft, without sputtering to a halt to remind yourself of what each says. Consult your notes and sources as you need them; otherwise, push them aside, and immerse yourself in your own writing.

CITING SOURCES

An Alternative to Colliding Footnotes

As did most people I knew, I took a typing class the summer between eighth grade and high school. Our instructional texts were long books with the bindings at the top, and we worked on standard Royal typewriters that were built like tanks. I got up to thirty words a minute, I think, which wasn't very good, but thanks to that class, I can still type without looking at the keyboard. But the one thing I never learned was how to turn the typewriter roller up a half space to type a footnote number that would neatly float above the line. In every term paper in high school, my footnotes collided with my sentences.

I'm certain that such technical difficulties were not the reason that most academic writers in the humanities and social sciences have largely abandoned the footnote method of citation for the parenthetical one, but I'm relieved, nonetheless. In the new system, borrowed material is parenthetically cited in the paper by indicating the author of the original work and the page it was taken from or the date it was published. These parenthetical citations are then explained more fully in the "Works Cited" page at the end of your paper where the sources themselves are listed. (See "Preparing the 'Works Cited' Page" in Chapter 5.)

When to Cite

Before further examining the details of how to use parenthetical citations, remember when you must cite a source in your paper:

1. Whenever you quote from an original source
2. Whenever you borrow ideas from an original source, even when you express them in your own words by paraphrasing or summarizing
3. Whenever you borrow factual information from a source that is *not common knowledge*

The Common Knowledge Exception

The business about *common knowledge* causes much confusion. Just what does this term mean? Basically, *common knowledge* means facts that are widely known and about which there is no controversy.

Sometimes, it's really obvious whether something is common knowledge. The fact that the Super Bowl occurs in late January and pits the winning teams from the American and National Football Conferences is common knowledge. The fact that former president Ronald Reagan was once an actor and starred in a movie with a chimpanzee is common knowledge, too. And the fact that most Americans get most of their news from television is also common knowledge, though this information is getting close to leaving the common knowledge domain.

But what about Christine's assertion that most dreaming occurs during rapid eye movement (REM) sleep? This is an idea about which all of her sources seem to agree. Does that make it common knowledge?

It's useful to ask next, How common to whom? Experts in the topic at hand or the rest of us? As a rule, consider the knowledge of your readers. What information will not be familiar to most of your readers or may even surprise them? Which ideas might even raise skepticism? In this case, the fact about REM sleep and dreaming goes slightly beyond the knowledge of most readers, so to be safe, it should be cited. Use common sense, but when in doubt, cite.

The MLA Author/Page System

Starting in 1984, the Modern Language Association (MLA), a body that, among other things, decides documentation conventions for papers in the humanities, switched from footnotes to the author/page parenthetical citation system. The American Psychological Association (APA), a similar body for the social sciences, promotes use of the author/year system.

You will find it fairly easy to switch from one system to the other once you've learned both. Since MLA conventions are appropriate for English classes, we will focus on the author/page system in the following sections. APA standards are explained more fully in Appendix C, which includes a sample paper.

The Basics of Using
Parenthetical Citation

The MLA method of in-text citations is fairly simple. (How to handle the "Works Cited" page is discussed more fully in the next chapter.) As close as possible to the borrowed material, you indicate in parentheses the original source (usually, the author's name) and the page number in the work that material came from. For example, here's how you'd cite a book or article with a single author using the author/page system:

```
From the very beginning of "Sesame Street" in
1969, kindergarten teachers discovered that
incoming students who had watched the program
already knew their ABC's (Chira 13).*
```

The parenthetical citation here tells readers two things: (1) This information about the success of "Sesame Street" does not originate with the writer but with someone named *Chira,* and (2) readers can consult the original source for further information by looking on page 13 of Chira's book or article, which is cited fully at the back of the paper in the "Works Cited." Here is what readers would find there:

```
                    Works Cited
Chira, Susan. "'Sesame Street' At 20: Taking
    Stock." New York Times. 15 Nov. 1989: 13.
```

Here's another example of parenthetical author/page citation from another research paper. Note the differences from the previous example:

```
"One thing is clear," writes Thomas Mallon,
"plagiarism didn't become a truly sore point with
writers until they thought of writing as their
trade . . . Suddenly his capital and identity were
at stake" (3-4).
```

The first thing you may have noticed is that the author's last name—*Mallon*—was omitted from the parenthetical citation. It didn't need to be included, since it had already been mentioned in the text. *If you mention the author's name in the text of your paper, then you only need to parenthetically cite the relevant page number(s).* This citation also tells us that the quoted passage comes from two pages rather than one.

---

*This and the following "Works Cited" example, along with those on pp. 163–164, are used with permission of Heidi R. Dunham.

Placement of Citations. Place the citation as close as you can to the borrowed material, trying to avoid breaking the flow of the sentences, if possible. To avoid confusion about what's borrowed and what's not—particularly in passages longer than a sentence—mention the name of the original author *in your paper*. For example, in the next example, the writer simply cites the source at the end of the paragraph, not naming the source in the text. Doing so makes it hard for the reader to figure out whether *Blager* is the source of the information in the entire paragraph or just part of it:

> Though children who are victims of sexual abuse
> seem to be disadvantaged in many areas, including
> the inability to forge lasting relationships, low
> self-esteem, and crippling shame, they seem
> advantaged in other areas. Sexually abused
> children seem to be more socially mature than
> other children of their same age group. It's a
> distinctly mixed blessing (Blager 994).

In the following example, notice how the ambiguity about what's borrowed and what's not is resolved by careful placement of the author's name and parenthetical citation in the text:

> Though children who are victims of sexual abuse
> seem to be disadvantaged in many areas, including
> the inability to forge lasting relationships, low
> self-esteem, and crippling shame, they seem
> advantaged in other areas. According to Blager,
> sexually abused children seem to be more socially
> mature than other children of their same age group
> (994). It's a distinctly mixed blessing.

In this latter version, it's clear that *Blager* is the source for one sentence in the paragraph, and the writer is responsible for the rest. Generally, use an authority's last name, rather than a formal title or first name, when mentioning her in your text. Also note that the citation is placed *inside* the period of the sentence (or last sentence) that it documents. That's almost always the case, except at the end of a blocked quotation, where the parenthetical reference is placed after the period of the last sentence (see earlier in this chapter). The citation can also be placed near the author's name, rather than at the end of the sentence, if it doesn't unnecessarily break the flow of the sentence. For example:

```
Blager (994) observes that sexually abused

children tend to be more socially mature than

other children of their same age group.
```

How to Cite When There Is No Author. Occasionally, you may encounter a source where the author is anonymous—the article doesn't have a byline, or for some reason, the author hasn't been identified. This isn't unusual with pamphlets, editorials, government documents, some newspaper articles, and short filler articles in magazines. If you can't parenthetically name the author, what do you cite?

Most often, cite the title (or an abbreviated version, if the title is long) and the page number. If you choose to abbreviate the title, begin with the word under which it is alphabetized in the "Works Cited." For example:

```
Simply put, public relations is "doing good and

getting credit" for it ("Getting Yours" 3).
```

Here is how the publication cited above would be listed at the back of the paper:

```
              Works Cited

Getting Yours: A Publicity and Funding Primer for

    Nonprofit and Voluntary Organizations.

  Lincoln: Contact Center, 1991.
```

For clarity, it's helpful to mention the original source of the borrowed material in the text of your paper. When there is no author's name, refer to the publication (or institution) you're citing or make a more general reference to the source. For example:

> An article in <u>Cuisine</u> magazine argues that the
> best way to kill a lobster is to plunge a knife
> between its eyes ("How to Kill" 56).

or

> According to one government report, with the
> current minimum size limit, most lobsters end up
> on dinner plates before they've had a chance to
> reproduce ("Size at Sexual Maturity" 3-4).

How to Cite Different Works by the Same Author. Suppose you end up using several books or articles by the same author. Obviously, a parenthetical citation that merely lists the author's name and page number won't do, since it won't be clear *which* of several works the citation refers to. In this case, include the author's name, an abbreviated title (if the original is too long), and the page number. For example:

> The thing that distinguishes the amateur from the
> experienced writer is focus; one "rides off in all
> directions at once," and the other finds one
> meaning around which everything revolves (Murray,
> "Write to Learn" 92).

The "Works Cited" list would show multiple works by one author as follows:

Works Cited

Murray, Donald M. <u>Write to Learn</u>. Third Ed. Fort
> Worth: Holt, 1990.

---. <u>A Writer Teaches Writing: A Practical Method
> of Teaching Composition</u>. Boston: Houghton,
> 1968.

It's obvious from the parenthetical citation which of the two Murray books is the source of the information. Note that, in the parenthetical reference, no punctuation separates the title and the page number but a comma follows the author's name. If Murray had been mentioned in the text of the paper, his name could have been dropped from the citation.

How to handle the "Works Cited" page is explained more fully in the next chapter, but for now, notice that the three hyphens used in the second entry are meant to signal that the author's name in this source is the same as in the preceding entry.

How to Cite Indirect Sources. Whenever you can, cite the original source for material you use. For example, if an article on television violence quotes the author of a book and you want to use the quote, try to hunt down the book. That way, you'll be certain of the accuracy of the quote and you may find some more usable information.

Sometimes, however, finding the original source is not possible. In those cases, use the term *qtd. in* to signal that you've quoted or paraphrased a quotation from a book or article that initially appeared elsewhere. In the following example, the citation signals that Bacon's quote was culled from an article by Guibroy, not Bacon's original work:

```
Francis Bacon also weighed in on the dangers of

imitation, observing that "it is hardly possible

at once to admire an author and to go beyond him"

(qtd. in Guibroy 113).
```

How to Cite Personal Interviews. If you mention the name of your interview subject in your text, no parenthetical citation is necessary. On the other hand, if you don't mention the subject's name, cite it in parentheses after the quote:

```
Instead, the recognizable environment gave

something to kids the could relate to. "And it had

a lot more real quality to it than say, 'Mister

Rogers' . . . ," says one educator. "Kids say the

reason they don't like 'Mister' Rogers is that

it's unbelievable" (Diamonti).
```

Regardless of whether you mention your subject's name, you should include a reference to the interview in the "Works Cited." In this case, the reference would look like this:

Works Cited

Diamonti, Nancy. Personal Interview. 5 November

1990.

Sample Parenthetical References for Other Sources

MLA format is pretty simple, and we've already covered some of the basic variations. You should also know four additional variations, as follow:

1. CITING AN ENTIRE WORK

If you mention the author's name in the text, no citation is necessary. The work should, however, be listed in the "Works Cited."

Leon Edel's <u>Henry James</u> is considered by many to

be a model biography.

2. CITING A VOLUME OF A MULTIVOLUME WORK

If you're working with one volume of a multivolume work, it's a good idea to mention which volume in the parenthetical reference. The citation below attributes the passage to the second volume, page 3, of a work by Baym and three or more other authors. The volume number always precedes the colon, which is followed by the page number:

By the turn of the century, three authors

dominated American literature: Mark Twain, Henry

James, and William Dean Howells (Baym et al. 2:3).

3. CITING SEVERAL SOURCES FOR A SINGLE PASSAGE

Occasionally, a number of sources may contribute to a single passage. List them all in one parenthetical reference, separated by semicolons:

```
American soccer may never achieve the popularity
it enjoys in the rest of the world, an unfortunate
fact that is integrally related to the nature of
the game itself (Gardner 12; "Selling Soccer" 30).*
```

4. CITING A LITERARY WORK

Because so many literary works, particularly classics, have been reprinted in so many editions, it's useful to give readers more information about where a passage can be found in one of these editions. List the page number and then the chapter number (and any other relevant information, such as the section or volume), separated by a semicolon. Use arabic rather than roman numerals, unless your teacher instructs you otherwise:

```
Izaak Walton warns that "no direction can be given
to make a man of a dull capacity able to make a
Flie well" (130; ch. 5).
```

When citing classic poems or plays, instead of page numbers, cite line numbers and other appropriate divisions (book, section, act, scene, part, etc.). Separate the information with periods. For example, (*Othello* 3.286) indicates scene 3, line 286 of Shakespeare's work.

Driving Through the First Draft

You have an opening, a lot of material in your notes—much of it, written in your own words—and maybe an outline. You've considered some general methods of development, looked at ways to write with sources, and completed a quick course in how to cite them. Finish the week by writing through the first draft.

Writing the draft may be difficult. All writing, but especially research writing, is a recursive process. You may find sometimes that you must circle back to a step you took before, discovering a gap in your information, a new idea for a thesis statement, or a better lead or focus. Circling back may be frustrating at times, but it's natural and even a good sign: It means you're letting go of your preconceived ideas and allowing the discoveries you make *through writing* to change your mind.

*Jason Pulsifer, University of New Hampshire, 1991. Used with permission.

A Draft Is Something
the Wind Blows Through

Remember, too, that a *draft* is something the wind blows through. It's too early to worry about writing a research paper that's airtight, with no problems to solve. Too often, student writers think they have to write a perfect paper in the first draft. You can worry about plugging holes and tightening things up next week. For now, write a draft, and if you must, put a reminder on a piece of paper and post it on the wall next to your thesis statement. Look at this reminder every time you find yourself agonizing over the imperfections of your paper. The reminder should say, "It Doesn't Count."

Keep a few other things in mind while writing your first draft:

1. *Focus on your tentative thesis.* Remember, the thesis is the controlling idea of your paper. The draft should be built around the thesis, from beginning to end.

2. *Vary your sources.* Offer a variety of different sources as evidence to support your assertions. Beware of a single page that cites only one source.

3. *Remember your audience.* What do your readers want to know about your topic? What do they need to know to understand what you're trying to say?

4. *Write with your notes.* If you took thoughtful notes during the third week—carefully transforming another author's words into your own, flagging good quotes, and developing your own analysis—then you've already written at least some of your paper. You may only need to fine-tune the language in your notes and then plug them into your draft.

5. *Be open to surprises.* The act of writing is often full of surprises. In fact, it should be, since *writing* is *thinking* and the more you think about something, the more you're likely to see. You might get halfway through your draft and discover the part of your topic that *really* fascinates you. Should that happen, you may have to change your thesis or throw away your outline. You may even have to reresearch your topic, at least somewhat. It's not necessarily too late to shift the purpose or focus of your paper (though you should consult your instructor before totally abandoning your topic at this point). Let your curiosity remain the engine that drives you forward.

5

□ ■ □

The Fifth Week

REVISING FOR PURPOSE

My high school girlfriend, Jan, was bright, warm hearted, and fun, and I wasn't at all sure I liked her much, at least at first. Though we had a lot in common—we both loved sunrise over Lake Michigan, bird watching, and Simon and Garfunkel—I found Jan a little intimidating, a little too much in a hurry to anoint us a solid "couple." But we stuck together for three years, and as time passed, I persuaded myself—despite lingering doubts—that I couldn't live without her. There was no way I was going to break my white-knuckled hold on that relationship. After all, I'd invested all that time.

As a writer, I used to have similar relationships with my drafts. I'd work on something very hard, finally finishing the draft. I'd know there were problems, but I'd developed such a tight relationship with my draft that the problems were hard to see. And even when I recognized some problems, the thought of making major changes seemed too risky. Did I dare ruin the things I loved about the draft? These decisions were even harder if the draft took a long time to write.

Revision doesn't necessarily mean you have to sever your relationship with your draft. It's probably too late to make a complete break with the draft and abandon your topic. However, revision does demand finding some way to step back from the draft and change your relationship with it, seeing it from the reader's perspective rather than just the writer's. Revision requires that you loosen your grip. And when you do, you may decide to shift your focus or rearrange the information. At the very least, you may discover gaps in in-

formation or sections of the draft that need more development. You
will certainly need to prune sentences.

The place to begin is *purpose.* You should determine whether
the purpose of your paper is clear and examine how well the information is organized around that purpose.

Revision, as the word implies, means "re-seeing" or "recon-
ceiving," trying to see what you failed to notice with the first look.
That can be hard. Remember how stuck I was on that one picture of
the lighthouse? I planted my feet in the sand, and the longer I stared
through the camera lens, the harder it was to see the lighthouse from
any other angle. It didn't matter that I didn't particularly like what I
was seeing. I just wanted to take the picture.

You've spent more than four weeks researching your topic and
the last few days composing your first draft. You may find that
you've spent so much time staring through the lens—seeing your topic
the way you chose to see it in your first draft—that doing a major revision is about as appealing as eating cold beets. How do you get the
perspective to "re-see" the draft and rebuild it into a stronger paper?

Using a Reader

If you wanted to save a relationship, you might ask a friend to
intervene. Then you'd get the benefit of a third-party opinion, a fresh
view that could help you see what you may be too close to to see.

A reader can do the same thing for your research paper draft.
She will come to the draft without the entanglements that encumber
the writer and provide a fresh pair of eyes through which you can see
the work.

What You Need from a Reader

Your instructor may be that reader, or you might exchange
drafts with someone else in class. You may already have someone
whom you share your writing with—a roommate, a friend. Whomever
you choose, try to find a reader who will respond honestly *and* make
you want to write again.

What will be most helpful from a reader at this stage? Comments about your spelling and mechanics are not critical right now.
You'll deal with those factors later. What the reader needs to point
out is if the *purpose* of your paper is clear and if your thesis is convincing. Is it clear what your paper is about, what part of the topic
you're focusing on? Does the information presented stay within that

focus? Does the information clarify and support what you're trying to say? It would also be helpful for the reader to tell you what parts of the draft are interesting and what parts seem to drag.

□ *EXERCISE 5-1*
Directing the Reader's Response

Though you could ask your reader for a completely open-ended reaction to your paper, the following questions might help her focus on providing comments that will help you tackle a revision:

1. After reading the draft, what would you say is the main question the paper is trying to answer or focus on?
2. In your own words, what is the main point?
3. What do you remember from the draft that is most convincing that the ideas in the paper are true? What is least convincing?
4. Where is the paper most interesting? Where does the paper drag?

How your reader responds to the first two questions will tell you a lot about how well you've succeeded in making the purpose and thesis of your paper clear. The answer to the third question may reveal how well you've *used* the information gleaned from research. The reader's response to the fourth question will give you a preliminary reading on how well you engaged her. Did you lose her anywhere? Is the paper interesting?

□ ■ □

A reader responding to Jeff's paper titled "The Alcoholic Family" helped him discover some problems that are typical of first drafts. His paper was inspired by his girlfriend's struggles to deal with her alcoholic father. Jeff wondered if he could do anything to help. Jeff's reader was touched by those parts of the paper where he discusses his own observations of the troubled family's behavior; however, the reader was confused about Jeff's purpose. "Your lead seems to say that your paper is going to focus on how family members deal with an alcoholic parent," the reader wrote to Jeff, "but I thought your main idea was that people outside an alcoholic family can help but must be careful about it. I wanted to know more about how you now think you can help your girlfriend. What exactly do you need to be careful about?"

This wasn't an observation Jeff could have made, given how close he is to the topic and the draft. But armed with objective and specific information about what changes are needed, Jeff is ready to attack the draft.

Attacking the Draft

The controlling idea of your paper—that thesis you posted on an index card above your desk a week or more ago—is the heart of your paper and should, in some way, be connected to everything else in the draft.

Though a good reader can suddenly help you see things you've missed, she will likely not give much feedback on what you should do to fix these problems. Physically attacking the draft might help. If you typed your first draft, then doing this may feel sacrilegious—a little like writing in books. One of the difficulties with revision is that writers respect the typewritten page too much. When the draft is typed up, with all those words marching neatly down the page, it is hard to mess it up again. As pages emerge from the typewriter or printer, you can almost hear the sound of hardening concrete. Breaking the draft into pieces can free you to clearly see them and how they fit together.

☐ *EXERCISE 5-2*
Cut-and-Paste Revision

Try this cut-and-paste revision exercise (another useful technique inspired by Peter Elbow and his book *Writing with Power**):

1. Make a photocopy of your first draft (one-sided pages only). Save the original; you may need it later.

2. Cut apart the photocopy of your research paper, paragraph by paragraph. (You may cut it into even smaller pieces later.) Once the draft has been completely disassembled, shuffle the paragraphs—get them wildly out of order so the original draft is just a memory.

3. Now go through the shuffled stack and find the *core paragraph,* the most important one in the whole paper. This is probably the

*Peter Elbow, *Writing with Power* (New York: Oxford University Press, 1981).

paragraph that contains your thesis, or main point. This paragraph is the one that gets to the heart of what you're trying to say. Set it aside.

4. With your core paragraph directly in front of you, work your way through the remaining stack of paragraphs and make two new stacks: one of paragraphs that are relevant to your core and one of paragraphs that don't seem relevant, that don't seem to serve a clear purpose in developing your main idea. Be as tough as a drill sergeant as you scrutinize each scrap of paper. What you are trying to determine is whether each piece of information, each paragraph, is there for a reason. Ask yourself these questions as you examine each paragraph:

- Does it *develop* my thesis or further the purpose of my paper, or does it seem an unnecessary tangent that could be part of another paper with a different focus?
- Does it provide important *evidence* that supports my main point?
- Does it *explain* something that's key to understanding what I'm trying to say?
- Does it *illustrate* a key concept?
- Does it help establish the *importance* of what I'm trying to say?
- Does it raise (or answer) a *question* that I must explore, given what I'm trying to say?

You might find it helpful to write on the back of each relevant paragraph which of these purposes it serves. You may also discover that *some* of the information in a paragraph seems to serve your purpose, while the rest strikes you as unnecessary. Use your scissors to cut away the irrelevant material, pruning back the paragraph to include only what's essential.

5. You now have two stacks of paper scraps: those that seem to serve your purpose and those that don't. For now, set aside your "reject" pile. Put your core paragraph back into the "save" pile, and begin to reassemble a very rough draft, using what you've saved. Play with order. Try new leads, new ends, new middles. As you spread out the pieces of information before you, see if a new structure suddenly emerges. *But especially, look for gaps—places where you should add additional information.* Jot down ideas for material you might add on a piece of paper; then cut up the paper and splice (with tape) each idea in the appropriate place when you reassemble the draft in the next step. You may rediscover uses for information in your "reject" pile, as well. Mine that pile, if you need to.

6. As a structure begins to emerge, begin taping together the fragments of paper and splicing ideas for new information. Don't worry about transitions; you'll deal with those later. When you're done with the reconstruction, the draft should look drafty—something the wind can blow through—and may be totally unlike the version you started with.

□ ■ □

Examining the Wreckage

As you deal with the wreckage your scissors have wrought on your first draft, you might notice other problems with it. For example, you may discover that your draft has no real core paragraph, no part that is central to your point and purpose. Don't panic. Just make sure that you write one in the revision.

To your horror, you may find that your "reject" pile of paragraphs is bigger than your "save" pile. If that's the case, you won't have much left to work with. You may need to reresearch the topic (returning to the library this week to collect more information) or shift the focus of your paper. Perhaps both.

To your satisfaction, you may discover that your reconstructed draft looks familiar. You may have returned to the structure you started with in the first draft. If that's the case, it might mean your first draft worked pretty well; breaking it down and putting it back together simply confirmed that.

When Jeff cut up "The Alcoholic Family," he discovered immediately that his reader was right: Much of his paper did not seem clearly related to his point about the role outsiders can play in helping alcoholic families. His "reject" pile had paragraph after paragraph of information about the roles that alcoholic family members assume when there's a heavy drinker in the house. Jeff asked himself, What does that information have to do with the roles of outsiders? He considered changing his thesis, rewriting his core paragraph to say something about how each family member plays a role in dealing with the drinker. But Jeff's purpose in writing the paper was to discover what *he* could do to help.

As Jeff played with the pieces of his draft, he began to see two things. First of all, he realized that some of the ways members behave in an alcoholic family make them resistant to outside help; this insight allowed him to salvage some information from his "reject" pile by more clearly connecting the information to his main point. Second, Jeff knew he had to go back to the well: He needed to return to the library and recheck his sources to find more information on what family friends can do to help.

REVISING FOR
INFORMATION

I know. You thought you were done digging. But as I said last week, research is a recursive process. (Remember, the word is *re-search,* or "look again.") You will often find yourself circling back to the earlier steps as you get a clearer sense of where you want to go.

As you stand back from your draft, looking again at how well your research paper accomplishes your purpose, you'll likely see holes in the information. They may seem more like craters. Jeff discovered he had to reresearch his topic, returning to the library to hunt for new sources to help him develop his point. Since he had enough time, he repeated some of the research steps from the third week, beginning with a first-level search (see "First-Level Searching" in Chapter 3). This time, though, he knew exactly what he needed to find.

You may find that you basically have what information you need but that your draft requires more development. Candy's draft on how child abuse affects language included material from some useful studies from the *Journal of Speech and Hearing Disorders,* which showed pretty conclusively that abuse cripples children's abilities to converse. At her reader's suggestion, Candy decided it was important to write more in her revision about what was learned from the studies, since they offered convincing evidence for her thesis. Though she could mine her notes for more information, Candy decided to recheck the journal indexes to look for any similar studies she may have missed. As you begin to see exactly what information you need, don't rule out another trip to the library, even this late in the game.

Finding Quick Facts

The holes of information in your research paper draft may not be large at all. What's missing may be an important but discrete fact that would really help your readers understand the point you're making. For example, in Janabeth's draft on the impact of divorce on father/daughter relationships, she realized she was missing an important fact: the number of marriages that end in divorce in the United States. This single piece of information could help establish the significance of the problem she was writing about. Janabeth could search her sources for the answer, but there's a quicker way: fact books.

736 *Entertainment and Culture*

Top 15 Regularly Scheduled Network Programs, Nov. 1990

Rank	Program name (network)	Total percent of TV households
1.	Cheers (NBC)	24.0
2.	60 Minutes (CBS)	21.8
3.	Murder, She Wrote (CBS)	18.2
3.	Roseanne (ABC)	18.2
5.	America's Funniest People (ABC)	18.0
5.	America's Funniest Home Videos (ABC)	18.0
7.	Murphy Brown (CBS)	17.8
8.	Designing Women (CBS)	17.7
9.	Empty Nest (NBC)	17.6
10.	Bill Cosby Show (NBC)	17.5
11.	Golden Girls (NBC)	17.2
12.	A Different World (NBC)	17.0
13.	NFL Monday Night Football (ABC)	16.7
14.	Unsolved Mysteries (NBC)	16.6
15.	Matlock (NBC)	16.3

Total U.S. TV households 93,100,000

NOTE: Percentages are calculated from average audience viewings, 5 minutes or longer and 2 or more telecasts. *Source:* Nielsen Media Research, copyright 1991, Nielsen Media Research.

Top 15 Syndicated TV Programs 1990–91 Season

Rank	Program	Rating (% U.S.)[1]
1.	Wheel of Fortune, M-F	13.4
2.	Jeopardy	12.0
3.	Star Trek	10.7[2]
4.	Oprah Winfrey Show	9.0
5.	Cosby Show	8.3[2]
5.	Entertainment Tonight	8.3[2]
7.	Warner Brothers Volume 26	8.2[2]
8.	A Current Affair	7.9[2]
9.	MGM Premiere Network III	7.5[2]
9.	Wheel of Fortune, Weekend	7.5
11.	Universal Pictures Debut Network	6.7[2]
12.	Orion Galaxy Network	6.2[2]
12.	Republic Color Movies	6.2[2]
12.	Warner Brothers Premiere Edition	6.2[2]
15.	Donahue	5.9

1. 8/27/90–12/30/90. 2. Includes multiple exposures. *Source:* Nielsen Syndication Service National TV Ratings. Copyright 1991, Nielsen Media Research.

Top Sports Shows 1990–91[1]

Rank	Program name (network)	Rating (% of TV households)
1.	Super Bowl XXV (ABC)	41.9
2.	NFC Championship Game (CBS)	26.5
3.	AFC Playoff Bengals vs. Raiders (NBC)	24.7
4.	NFC Playoff Saints vs. Bears (CBS)	24.2
5.	NFC Playoff Bears vs. Giants (CBS)	22.6

1. Sept. 17, 1990, through July 14, 1991. *Source:* Nielsen Media Research, copyright 1991, Nielsen Media Research.

Top Specials 1990–91[1]

Rank	Program name (network)	Rating (% of TV households)
1.	63rd Academy Awards (ABC)	28.4
2.	Best of Ed Sullivan (CBS)	21.3
3.	American Music Awards (ABC)	20.4
4.	Grammy Awards (CBS)	18.8
5.	Barbara Walters Special with Jeremy Irons, Sophia Loren, and Whoopi Goldberg (ABC)	18.5

1. Sept. 17, 1990, through June 9, 1991. *Source:* Nielsen Media Research, copyright 1991, Nielsen Media Research.

Persons Viewing Prime Time[1]
(in millions)

	Total persons
Monday	99.2
Tuesday	97.2
Wednesday	89.7
Thursday	95.9
Friday	86.7
Saturday	87.8
Sunday	107.2
Total average	95.4

1. Average minute audiences Nov. 1990. NOTE: Prime time is 8–11 p.m. (EST) except Sun. 7–11 pm. *Source:* Nielsen Media Research, copyright 1991, Nielsen Media Research.

Top Rated Movies 1990–91[1]

Rank	Program name (network)	Rating (% of TV households)
1.	Sarah, Plain and Tall (CBS)	23.1
2.	Stephen King's "It" (Part 2) (ABC)	20.6
3.	Kaleidoscope (NBC)	20.3
4.	Love, Lies and Murder (Part 2) (NBC)	20.3
5.	And the Sea Will Tell (Part 1) (CBS)	20.1

1. Sept. 17, 1990, through April 14, 1991. *Source:* Nielsen Media Research, copyright 1991, Nielsen Media Research.

FIGURE 5-1 *Information Please Almanac* is one of several good sources for information on popular culture.

Source: From *1992 Information Please Almanac.* Copyright © 1991 by Houghton Mifflin Company. All rights reserved.

Fact books are references loaded with specific, factual information that can answer most any question that is statistical in nature. Here are several key sources in which you can find fast answers to questions of fact. All are published annually, so the information is likely to be current:

> *Statistical Abstracts of the United States*. U.S. Bureau of the Census. Washington DC: GPO. *An astonishingly wide range of economic, social, and political statistics, culled largely from government sources. A gold mine!*
>
> *World Almanac and Book of Facts: 1992*. New York: Pharos Books. *Published since 1868, so it's useful for historical information, as well.*
>
> *Information Please Almanac, Atlas and Yearbook: 1992*. 45th edition. Boston: Houghton Mifflin. *In addition to statistical information, contains material on popular culture, as well* (see Figure 5-1).
>
> *Facts on File: A Weekly World News Digest*. New York: Facts on File. *Published twice monthly, a useful source of information on dates of events, names of people involved, and so on. Extremely timely information.*

Any one of the yearbooks listed above could have answered Janabeth's question about U.S. divorce rates, but she decided to check *Statistical Abstracts*. A quick look at the index in the front of the book led her to a page of tables on divorce and marriage, loaded with useful facts (see Figure 5-2). Janabeth accidently discovered another table on the same page in *Statistical Abstracts* that proved equally useful: divorce rates among specific age groups.

Fact books can be valuable sources of information that will plug small holes in your draft. These references are especially useful during revision, when you often know exactly what fact you need. But even if you're not sure whether you can glean a useful statistic from one of these sources, they might be worth checking anyway. There's a good chance you'll find something useful.

REVISING FOR LANGUAGE

Most of my students have the impression that revision begins and ends with concerns about language—about *how* they said it rather than *what* they said. Revising for language is really a tertiary concern (though an important one), to be addressed after the writer has struggled with the purpose and design of a draft.

Once you're satisfied that your paper's purpose is clear, that it provides readers with the information they need to understand what

42   Population

No. 48. Population by Selected Ancestry Group and Region: 1980

[As of April 1. Covers persons who reported single and multiple ancestry groups. Persons who reported a multiple ancestry group may be included in more than one category. Major classifications of ancestry groups do not represent strict geographic or cultural definitions. The European ancestry groups shown are those with one million or more persons and other groups shown are those with 75,000 or more persons. Based on a sample and subject to sampling variability; see text, section 1 and Appendix III. For composition of regions, see fig. I, inside front cover]

ANCESTRY GROUP	Number (1,000)	PERCENT DISTRIBUTION, BY REGION				ANCESTRY GROUP	Number (1,000)	PERCENT DISTRIBUTION, BY REGION			
		North-east	Mid-west	South	West			North-east	Mid-west	South	West
European: [1]						Chinese	894	25	9	12	55
English	49,596	16	23	40	21	Filipino	795	10	11	11	68
German	49,224	19	41	22	18	Japanese	791	7	8	9	77
Irish	40,166	24	26	32	18	Korean	377	18	18	20	43
French [2]	12,892	26	27	27	19	Asian Indian	312	35	23	23	19
Italian	12,184	57	16	13	14	Vietnamese	215	9	14	33	44
Scottish	10,049	19	23	35	24						
Polish	8,228	41	38	11	10						
Dutch	6,304	18	35	26	20	Jamaican	253	70	6	18	5
Swedish	4,345	15	43	12	31	Haitian	90	72	4	21	2
Norwegian [3]	3,454	7	55	7	31						
Russian [3]	2,781	48	17	16	19	Mexican	7,693	1	9	35	55
Czech [4]	1,892	18	49	18	15	Spanish/					
Hungarian	1,777	39	33	13	14	Hispanic [5]	2,687	23	8	26	43
Welsh	1,665	25	27	22	27	Puerto Rican	1,444	73	11	8	7
Danish	1,518	9	38	10	43	Cuban	598	24	4	63	9
Portuguese	1,024	50	3	6	41	Dominican	171	91	1	6	2
						Colombian	156	54	7	26	13
Other:						Spaniard	95	36	6	36	22
Lebanese	295	31	27	26	16	Ecuadoran	88	64	7	11	18
Armenian	213	39	14	5	42	Salvadoran	85	13	3	9	75
Iranian	123	17	15	26	42						
Syrian	107	47	20	18	15	Hawaiian	202	2	3	6	89
Arab/Arabian [5]	93	19	29	21	30						
						American Indian	6,716	9	24	44	24
Afro-American	20,965	17	22	53	9	French Canadian	780	47	23	13	17
African [5]	204	33	19	33	1	Canadian	456	42	19	15	23

[1] Excludes Spaniard.   [2] Excludes French Basque.   [3] Represents persons who reported as "Russian," "Great Russian," "Georgian," and other related European or Asian groups. Excludes Ukrainian, Ruthenian, Belorussian and some other distinct ethnic groups. See source for further information.   [4] Includes persons who reported as "Czech," "Bohemian," and "Moravian," as well as the general response of "Czechoslovakian."   [5] Represents a general type of response which may encompass several ancestry groups.

Source: U.S. Bureau of the Census, *1980 Census of Population, Supplementary Report,* series PC80-S1-10.

No. 49. Marital Status of the Population, by Sex and Age: 1989

[As of March. Persons 18 years old and over. Excludes members of Armed Forces except those living off post or with their families on post. Based on Current Population Survey; see text, section 1, and Appendix III. See *Historical Statistics, Colonial Times to 1970,* series A 160-171, for decennial census data]

SEX AND AGE	NUMBER OF PERSONS (1,000)					PERCENT DISTRIBUTION				
	Total	Single	Married	Widowed	Divorced	Total	Single	Married	Widowed	Divorced
Male	85,799	22,195	55,279	2,282	6,044	100.0	25.9	64.4	2.7	7.0
18-19 years old	3,635	3,533	95	2	5	100.0	97.2	2.6	0.1	0.1
20-24 years old	8,939	6,915	1,912	6	105	100.0	77.4	21.4	0.1	1.2
25-29 years old	10,650	4,890	5,243	-	518	100.0	45.9	49.2	-	4.9
30-34 years old	10,811	2,789	7,157	23	842	100.0	25.8	66.2	0.2	7.8
35-39 years old	9,595	1,461	7,091	33	1,009	100.0	15.2	73.9	0.3	10.5
40-44 years old	8,086	673	6,432	38	943	100.0	8.3	79.5	0.5	11.7
45-54 years old	11,917	801	9,661	164	1,291	100.0	6.7	81.1	1.4	10.8
55-64 years old	10,088	563	8,385	328	812	100.0	5.6	83.1	3.3	8.0
65-74 years old	7,880	386	6,387	704	402	100.0	4.9	81.1	8.9	5.1
75 years old and over	4,199	184	2,915	982	118	100.0	4.4	69.4	23.4	2.8
Female	93,984	17,775	56,195	11,492	8,522	100.0	18.9	59.8	12.2	9.1
18- 9 years old	3,719	3,366	333	8	11	100.0	90.5	9.0	0.2	0.3
20-24 years old	9,336	5,838	3,231	11	256	100.0	62.5	34.6	0.1	2.7
25-29 years old	10,827	3,184	6,755	31	858	100.0	29.4	62.4	0.3	7.9
30-34 years old	10,950	1,854	7,868	67	1,161	100.0	16.9	71.9	0.6	10.6
35-39 years old	9,775	969	7,391	133	1,281	100.0	9.9	75.6	1.4	13.1
40-44 years old	8,418	530	6,311	250	1,327	100.0	6.3	75.0	3.0	15.8
45-54 years old	12,705	692	9,518	697	1,798	100.0	5.4	74.9	5.5	14.2
55-64 years old	11,311	492	7,716	2,035	1,067	100.0	4.4	68.2	18.0	9.4
65-74 years old	9,867	441	5,251	3,614	560	100.0	4.5	53.2	36.6	5.7
75 years old and over	7,077	410	1,819	4,646	203	100.0	5.8	25.7	65.6	2.9

- Represents or rounds to zero.

Source: U.S. Bureau of the Census, *Current Population Reports,* series P-20, No. 445.

FIGURE 5-2 *Statistical Abstracts of the United States* is a rich source of facts on economic, political, and social subjects.

you're trying to say, and that it is organized in a logical, interesting way, *then* focus your attention on the fine points of *how* it is written. Begin with voice.

Listening to the Voice

Listen to your paper by reading it aloud to yourself. You may find the experience a little unsettling. Most of us are not used to actively listening to our writing voices. But your readers will be listening.

As you read, ask yourself: Is this the voice you want readers to hear? Does it seem appropriate for this paper? Does it sound flat or wooden or ponderous in any places? Does it sound anything like you?

If revising your writing voice is necessary for any reason, begin at the beginning—the first line, the first paragraph—and rely on your ears. What sounds right?

You may discover that you begin with the right voice but lose it in places. That often happens when you move from anecdotal material to exposition, from telling a story to explaining research findings. To some extent, a shift in voice is inevitable when you move from one method of development to another, especially from personal material to factual material. But examine your word choices in those passages that seem to go flat. Do you sometimes shift to the dry language used by your sources? Can you rewrite that language in your own voice? When you do, you will find yourself cutting away unnecessary, vague, and pretentious language.

Rewriting in your own voice has another effect, too: It brings the writing to life. Readers respond to an individual writing voice. When I read David Quammen or Richard Conniff, he rises up from the page, like a hologram, and suddenly, I can see him as a distinct person. I also become interested in how each man sees the things he's writing about.

Avoid Sounding Glib

Beware, though, of a voice that calls more attention to itself than the substance of what you're saying. As you've no doubt learned from reading scholarly sources, much academic writing is voiceless, partly because what's important is not *who* the writer is but *what* he has to say.

Sometimes, in an attempt to sound natural, a writer will take on a folksy or overly colloquial voice, which is much worse than sounding lifeless. What impression does this passage give you?

> The thing that really blew my mind was that
> marijuana use among college students had actually
> declined in the past ten years! I was psyched to
> learn that.

Ugh!

As you search for the right voice in doing your revision, look for a balance between flat, wooden prose, which sounds as if it were manufactured by a machine, and forced, flowery prose, which distracts the reader from what's most important: what you're trying to say.

Scrutinizing Paragraphs

How Well Do You Integrate Sources?

Last week, we looked at how to fluently blend quotation, paraphrase, and summary with your own analysis. When you achieve the right blend, the reader senses that you are in control, that the information serves your purpose. When the blend isn't quite right, you—your voice and your purpose—may disappear behind the information. As a result, your paper will seem roughly stitched together. That's the problem in the following paragraph from a research paper on the conflict with Iraq:

> George Bush and Saddam Hussein acted during the
> Gulf War in response to their own upbringing
> (Steinem 25). "Somehow, the Gulf War had turned
> into a conflict that both men carried out in ways
> that were the essence of their childhoods; one
> killing close up, the other from a distance; one
> lashing out against the world as if his life
> depended on it, the other striving to gain its
> approval with a victorious game" (Steinem 26). How
> we were treated as children has a great affect on
> how we treat the world. "Socialization determines
> the way this self-hatred is played out" (Steinem
> 26). Girls tend to respond differently than boys.

   This information seems interesting enough, but it is so lifelessly woven into the paragraph that it's downright dull. The writer summarizes, then quotes, then summarizes, then quotes—without flagging who said what or even being selective about what's said. Parenthetical citations are scattered throughout, breaking the flow of the paragraph. And though the paragraph does seem to have some unity, there's no clear sense of the writer's purpose in sharing the information. The writer is "missing in action": no voice, no analysis or commentary, no sense of emphasis on what's important.

   Now consider this rewrite of the same paragraph:

```
One of the most interesting theories about how the

Gulf War was waged has to do with the two men who

waged it--George Bush and Saddam Hussein. In

Revolution from Within, feminist Gloria Steinem

argues that "both men carried out [the war] in

ways that were the essence of their childhoods:

one killing close up, the other from a distance;

one lashing out against the world . . . the other

striving to gain its approval with a victorious

game" (26). If Steinem is right, then the fate of

the world is, and maybe always has been,

determined by how well international leaders were

treated by their parents.
```

   Notice the difference? Attributing the quote—and the idea—to its source, Gloria Steinem, is one key difference in the revised paragraph. Suddenly, the voice has a name, and a well-known one at that. But the writer is more involved here, as well, from the very first sentence, noting that the theory seems interesting and concluding with a remark about why it may be important. The rewrite is also much less cluttered with parenthetical references.

   Go over your draft, paragraph by paragraph, and look for ways to *use* the information from your research more smoothly. Be especially alert to "hanging quotes" that appear unattached to any source. Attribution is important. To anchor quotes and ideas to people or publications in your paper, use words such as *argues, observes, says, contends, believes,* and *offers* and phrases such as *according to.* Also look for ways to use quotes selectively, lifting key words or phrases and weaving them into your own writing. What can you add that highlights what you believe is significant about the information? How does it relate to your thesis and the purpose of your paper?

Is Each Paragraph Unified?

Each paragraph should be about one idea and organized around it. You probably know that already. But applying this notion is a particular problem in a research paper, where information abounds and paragraphs sometimes approach marathon length.

If any of your paragraphs are similar to that—that is, they seem to run nearly a page or more—look for ways to break them up into shorter paragraphs. Is more than one idea embedded in the long version? Are you explaining or examining more than one thing?

Also take a look at your shorter paragraphs. Do any present minor or tangential ideas that belong somewhere else? Are any of these ideas irrelevant? Should the paragraph be cut? The cut-and-paste exercise (5-2) done earlier this week may have helped you with this already.

Scrutinizing Sentences

Using Active Voice

Which of these two sentences seems more passive, more lifeless?

```
Steroids have been used by many high school

athletes.
```

or

```
Many high school athletes use steroids.
```

The first version, written in the passive voice, is clearly the more limp of the two. It's not grammatically incorrect. In fact, you may have found texts written in the passive voice to be pervasive in the reading you've done for your research paper. Research writing is plagued by passive voice, and that's one of the reasons it can be so mind numbing to read.

Passive voice construction is simple: The subject of the sentence—the thing doing the action—becomes the thing *acted upon* by the verb: for instance, *Clarence kicked the dog* versus *The dog was kicked by Clarence.* Sometimes, the subject may be missing altogether, as in *The study was released: Who* or *what* released it?

Active voice remedies the problem by pushing the subject up front in the sentence or adding the subject if he, she, or it is missing: for example, ***High school athletes*** *use steroids.* Knowing exactly who is using the drugs makes the sentence livelier.

Another tell-tale sign of passive voice is that it usually requires a *to be* verb: *is, was, are, were, am, be, being, been.* For example, *Alcoholism among women **has been** extensively studied.* Search your draft for *be's,* and see if any sentences are written in the passive voice. (If you write on a computer, some word-processing programs will search for you.) To make a sentence active, replace the missing subject: ***Researchers*** *have extensively studied alcoholism among women.*

See the box entitled "Active Verbs for Discussing Ideas," which was compiled by a colleague of mine, Cynthia Gannett. If you're desperate for an alternative to *says* or *argues,* this list offers 138 alternatives.

Using Strong Verbs

Though this may seem like nit-picking, you'd be amazed how much writing in the active voice can revitalize research writing. The use of strong verbs can have the same effect.

As you know, verbs make things happen. Some verbs can make the difference between a sentence that crackles and one that merely hums. Instead of this—*The league **gave** Roger Clemens, the Boston Red Sox pitcher, a $10,000 fine for arguing with an umpire*—write this—*The league **slapped** Roger Clemens, the Boston Red Sox pitcher, with a $10,000 fine for arguing with an umpire.*

Varying Sentence Length

Some writers can sustain breathlessly long sentences, with multiple subordinate clauses, and not lose their readers. Joan Didion is one of those writers. Actually, she also knows enough not to do it too often. She carefully varies the lengths of her sentences, going from a breathless one to one that can be quickly inhaled and back again. For example, here is how her essay "Dreamers of the Golden Dream" begins. Notice the mix of sentence lengths.

This is the story about love and death in the golden land, and begins with the country. The San Bernadino Valley lies only an hour east of Los Angeles by the San Bernadino Freeway but is in certain ways an alien place: not the coastal California of the

ACTIVE VERBS
FOR DISCUSSING IDEAS

informs	protects	cautions	confronts
reviews	insists	shares	regards
argues	handles	convinces	toys with
states	confuses	declares	hypothesizes
synthesizes	intimates	ratifies	suggests
asserts	simplifies	analyzes	contradicts
claims	narrates	affirms	considers
answers	outlines	exaggerates	highlights
responds	allows	observes	disconfirms
critiques	initiates	substitutes	admires
explains	asserts	perceives	endorses
illuminates	supports	resolves	uncovers
determines	compares	assaults	hesitates
challenges	distinguishes	disputes	denies
experiments	describes	conflates	refutes
experiences	assists	retorts	assembles
pleads	sees	reconciles	demands
defends	persuades	complicates	criticizes
rejects	lists	urges	negates
reconsiders	quotes	reads	diminishes
verifies	exposes	parses	shows
announces	warns	concludes	supplements
provides	believes	stresses	accepts
formulates	categorizes	facilitates	buttresses
qualifies	disregards	contrasts	relinquishes
hints	tests	discusses	treats
repudiates	postulates	guides	clarifies
infers	acknowledges	proposes	grants
marshalls	defies	points out	insinuates
summarizes	accepts	judges	identifies
disagrees	emphasizes	enumerates	explains
rationalizes	confirms	reveals	interprets
shifts	praises	condemns	adds
maintains	supplies	implies	
persists	seeks	reminds	

Source: Reproduced with permission of Cynthia Gannett.

subtropical twilights and the soft westerlies off the Pacific but a harsher California, haunted by the Mojave just beyond the mountains, devastated by the hot dry Santa Ana wind that comes down through the passes at 100 miles an hour and whines through the eucalyptus windbreaks and works on the nerves. October is a bad month for the wind, the month when breathing is difficult and the hills blaze up spontaneously. There has been no rain since April. Every voice seems a scream. It is the season of suicide and divorce and prickly dread, wherever the wind blows.*

The second sentence of Didion's lead is a whopper, but it works, especially since it's set among sentences that are more than half its length. Didion makes music here.

Examine your sentences. Are the long ones too long? You can usually tell if, when you read a sentence, there's no sense of emphasis or it seems to die out. Can you break an unnecessarily long sentence into several shorter ones? More common is a string of short, choppy sentences. For example:

```
Babies are born extrasensitive to sounds. This

unique sensitivity to all sounds does not last.

By the end of the first year, they become deaf

to speech sounds not a part of their native

language.
```

This isn't horrible, but with some sentence combining, the passage will be more fluent:

```
Though babies are born extrasensitive to sounds,

this unique sensitivity lasts only through the end

of the first year, when they become deaf to speech

sounds not a part of their native language.
```

Look for short sentences where you are repeating words or phrases and also for sentences that begin with pronouns. Experiment with sentence combining. The result will not only be more fluent prose but a sense of emphasis, a sense of the relationship between the information and your ideas about it.

*Joan Didion, *Slouching Toward Bethlehem* (New York: Pocket, 1968).

Editing for Simplicity

Thoreau saw simplicity as a virtue, something that's obvious not only by the time he spent beside Walden Pond but also by the prose he penned while living there. Thoreau writes clearly and plainly.

Somewhere, many of us got the idea that simplicity in writing is a vice—that the long word is better than the short word, that the complex phrase is superior to the simple one. The misconception is that to write simply is to be simple minded. Research papers, especially, suffer from this mistaken notion. They are often filled with what William Zinsser calls *clutter.*

☐ **EXERCISE 5-3**
Cutting Clutter

The following passage is an example of cluttered writing at its best (worst?). It contains phrases and words that often appear in college research papers. Read the passage once. Then take a few minutes and rewrite it, cutting as many words as you can without sacrificing the meaning. Look for ways to substitute a shorter word for a longer one and to say in fewer words what is currently said in many. Try to halve the word count.

```
The implementation of the revised alcohol policy

in the university community is regrettable at the

present time due to the fact that the

administration has not facilitated sufficient

student input, in spite of the fact that there

have been attempts by the people affected by this

policy to make their objections known in many

instances.
```
(55 words)

If you found yourself getting a little ruthless as you edited this rather dead passage, it's all right. The passage needed some machete work. A stock phrase such as *due to the fact that,* which often appears in research papers, can be resurrected quite simply by using the word *because.* A fancy word such as *implementation* can be replaced with a simple one such as *start.* There's a lot of clutter like this in the previous passage.

I hope you will also see that simplifying the prose here does not make it more simple minded but simply more clear. Cluttered writing, which is often intended to impress readers, ends up turning them off.

Of course, it's easy to be ruthless editing someone else's work. Can you be equally ruthless with your own? Take a random page of your draft research paper, and cut *at least* seven words. Look at the kinds of clutter you cut away. Do you use long words when short ones will do just as well? Do you resort to stock phrases, such as *at the present time (now)*? Do you signal to the reader what should be obvious with phrases such as *In conclusion* or *It should be pointed out* or *It is my opinion that?*

After you study a page of your draft and see the kinds of clutter that creeps into your writing, edit the rest. The rule is to simplify, simplify, making every word count.

□ ■ □

PREPARING THE FINAL MANUSCRIPT

I wanted to title this section "Preparing the Final Draft," but it occurred to me that *draft* doesn't suggest anything final. I always call my work a draft because, until it's out of my hands, it never feels finished. You may feel that way, too. You've spent five weeks on this paper—and the last few days, disassembling it and putting it back together again. How do you know when you're finally done?

For many students, the deadline dictates that: The paper is due tomorrow. But you may find that your paper really seems to be coming together in a satisfying way. You may even like it, and you're ready to prepare the final manuscript.

Considering "Reader-Friendly" Design

Later in this section, we'll discuss the format of your final draft. Research papers in some disciplines have prescribed forms. Some papers in the social sciences, for example, require an abstract, an introduction, a discussion of method, a presentation of results, and a discussion of those results. These sections are clearly defined using subheadings, making it easier for readers to examine those parts of the paper they're most interested in. You probably discovered that in your own reading of formal research. You'll likely learn the formats research papers should conform to in various disciplines as you take upper-level courses in those fields.

While you should document this paper properly, you may have some freedom to develop a format that best serves your purpose. As you consider the format of your rewrite, keep readers in mind. How can you make your paper more readable? How can you signal your plan for developing the topic and what's important?

Some visual devices might help, including:

- Subheadings
- Graphs, illustrations, tables
- "Bulleted" lists (like the one you're reading now)
- "Block" quotes
- Underlining and paragraphing for emphasis
- "White space"

Long, unbroken pages of text can appear to be a gray, uninviting mass to the reader. All of the devices listed help break up the text, making it more "reader friendly." Subheadings, if not overly used, can also cue your reader to significant sections of your paper and how they relate to the whole. Long quotes, those over four lines, can be "blocked," or indented ten spaces (rather than the usual five spaces customary for indenting paragraphs), separating them from the rest of the text. (See Chapter 4, "Writing with Sources," for more on blocking quotes.) "Bullets"—dots or asterisks preceding brief items—can be used to highlight a quick list of important information. Graphs, tables, and illustrations also break up the text, but even more important, they can help clarify and explain information. (See "Placement of Tables, Charts, and Illustrations," later in this chapter.)

The format of the book you're reading is intended, in part, to make it accessible to readers. As you revise, consider how the "look" of your paper can make it more inviting and easily understood.

Following MLA Conventions

I've already mentioned that formal research papers in various disciplines may have prescribed formats. If your instructor expects a certain format, he has probably detailed exactly what that format should be. But in all likelihood, your paper for this class need not follow a rigid form. It will probably adhere to the basic MLA (Modern Language Association) guidelines described in the following sections. (For an explanation and sample of the format of an APA-style paper, see Appendix C.)

Printing or Typing

Type your paper on white, 8½" × 11" bond paper. Avoid the erasable variety, which smudges. If you write on a computer, make sure the printer has a fresh ribbon or sufficient toner. That is especially important if you have a dot-matrix printer, which can produce barely legible pages on an old ribbon.

Margins and Spacing

The old high school trick is to have big margins. That way, you can get the length without the information. Don't try that trick with this paper. Leave one-inch margins at the top, bottom, and sides of your pages. Indent paragraphs five spaces and blocked quotes ten spaces. Double-space all of the text, including blocked quotes and "Works Cited."

Title Page

Your paper doesn't need a separate title page. Begin with the first page of text. One inch below the top of the page, type your name, your instructor's name, the course number, and the date (see following). Below that, type the title, centered on the page. Begin the text of the paper below the title.

```
Karoline Ann Fox

Professor Dethier

English 401

15 December 1991

          Metamorphosis, the Exorcist,

                and Oedipus

     Ernst Pawel has said that Franz Kafka's "The

Metamorphosis" . . .
```

Note that every line is double-spaced. The title is not underlined (unless it includes the name of a book or some other work that should be underlined) or boldfaced.

Pagination

Make sure that every page after the first one is numbered. That's especially important with long papers. Type your last name and the page number in the upper-righthand corner, flush with the right margin: *Ballenger 3.* Don't use the abbreviation *p.* or a hyphen between your name and the number.

Placement of Tables, Charts, and Illustrations

With MLA format, papers do not have appendixes. Tables, charts, and illustrations are placed in the body of the paper, close to the text that refers to them. Number illustrations consecutively (*Table 1* or *Figure 3*), and indicate sources below. If you use a chart or illustration from another text, give the full citation. Place any table caption above the table, flush left. Captions for illustrations or diagrams are usually placed below them.

Preparing the "Works Cited" Page

The "Works Cited" page ends the paper. (This may also be called the "References Cited" or "Sources Cited" page, depending on the nature of your sources or the preferences of your instructor.) In the old footnote system (which, by the way, is still used in some humanities disciplines), this section used to be called "Endnotes" or "Bibliography." There are also several other lists of sources that may appear at the end of a research paper. An "Annotated List of Works Cited" not only lists the sources used in the paper but includes a brief description of each. A "Works Consulted" list includes sources that may or may not have been cited in the paper but shaped your thinking. A "Content Notes" page, keyed to superscript numbers in the text of the paper, lists short commentaries or asides that are significant but not central enough to the discussion to be included in the text of the paper.

The "Works Cited" page is the workhorse of most college papers. The other source lists are used less often. "Works Cited" is essentially an alphabetical listing of all the sources you quoted, paraphrased, or summarized in your paper. If you have used MLA format for citing sources, your paper has numerous parenthetical references to authors and page numbers. The "Works Cited" page provides complete information on each source cited in the text for the reader who wants to know. (In APA format, this page is called "References" and is only slightly different in how items are listed. See Appendix C for APA guidelines.)

If you've been careful about collecting complete bibliographic information—author, title, editor, edition, volume, place, publisher, date, page numbers—then preparing your "Works Cited" page will be easy. If you've recorded that information on notecards, all you have to do is put them in alphabetical order and then transcribe them into your paper. If you've been careless about collecting that information, you may need to take a hike back to the library.

Format

Alphabetizing the List. "Works Cited" follows the text of your paper on a separate page. After you've assembled complete information about each source you've cited, put the sources in alphabetical order by the last name of the author. If the work has multiple authors, use the last name of the first listed. If the source has no author, then alphabetize it by the first key word of the title. If you're citing more than one source by a single author, you don't need to repeat the name for each source; simply place three dashes followed by a period ("---.") for the author's name in subsequent listings.

Indenting and Spacing. Type the first line of each entry flush left, and indent subsequent lines of that entry (if any) five spaces. Double-space between each line and each entry. For example:

Berquist 12

Works Cited

Bierman, Dick, and Oscar Winter. "Learning During
  Sleep: An Indirect Test of the Erasure Theory
  of Dreaming." Perceptual and Motor Skills 69
  (1989): 139-144.

Berquist, Christine. Survey. Durham, NH:
  University of New Hampshire.

Boxer, Sarah. "Inside Our Sleeping Minds." Modern
  Maturity October-November 1989: 48-54.

Brook, Stephen. The Oxford Book of Dreams. New
  York: Oxford U P, 1983.

Carlson, Neil R. Psychology: The Science of
  Behavior. Boston: Allyn, 1990.

Chollar, Susan. "Dreamchasers." <u>Psychology Today</u>

    April 1989: 60-61.

Foulkes, David, and Wilse B. Webb. "Sleep and

    Dreams." <u>Encyclopedia Britannica</u>. 1986 ed.

Hobson, J. Allan. <u>The Dreaming Brain</u>. New York:

    Basic Books, 1988.

Hudson, Liam. <u>Night Life: The Interpretation of</u>

    <u>Dreams</u>. New York: St. Martin's, 1985.

Long, Michael E. "What Is This Thing Called

    Sleep?" <u>National Geographic</u> December 1987:

    787-821.

Citing Books

You usually need three pieces of information to cite a book: the name of the author or authors, the title, and the publication information. Occasionally, other information is required. The *MLA Handbook** lists this additional information in the order it would appear in the citation. Remember, any single entry will include a few of these things, not all of them. Use whichever are relevant to the source you're citing.

1. Name of the author
2. Title of the book (or part of it)
3. Number of edition used
5. Number of volume used
6. Name of the series
7. Where published, by whom, and the date
8. Page numbers used
9. Any annotation you'd like to add

Each piece of information in a citation is followed by a period and two spaces.

Title. As a rule, the titles of books are underlined, with the first letters of all principle words capitalized, including those in any subtitles. Titles that are not underlined are usually those of pieces

---

**MLA Handbook for Writers of Research Papers,* 3d ed. (New York: MLA, 1988).

found within larger works, such as poems and short stories in anthologies. These titles are set off by quotation marks. Titles of religious works (the Bible, the Koran, etc.) are neither underlined nor enclosed within quotation marks.

Edition. If a book doesn't indicate any edition number, then it's probably a first edition, a fact you don't need to cite. Look on the title page. Signal an edition like this: *2nd Ed., 3rd Ed.,* and so on.

Publication Place, Publisher, and Date. Look on the title page to find out who published the book. Publishers' names are usually shortened in the "Works Cited" list: for example, *St. Martin's Press, Inc.* is shortened to *St. Martin's.*

It sometimes confusing to know what to cite about the publication place, since several cities are often a listed on the title page. Cite the first. For books published outside the United States, add the country name along with the city to avoid confusion.

The date a book is published is usually indicated on the copyright page. If several dates or several printings by the same publisher are listed, cite the original publication date. However, if the book is a revised edition, give the date of that edition. One final variation: If you're citing a book that's a reprint of an original edition, give both dates. For example:

```
Stegner, Wallace. Recapitulation. 1979. Lincoln:

    U of Nebraska P, 1986.
```

This book was first published in 1979 and then republished in 1986 by the University of Nebraska Press.

Page Numbers. Normally, you don't list page numbers of a book. The parenthetical reference in your paper specifies that. But if you use only part of a book—an introduction or an essay—list the appropriate page numbers following the publication date. Use periods to set off the page numbers. If the author or editor of the entire work is also the author of the introduction or essay you're citing, list her by last name only the second time you cite her. For example:

```
Lee, L. L., and Merrill Lewis. Preface. Women,

    Women Writers, and the West. Ed. Lee and

    Lewis. Troy: Whitston, 1980. v-ix.
```

Sample Book Citations

1. A BOOK BY ONE AUTHOR

Keen, Sam. <u>Fire in the Belly</u>. New York: Bantam,

    1991.

2. A BOOK BY TWO AUTHORS

Ballenger, Bruce, and Barry Lane. <u>Discovering the</u>

    <u>Writer Within</u>. Cincinnati: Writer's Digest,

    1988.

3. A BOOK WITH MORE THAN THREE AUTHORS

If a book has more than three authors, list the first and substitute the term *et al.* for the others.

Jones, Hillary et al. <u>The Unmasking of Adam</u>.

    Highland Park: Pegasus, 1992.

4. SEVERAL BOOKS BY THE SAME AUTHOR

Baldwin, James. <u>Tell Me How Long the Train's Been</u>

    <u>Gone</u>. New York: Dell—Doubleday, 1968.

———. <u>Going to Meet the Man</u>. New York: Dell—

    Doubleday, 1948.

5. A COLLECTION OR ANTHOLOGY

Crane, R. S., ed. <u>Critics and Criticism: Ancient</u>

    <u>and Modern</u>. Chicago: U of Chicago P, 1952.

6. A WORK IN AN ANTHOLOGY OR COLLECTION

The title of a work that is part of a collection but was originally published as a book should be underlined. Otherwise, the title of a work in a collection should be enclosed in quotation marks.

Bahktin, Mikhail. <u>Marxism and the Philosophy of</u>

    <u>Language. The Rhetorical Tradition</u>. Ed.

    Patricia Bizzell and Bruce Herzberg. New

    York: St. Martin's, 1990. 928—944.

Jones, Robert F. "Welcome to Muskie Country." <u>The</u>
   <u>Ultimate Fishing Book</u>. Ed. Lee Eisenberg and
   DeCourcy Taylor. Boston: Houghton, 1981.
   122–134.

7. AN INTRODUCTION, PREFACE, FOREWORD, OR PROLOGUE

Scott, Jerie Cobb. Foreword. <u>Writing Groups:</u>
   <u>History, Theory, and Implications</u>. By Ann
   Ruggles Gere. Carbondale, IL: SIU P, 1987.
   ix–xi.

Rich, Adrienne. Introduction. <u>On Lies, Secrets,</u>
   <u>and Silence</u>. By Rich. New York: Norton.
   9–18.

8. A BOOK WITH NO AUTHOR

<u>Standard College Dictionary</u>. New York: Funk &
   Wagnalls, 1990.

9. AN ENCYLOPEDIA

"City of Chicago." <u>Encyclopaedia Britannica</u>.
   1989 ed.

10. A BOOK WITH AN INSTITUTIONAL AUTHOR

Hospital Corporation of American. <u>Employee</u>
   <u>Benefits Handbook</u>. Nashville: HCA, 1990.

11. A BOOK WITH MULTIPLE VOLUMES

Include the number of volumes in the work between the title
and publication information.

Baym, Nina et al., eds. <u>The Norton Anthology of</u>
   <u>American Literature</u>. 3rd Ed. 2 vols. New
   York: Norton, 1989.

If you use one volume of a multivolume work, indicate which one along with the page numbers followed by the total number of volumes in the work.

```
Anderson, Sherwood. "Mother." The Norton Anthology

    of American Literature. Ed. Nina Baym et al.

    Vol 2. New York: Norton, 1989. 1115-1131.

    2 Vols.
```

12. A TRANSLATION

```
Montaigne, Michel de. Essays. Trans. J. M. Cohen.

    Middlesex, England: Penguin, 1958.
```

13. GOVERNMENT DOCUMENTS

Because of the enormous variety of government documents, proper citation can be a challenge. Since most government documents do not name authors, begin an entry for such a source with the level of government (U.S. Government, State of Illinois, etc., unless it is obvious from the title), followed by the sponsoring agency, the title of the work, and the publication information. Look on the title page to determine the publisher. If it's a federal document, then the Government Printing Office (abbreviated GPO) is usually the publisher.

```
United States. Bureau of the Census. Statistical

    Abstract of the United States. Washington:

    GPO, 1990.
```

Citing Periodicals

Periodicals—magazines, newspapers, journals, and similar publications that appear regularly—are cited similarly to books but sometimes involve different information, such as date, volume, and page numbers. The *MLA Handbook* lists the information to include in a periodical citation in the order in which it should appear:

1. Name of the author
2. Article title
3. Periodical title
4. Series number or name

5. Volume number
6. Date
7. Page numbers

Author's Name. List the author(s) as you would for a book citation.

Article Title. Unlike book titles, article titles are usually enclosed in quotation marks.

Periodical Title. Underline periodical titles, dropping introductory articles (*Aegis* not *The Aegis*). If you're citing a newspaper your readers may not be familiar with, include in the title—enclosed in brackets but not underlined—the city in which it was published. For example:

```
MacDonald, Mary. "Local Hiker Freezes to Death."
     Foster's Daily Democrat [Dover, NH] 28
     Jan. 1992: 1.
```

Volume Number. Most academic journals are numbered as volumes (or occasionally feature series numbers); the volume number should be included in the citation. Popular periodicals sometimes have volume numbers, too, but these are not included in the citation. Indicate the volume number immediately after the journal's name. Omit the tag *vol.* before the number.

There is one important variation: Though most journals number their pages continuously, from the first issue every year to the last, a few don't. These journals feature an issue number as well as a volume number. In that case, cite both by listing the volume number, a period, and then the issue number: for example *12.4,* or volume number *12* and issue *4.*

Date. When citing popular periodicals, include the day, month, and year of the issue you're citing—in that order—following the periodical name. Academic journals are a little different. Since the volume number indicates when the journal was published within a given year, just indicate that year. Put it in parentheses following the volume number and before the page numbers (see examples following).

Page Numbers. Include the page numbers of the article at the end of the citation, followed by a period. Just list the pages of the entire article, omitting abbreviations such as *p.* or *pp.* It's common for articles in newspapers and popular magazines *not* to run on consecutive pages. In that case, indicate the page on which the article begins, followed by a "+" (*12+*).

Newspaper pagination can be peculiar. Some papers wed the section (usually a letter) with the page number (*A4*); other papers simply begin numbering anew in each section. Most, however, paginate continuously. See the following sample citations for newspapers for how to deal with these peculiarities.

Sample Periodical Citations

1. A MAGAZINE ARTICLE

Probasco, Steve. "Nymphing Tactics for Winter

    Steelhead." <u>Fly Fisherman</u>. February 1992:

    36–39.

Jones, Thom. "The Pugilist At Rest." <u>New Yorker</u> 12

    Dec. 1991: 38–47.

2. A JOURNAL ARTICLE

For an article that is paginated continuously, from the first issue every year to the last, cite as follows:

Allen, Rebecca E., and J. M. Oliver. "The Effects

    of Child Maltreatment on Language

    Development." <u>Child Abuse and Neglect</u> 6

    (1982): 299–305.

For an article in a journal that begins pagination with each issue, include the issue number along with the volume number.

Goody, Michelle M., and Andrew S. Levine.

    "Healthcare Workers and Occupational Exposure

    to AIDS." <u>Nursing Management</u> 23.1 (1992):

    59–50.

3. A NEWSPAPER ARTICLE

Some newspapers have several editions (morning edition, late edition, national edition), and each may feature different articles. If an edition is listed on the masthead, include it in the citation.

Gelbspan, Ross. "NRC Staff Lied About Seabrook,
Study Says." <u>Boston Globe</u> 29 Jan. 1992,
morning ed.: 1+.

Some papers begin numbering pages anew in each section. In
that case, include the section number if it's not part of pagination.

Brooks, James. "Lobsters on the Brink." <u>Portland
Press</u> 29 Nov. 1988, sec. 2: 4.

4. AN ARTICLE WITH NO AUTHOR

"The Understanding." <u>New Yorker</u> 2 Dec. 1991:
34–35.

5. AN EDITORIAL

"The Star Search." Editorial. <u>Boston Globe</u> 29
Jan. 1992: 10.

6. A LETTER TO THE EDITOR

Levinson, Evan B. "Paying Out of Pocket for
Student Supplies." Letter. <u>Boston Globe</u> 29
Jan. 1992: 10.

7. A REVIEW

Page, Barbara. Rev. of Allegories of Cinema:
American Film in the Sixties by
David E. James. <u>College English</u> 54 (1992):
945–954.

8. AN ABSTRACT FROM
DISSERTATION ABSTRACTS INTERNATIONAL

McDonald, James C. "Imitation of Models in the
History of Rhetoric: Classical, Belletristic,
and Current-traditional." <u>DAI</u> 48 (1988):
2613A. U of Texas, Austin.

Citing Nonprint and Other Sources

1. AN INTERVIEW

If you conducted the interview yourself, list your subject's name first, indicate what kind of interview it was (telephone interview or personal interview), and provide the date.

```
Diamonti, Nancy. Personal interview. 5 Nov. 1990.
```

If you're citing an interview done by someone else (perhaps from a book or article) and the title does not indicate that it was an interview, you should, after the subject's name. Always begin the citation with the subject's name.

```
Stegner, Wallace. Interview. Conversations with
    Wallace Stegner. By Richard Eutlain and
    Wallace Stegner. Salt Lake: U of Utah P, 1990.
```

2. SURVEYS, QUESTIONNAIRES, AND CASE STUDIES

If you conducted the survey or case study, list it under your name and give it an appropriate title.

```
Berquist, Christine. "Dream Questionnaire."
    Durham: U of New Hampshire, 1990.
```

3. RECORDINGS

Generally, list a recording by the name of the performer and underline the title. Also include the recording company, catalog number, and year. (If you don't know the year, use the abbreviation *n.d.*)

```
Orff, Carl. Carmina Burana. Cond. Seiji Ozawa.
    Boston Symphony. RCA, 6533-2-RG, n.d.
```

4. TELEVISION AND RADIO PROGRAMS

List the title of the program (underlined), the station, and the date. If the episode has a title, list that first in quotation marks. You may also wish to include the name of the narrator or producer after the title.

```
All Things Considered. Interview with Andre Dubus.
    NPR. WBUR, Boston. 12 Dec. 1990.
```

5. FILMS AND VIDEOTAPES

Begin with the title (underlined), followed by the director, the distributor, and the year. You may also include names of writers, performers, or producers. End with the date and any other specifics about the characteristics of the film or videotape that may be relevant (length and size).

<u>Touchstone</u>. Videocassette. Dir. Jim Stratton.

Alaska Conservation Foundation, 1990. 25 min.

You can also list a video or film by the name of a contributor you'd like to emphasize.

Capra, Francis, dir. <u>It's a Wonderful Life</u>. With

Jimmy Stewart and Donna Reed.

6. ARTWORKS

List each work by artist. Then cite the title of the work (underlined) and where it's located (institution and city). If you've reproduced the work from a published source, include that information, as well.

Homer, Winslow. <u>Casting for a Rise</u>. Hirschl and

Adler Galleries, New York. Illus. in <u>Ultimate</u>

<u>Fishing Book</u>. Ed. Lee Eisenberg and Decourcy

Taylor. Boston: Houghton, 1981.

7. LECTURES AND SPEECHES

List each by the name of the speaker, followed by the title of the address (if any) in quotation marks, the name of the sponsoring organization, the location, and the date. Also indicate what kind of address it was (lecture, speech, etc.).

Tsongas, Paul. Speech. Tsongas for President

Campaign. Durham, 28 Jan. 1992.

8. A PAMPHLET

Cite a pamphlet as you would a book.

<u>New Challenges for Wilderness Conservationists</u>.

Washington D.C.: Wilderness Society, 1973.

Proofreading Your Paper

You've spent weeks researching, writing, and revising your paper. You want to stop now. That's understandable, no matter how much you were driven by your curiosity. Before you sign off on your research paper, placing it in someone else's hands, take the time to proofread it.

I was often so glad to be done with a piece of writing that I was careless about proofreading it. That changed about ten years ago, after I submitted a portfolio of writing to complete my master's degree. I was pretty proud of it, especially an essay about dealing with my father's alcoholism. Unfortunately, I misspelled that word—*alcoholism*—every time I used it. It was pretty humiliating.

Proofreading on a Computer

Proofreading used to involve gobbing on correction fluid to cover up mistakes and then trying to line up the paper and type in the change. If you write on a computer, you're spared from that ordeal. The text can be easily manipulated on the screen.

Software programs can also help with the job. Most word-processing programs, for example, come with spell-checkers. These programs don't flag problems with sentence structure or the misuse of words, but they do catch typos and consecutive repetitions of words. A spell-checker is mighty handy. Learn how to use it.

Some programs, like RightWriter, will count the number of words in your sentences, alerting you to particularly long ones, and will even point out uses of passive voice. I find some of these programs irritating because they evaluate writing ability based on factors like sentence length, which may not be a measure of the quality of your work at all. But for a basic review, these programs can be extremely useful, particularly for flagging passive construction.

A lot of writers find they need to print out their paper and proofread the "hard copy." They argue that they catch more mistakes if they proofread on paper than if they proofread onscreen. It makes sense, especially if you've been staring at the screen for days. A printed copy of your paper *looks* different, and I think you see it differently, maybe with fresher eyes and attitude. You might notice things you didn't notice before. You decide for yourself how and when to proofread.

Looking Closely

You've already edited the manuscript, pruning sentences and tightening things up. Now hunt for the little errors in grammar and mechanics that you missed. Aside from misspellings (usually typos), some pretty common mistakes appear in the papers I see. For practice, see if you can catch some of them in the following exercise, where you proofread an excerpt from a student paper.

☐ *EXERCISE 5-4*
Picking Off the Lint

I have a colleague who compares proofreading to picking the lint off an outfit, which is often your final step before heading out the door. Examine the following excerpt from a student paper. Proofread it, catching as many mechanical errors as possible. Note punctuation mistakes, agreement problems, misspellings, and anything else that seems off.

In an important essay, Melody Graulich notes how
"rigid dichotomizing of sex roles" in
most frontier myths have "often handicapped
and confused male as well as female writers
(187)," she wonders if a "universel mythology"
(198) might emerge that is less confining for both
of them. In Bruce Mason, Wallace Stegner seems to
experiment with this idea; acknowledgeing the
power of Bo's male fantasies <u>and</u> Elsa's ability to
teach her son to feel. It is his strenth. On the
other hand, Bruces brother chet, who dies young,
lost and broken, seems doomed because he lacked
sufficient measure of both the feminine and
masculine. He observes that Chet had "enough of
the old man to spoil him, ebnough of his mother to
soften him, not enough of either to save him (<u>Big
Rock</u>, 521)."

If you did this exercise in class, compare your proofreading of this passage with that of a partner. What did each of you find?

☐ ■ ☐

Ten Common Mistakes

The following is a list of the ten most common errors (besides misspelled words) made in research papers that should be caught in careful proofreading. A number of these errors occurred in the previous exercise.

1. Beware of commonly confused words, such as *your* instead of *you're*. Here's a list of others:

> *their/there*
> *know/now*
> *accept/except*
> *all ready/already*
> *advice/advise*
> *lay/lie*
> *its/it's*
> *passed/past*

2. Watch for possessives. Instead of *my fathers alcoholism,* the correct style is *my father's alcoholism.* Remember that if a noun ends in *s,* still add *'s: Tess's laughter.* If a noun is plural, just add the apostrophe: *the scientists' studies.*

3. Avoid vague pronoun references. The excerpt in Exercise 5-4 ends with the sentence beginning with *He observes that Chet . . .* Who's *he?* The sentence should read, *Bruce observes that Chet . . .* Whenever you use the pronouns *he, she, it, they,* and *their,* make sure each clearly refers to someone or something.

4. Subjects and verbs must agree. If the subject is singular, its verb must be, too: *The **perils** of acid rain **are** many.* What confuses writers sometimes is the appearance of a noun that is not really the subject near the verb. Exercise 5-4 begins, for example, with this sentence: *In an important essay, Melody Graulich notes how "rigid dichotomizing of sex roles" in most frontier myths **have** "often handicapped and confused male as well as female writers."* The subject here is not *frontier myths* but *rigid dichotomizing,* a singular subject. The sentence should read . . . *most frontier myths **has** "often handicapped and confused . . ."* The verb *has* may sound funny, but it's correct.

5. Punctuate quotes properly. Note that commas belong inside quotation marks, not outside. Periods belong inside, too. Colons and semicolons are exceptions—they belong *outside* quotation marks. Blocked quotes don't need quotation marks at all.

6. Scrutinize use of commas. Could you substitute periods or semi-colons instead? If so, you may be looking at *comma splices* or *run-on sentences.* Here's an example: *Since 1980, the use of marijuana by college students has steadily declined, this was something of a surprise to me and my friends.* The portion after the comma, *this was . . . ,* is another sentence. The comma should be a period, and *this* should be capitalized.

7. Make sure each parenthetical citation *precedes* the period in the sentence you're citing but *follows* the quotation mark at the end of a sentence. In MLA style, there is no comma between the author's name and page number: *(Marks 99).*

8. Use dashes correctly. Though they can be overused, dashes are a great way to break the flow of a sentence with a related bit of information. You've probably noticed I like them. In a manuscript, type dashes as *two* hyphens (--) not one.

9. After mentioning the full name of someone in your paper, normally use her *last name* in subsequent references. For example, this is incorrect: *Denise Grady argues that people are genetically predisposed to obesity.* **Denise** *also believes that some people are "programmed to convert calories to fat."* Unless you know Denise or for some other reason want to conceal her last name, change the second sentence to this: **Grady** *also believes that some people are "programmed to convert calories to fat."* One exception to this is when writing about literature. It is often appropriate to refer to characters by their first names, particularly if characters share last names (as in Exercise 5-4).

10. Scrutinize use of colons and semicolons. A colon is usually used to call attention to what follows it: a list, quotation, or appositive. A colon should follow an independent clause. For example, this won't do: *The most troubling things about child abuse are: the effect on self-esteem and language development.* In this case, eliminate the colon. A semicolon is often used as if it were a colon or a comma. In most cases, a semicolon should be used as a period, separating two independent clauses. The semicolon simply implies the clauses are closely related.

Using the "Search" Function

If you're writing on a computer, use the "search" function—a feature in most word-processing programs—to help you track down consistent problems. You simply tell the computer what word or punctuation to look for, and it will locate all occurrences in the text.

For example, if you want to check for comma splices, search for commas. The cursor will stop on every comma, and you can verify if it is correct. You can also search for pronouns to locate vague references or for words (like those listed in #1 above) you commonly misuse.

Avoiding Sexist Language

One last proofreading task is to do a *man* and *he* check. Until recently, sexism wasn't an issue in language. Use of words such as *mankind* and *chairman* was acceptable; the implication was that the terms applied to both genders. At least, that's how use of the terms was defended when challenged. Critics argued that words such as *mailman* and *businessman* reinforced ideas that only men could fill these roles. Bias in language is subtle but powerful. And it's often unintentional. To avoid sending the wrong message, it's worth making the effort to avoid sexist language.

If you need to use a word with a *man* suffix, check to see if there is an alternative. *Congressperson* sounds pretty clunky, but *representative* works fine. Instead of *mankind,* why not *humanity?* Substitute *camera operator* for *cameraman.*

Also check use of pronouns. Do you use *he* or *his* in places where you mean both genders? For example, *The writer who cares about his topic will bring it to life for his readers.* Since a lot of writers are women, this doesn't seem right. How do you solve this problem?

1. Use *his or her, he or she,* or that mutation *s/he.* For example, *The writer who cares about his or her topic will bring it to life for his or her readers.* This is an acceptable solution, but using *his or her* repeatedly can be awkward.

2. Change the singular subject to plural. For example, *Writers who care about their topics will bring them to life for their readers.* This version is much better and avoids discriminatory language altogether.

3. Alternate *he* or *she, his* or *hers* whenever you encounter an indefinite person. If you have referred to a writer as *he* on one page, make the writer *she* on the next page. Alternate throughout.

☐ EXERCISE 5-5
Revision Practice

I began this chapter by observing how hard it is to find distance from your own draft as you try to revise. That's not a problem when you read other writers' drafts. You naturally bring a fresh pair of eyes to another person's work, and that's why it's so helpful to use a reader in proofing a draft.

For practice, read Heidi's draft of "Is The *Sesame Street* Education A Good One?" in Appendix B. Don't look at the annotated version of Heidi's paper, which follows the draft, until later.

Heidi's first draft is strong, but it has some problems. What do you think they are? If you were advising Heidi on her rewrite of this paper, what would you suggest? Review the paper for the three reasons I discussed this week—looking at purpose, information, and language—and also be alert to any format problems.

This would be a great exercise to do in class, reading the paper together and sharing your reactions as a group. After you're done, compare your suggestions with those on the annotated version of Heidi's paper that follows her draft (see Appendix B).

□ ■ □

LOOKING BACK
AND MOVING ON

This book began with your writing, and it also will end with it. Before you close your research notebook on this project, open it one last time and fastwrite your response to the following questions. Keep your pen moving for seven minutes.

How was your experience writing this research paper different from that writing others? How was it the same?

When students share their fastwrites, this comment is typical: "It was easier to sit down and write this research paper than others I've written." One student last semester added, "I think it was easier because before writing the paper, I got to research something I wanted to know about and learn the answers to questions that mattered to me." If this research project was successful, you took charge of your own learning, as this student did.

Your research paper wasn't necessarily fun. Research takes time, and writing is work. Every week, you had new problems to solve. But if the questions you asked about your topic mattered, then you undoubtedly had moments, perhaps late at night in the library, when you encountered something that suddenly cracked your topic open and let the light come pouring out. The experience can be dazzling. It's even great when it's merely interesting.

What might you take away from this research paper that will prepare you for doing the next one? At the very least, I hope you've cultivated basic research skills: how to find information efficiently, how to document, how to avoid plagiarism, and how to take notes. But hopefully, you've learned more. Perhaps you've recovered a part of you that may have been left behind when you turned eleven or twelve—the curiosity that drove you to put bugs in mayonnaise jars, read about China, disassemble a transistor radio, and wonder about Mars. Curiosity is a handy thing in college. It gets you thinking. And that's the idea.

APPENDIX A

□ ■ □

Sample Undocumented Research Essay

Lemmings fight dirty, says Jennifer, and so do we. In the following research essay, Jennifer does a masterful job of weaving together information about lemmings, AIDS, rain forest destruction, divorce, folktales, one-night stands, desk graffiti, and manifest destiny. She carefully winds these threads around the core of her essay: the suggestion that human beings may not be much wiser about survival than the lowly lemming.

As you read Jennifer's piece, notice how unobtrusively she integrates the factual information from her research, never losing her voice or her direction. The essay just keeps building to its conclusion, ending with that powerful last line: *Are we ever going to quit fighting dirty?* This is one of the best student research essays I've come across.

Jennifer's "Lemming Death," as well as the essay "Why God Created Flies" earlier in this book (see Introduction), is an undocumented research essay. The writer does not make any formal effort to cite her sources in the text or at the end in a "Works Cited" page, though she does sometimes attribute her information to its source. Because of this lack of documentation, "Lemming Death" is less scholarly than most academic-type papers. Readers are unable to review her sources. While this does make her essay less authoritative as an academic paper, I think Jennifer succeeds in earning readers' trust through her strong writing and provocative point of view.

The lack of formal documentation is typical of essays published in magazines for more general audiences. Writers in academic disciplines, who write for more specialized audiences, are obliged to follow the conventions for citing sources. Your instructor, however, may encourage you to write a less formal research essay such as Jennifer's.

Consider personal essays you've already written. Might they be revised to use research in some of the ways that Jennifer used such information in "Lemming Death"? Of course, this essay could have easily included parenthetical citations and "Works Cited."

Even if you've been asked to use documentation, Jennifer White's essay should be an inspiring example of how you can approach your topic in a lively and personal way.

Source: "Lemming Death" is reprinted with permission of Jennifer White.

Lemming Death

by Jennifer White

Lemmings. I have become fascinated
with them since I heard that they
commit mass suicide by plunging into
the sea. Lemmings are tiny rodents.
They are black with grey bellies and a
skunk stripe down their backs. They are
round and fuzzy and their long hair
covers the soles of their feet. It
nearly covers their ears. Imagine a
group of these round and fuzzy rodents
congregated by the edge of the sea.
Would they contemplate death if they
could? Would they question the death of
their lemming souls before taking that
final jump? Before dooming themselves
to the wind and the waves?

What brings them to this end? What
pressures urge them to embark on these
suicidal processions? The ominous
presence of too many snowy owls? Not
enough moss and grass to feed
everybody? No. The pressure that

compels the lemmings to undertake such
journeys to the sea is not from
predatorial threats or hunger pangs. It
comes from each other. They don't like
each other. And there are lots of them
not to like.

So it is dislike that brings them
to the edges of rivers, ravines, lakes,
the sea, and streams. But once the
procession has halted at its obstacle,
is it dislike that makes them jump? Is
it dislike that makes the lemmings, as
more and more of them accumulate at the
water's edge, take flight?

A Scandinavian folktale tells of
lemming origin. They don't get here
like the rest of us; they rain down on
earth after they are spontaneously
generated in the clouds.

Too bad it's not true, because
maybe if it were there wouldn't be so
many of them.

Since lemmings find cohabitation
to be unbearable, you'd think that

population control wouldn't be a
problem. They love each other and they
leave each other. Mutually. They
fulfill each other's urges, and nobody
gets hurt. But they love and leave each
other a lot. In fact, female lemmings
can give birth, mate immediately, and
then give birth again three weeks
later. And they don't waste any time
getting started; they are sexually
active when they're three to five weeks
old.

However, when they are not
procreating and they do run into one
another, they fight dirty. They bristle
their fur, bare their teeth, and spit
at each other. They are intolerant.
They are aggressive. Or at least they
try to be.

They sound a lot like human
beings.

There are lots of human beings who
love each other and leave each other.

White 4

We call these interludes one-night
stands. Flings. In the movies they
happen when two glamorous people see
each other across a crowded room. In
real life they happen after we've had
one-too-many drinks. But even though we
love each other and leave each other
like the lemmings, we are not so mutual
about it. Usually one of us humans
wants to keep loving, while the other
is leaving. Sometimes the male is
afraid of commitment, or the female is
finding herself, or one or the other
has just come out of a relationship and
does not want to be tied down. We
humans are always coming out of
relationships, because like the
lemmings, there are lots of us who find
cohabitation unbearable. The divorce
rate is proof of that. Over half of the
2.5 million couples who get married
each year, with the intention of
spending the rest of their live with
one another, get divorced.

White 5

And, like the lemmings, we have a bit of a problem with population control. We're making too many babies and it will be the death of us, the death of everything on earth. There were 500 million people on the planet in 1650; from 1650 to 1850, the population doubled. Since then it has more than quadrupled. That's not good.

The rain forests, which contain half the world's plant and animal species--many of which haven't even been discovered--are being destroyed at a rate of 55 million acres per year. What are we thinking? Or aren't we?

Our history tells us that we are aggressive, and we can be intolerant, like the lemmings. The AIDS epidemic has brought gay-bashing to a new high. AIDS has, in fact, tripled in recent years. The camcorder revolution showed us that racism and police brutality really do exist; someone got it all on video when four officers of the Los

White 6

Angeles Police Department beat up
motorist Rodney King.

Sexism is still rampant, too: the
1980 United Nations report told us that
women constitute half the world's
population, perform two-thirds of its
work hours, receive one-tenth of its
income, and own less than one hundredth
of its property. Twelve years later,
little has changed. What's wrong with
this picture?

Some of us fight dirty, too, when
someone is in the way of something, or
even someone, we want. Remember Wanda
Holloway of Texas, who hired someone to
kill the mother of her daughter's
cheerleading rival so that the grief-
stricken girl wouldn't be able to
compete? Yikes. Some of us do bristle
our hair, bare our teeth, and spit like
lemmings, which is relatively harmless,
compared to some of the other things we
do. Some of us pull out guns and shoot.
There were 23,000 people who died in

1990 because of gunshot wounds. Some of
us lie, kiss ass, cheat, and steal.
Some of us employ other tactics. Some
tactics are more effective than others.

Yet you don't find groups of us
making tracks to the nearest large body
of water. You don't find us committing
mass suicide. Or do you?

I was sitting in class at a desk
that was covered with graffiti. I mean,
it was so covered that barely any brown
peaked through. And it was covered with
the usual stuff: fraternity insignias,
quotations and lyrics, obscenities,
declarations of undying love. The guy
next to me quietly inspected my desk
and its battle scars—"THIS SUCKS,"
"JERRY RULES," and "i luv mark," among
others—pondered for a moment, and
said, "It's like a human soul turned
inside out. No wonder people kill
themselves."

White 8

The human race is committing mass
suicide. We may not be flinging
ourselves off cliffs and embankments,
but we are doing it, we are killing
ourselves. The way we treat the planet,
and the way we treat each other, is
evidence of a slow death--slow and
intentional, because we know what we're
doing, and yet we aren't taking enough
measures to change.

Lemmings aren't afraid of change,
and since they can't change their
behavior, they change their location.
When there are too many of them in a
given area to prevent them from living
their preferred solitary existence,
some of them move. It's not an inner
compulsion, it's not a death drum
beating in their heads that urges them
on. It's a desire to ensure their
survival. They would kill each other if
they stayed. It's their Manifest
Destiny.

We've used ours up. We've reached our limits. We have no place else to go, unless you buy into the theory that we will one day civilize the moon and other planets, so we can do with the earth as we please. I can hear it now: "Yeah, that's it, we'll just trash the earth until we can't live here anymore and then start over somewhere else!" What's the point if we can't live together anyway?

Lemming deaths are unintentional. Sometimes their path to a promised land is blocked by a body of water; they do not seek the water. The lemmings at the front of the procession stop, but their followers keep coming. And coming. A mass panic results, and the animals throw themselves to their watery graves as an escape. Or, when they come to a body of water, they jump in because they think they can make it to the other side. They can swim, and they think they can make it.

The difference between humans and
the animals is that we have the ability
to reason. Lemmings act on instinct.
Humans are rational. Our behavior is
certainly not demonstrative of this
fact.

We've reached our limits. Are we
going to jump in, jump past our limits,
intending to make it? Are we going to
commit lemming death? Are we going to
change our behavior because we can no
longer "go West young man," or are we
going to ruin our lives, our planet,
our home? Are we ever going to quit
fighting dirty?

APPENDIX B

□ ■ □

Sample Research Paper Draft in MLA Style

Like a lot of people, Heidi grew up with "Sesame Street," the children's program on public television. Now, her younger sister is an avid fan of the show. When searching for a research topic, Heidi began to wonder just how effective "Sesame Street" is as an educational program. With that question as her focus, Heidi was surprised to discover that not everyone thinks Big Bird and Kermit and the rest of the gang always do such a good job educating young viewers.

The draft that follows, written in MLA (Modern Language Association) style, explores several criticisms of "Sesame Street" and Heidi's response to them. This is a strong paper—interestingly written, with some informative sources, including an interview—but it also has some weaknesses that should be ironed out through revision.

If you haven't already done so, complete Exercise 5-5 in Chapter 5. Be sure to read the unmarked draft that follows before you look at the annotated draft on page 242, which includes editorial comments about the writer's plans for revision as well as proofreading notations.

Also use this review to practice your knowledge of MLA conventions. Did you catch any problems with how Heidi cites sources or with the format she follows in her paper?

When you're done reading the clean draft, compare your suggestions with those in the marked-up version. Do you agree with the reader's comments? What additional suggestions would you make if you were Heidi's reader?

Source: "Is the 'Sesame Street' Education a Good One?" is reprinted with permission of Heidi R. Dunham.

Dunham 1

Heidi Dunham

Professor Williams

English 401

20 November 1990

Is The <u>Sesame Street</u>

Education A Good One?

It is inconceivable that

[Jim] Henson died for lack of

caring for himself. He took such

good care of those most precious

to us. He and his creatures taught

our children about exit signs, the

rules of street crossing, how

babies are born, how to distinguish

near and far, and how to count.

They taught the joy of friendship,

the importance of perservering,

the grace of tolerance, and the

beauty of diversity. Everything

kids need to know, they learned

from the muppets. We can hope that

<u>Sesame Street</u> will be the first

bond of their generation. . . .

(Rainie p. 12)

Dunham 2

And so continues a tribute to the
late Jim Henson, creator of the ever-
popular Muppet clan, a crowd in full-
scale play in the television series
<u>Sesame Street</u>. Harrison Rainie couldn't
have said it better than he did in the
passage above, which appeared in the
May 28, 1990 issue of <u>U.S. News and
World Report</u>. Now that Henson has
passed away, Kermit the Frog is without
his originator's voice, and millions of
devoted viewers of <u>Sesame Street</u> are
without the man who brought them into
his very special world. Fortunately,
and partly through Henson's own grace
and caring, <u>Sesame Street</u> will continue
to teach, and young children will
continue to learn from it.

Through the incredible dedication
of everyone involved with the program,
and the unique way the series is strung
together, <u>Sesame Street</u> has become one
of television's most popular shows.
Despite this known fact, there are

Dunham 3

those who argue the other side,
claiming that <u>Sesame Street</u> provides
an unsuitable education. After you've
heard the critics, see if you agree
with me that children who are such
dedicated viewers of this program
should be the true judges of its
success. In my opinion, they know best.

Though I'm now eighteen years old,
I was once a great fan of the show, an
interest that hasn't completely burned
out. You can still find me caught up in
a daily morning episode as I finish my
breakfast and prepare to begin the day.
As an adult, I view the silly skits and
furry characters with a different
perspective. I obviously don't watch to
learn how to tell time or tie my
shoelaces. Instead today I watch my own
sister as she is taught these same
things, and I am struck by the enormous
effects that the show has had on her.

I'm fascinated by how much delight
Mitzi has felt watching <u>Sesame Street</u>

over the years, and to realize how her
delight is most assuredly a reflection
of my own not too long ago. Most
interesting of all, perhaps, is she has
learned all along as she watches the
show, and it has captured her attention
from the start. While entertaining her,
it has also educated her.

Begun in 1969, the brainchild of
co-founder Joan Cooney, <u>Sesame Street</u>
is a children's educational television
show broadcast several times a day to
over 11 million homes in the United
States. There are also over 80
foreign countries whose young generations benefit from the carefully
planned out series (Rachlin 50).

Each <u>Sesame Street</u> program is a
combination of previously-recorded, and
new one to two minute segments, each
with a particular educational purpose.
The cast of characters who together
"run the show" run the gamut, from a
lovable, fuzzy orange and yellow

striped worm named Slimy, pet to Oscar
the Grouch who makes his home in a
trash can, to live personalities such
as Gordon and Olivia, a married couple
residing on Sesame Street with their
adopted son Myles.

Some actors and actesses who
contribute to the show's success have
done so by merely remaining a part of
the series most of their professional
lives. Sonia Manzano, for instance, the
actress who plays Maria, the Hispanic
who runs the fix-it shop with her TV
husband Luis, has been her character
ever since her start as a teenager
living on Sesame Street seventeen
years ago (Seligman 71). Today,
Sonia's own baby plays the role of
Maria and Luis's child on the
program, a birth that coincided with
the show's twentieth anniversary and a
focus of anticipation and celebration
for people of all ages across the
country.

Dunham 6

Seeing a pregnant Maria on the screen taught young viewers the basics of fetal growth and development, and introduced the process parents go through when expecting a child. Valerie Lovelace, research director for the show, explained that "we especially wanted to show that fathers have an important role both before and after birth, which reflects what's going on in real life" (Seligman). In preparing for their baby by attending birth classes together and reading books on child care, Luis and Maria showed kids across the country what it meant to become parents.

Another reason for the shows success is the dedication with which the producers plan the segments which will be shown. In response to criticism in recent years that the two minute segments discourage lengthy attention span among young children, many of the segments have been lengthened up to

Dunham 7

three times, allowing for a more drawn
out focus. (Rachlin p. 55) But some
would argue that this isn't altogether
necessary to a good show. A team of
serious researchers is dedicated to
observing children of different ages to
find out their interests and levels of
cognitive ability as a preliminary
measure to beginning any new idea on
the show. The findings help them to
decide the exact ways in which kids
will best benefit from television
taught learning, and the very areas in
which that teaching is most needed.

In addition to a seventeen-year
$1.2 million study which has just been
launched to study the long-term effects
of Sesame Street on its viewers, many
smaller experiments have been done to
determine routes for daily programming
(Wood 10). These folk are serious
about what they're doing. Currently,
Children's Television Workshop employs
a staff of five full-time researchers

Dunham 8

for the show who are ever on the move
to examine and evaluate the successes
of each "Street" episode by taping
children as they watch and asking
opinions of various educators (Wood
10). For example, when planning the
programming of Maria's pregnancy,
Lovelace and her coleagues spent six
months on a project, interviewing sixty
New York schoolchildren to determine
what they did and didn't know about
pregnancy (Seligman 71). As Lovelace
explained, "Most of the kids couldn't
define the word "pregnant", so we had
to explain it. Neither was the word
'womb' understood by many; in fact,
most of the kids confused it with
'room'. This led researchers to
recommend eliminating use of the word
in future episodes (Seligmann 71)."

Many who have doubts about Sesame
Street worry about the rapidly-
shifting scenes in any give episode.
Claims Jerome L. Singer, professor of

psychology at Yale, "If this is
intended seriously to be an education
show, I question whether the fast pace,
the interruptions, the fragmentation of
presentation is sufficient. Unless
counting is demonstrated in a concrete
way, just knowing the names of numbers
doesn't mean anything." (Chira 13) In
response to this criticism, University
of Massachusetts pyschology professor
Daniel A. Anderson claims that while it
may be the case that segments are
rather short, this characteristic may
actually be a plus to the show's
success at maintaing a childs interest.
He said that a recent study shows the
average child looks at and away from
Sesame Street 150 times over the hour,
and that he tends to zero in and focus
on those segments which interest him
most and which he is best able to
relate to and comprehend (Chira 13).

Nancy Diamonti, a local elementary
school principal and mother of three,

Dunham 10

remembers as I do a few of these <u>Sesame</u>
<u>Street</u> segments, recalling the
significance of what each meant and
taught. As she pointed out, there was
one segment "that kids absolutely
loved. . . it was on the manufacturing
process, and they went to a crayon
factory. Now they could have gone to
any kind of factory and bored people
silly but instead they went to a crayon
factory and kids were thrilled. . ."

In yet another instance, she
recalls, kids are taught all kinds of
sequencing skills. . . all kinds of
problem-solving skills." It is the one
in which the baby screams out for her
bottle, and the scene switches
instantaneously back ot the cows on the
farm. As viewers we are taken through
the whole process, from cow to the
factory where the milk is pasteurized
and homogenized, to the bottle factory
where the bottles are filled, to the
milk truck making its delivery, and

Dunham 11

finally to the baby, who receives her
bottle, stops her crying, and sits up
giggling contentedly in her crib. It is
this kinds of lessons which <u>Sesame
Street</u> is well known for and which are
most beneficial to kids because they
are entertaining at the same time.

Studies, including one by Dolf
Zillerman and his co-workers in 1980,
have also shown that children respond
better to programs which grab their
attention and hold it there by
including humorous inserts between the
serious (Rubin 150). In this study it
was discovered that while the average
college student would find this method
both illogical and be unable to relate
it to his learning, young kids in fact
benefit from it. A program such as
<u>Sesame Street</u>, where Cookie Monster
may suddenly interrupt Grover
explaining the meaning of "near" and
"far" demanding a cookie is much more
attention-grabbing than a serious

Dunham 12

lesson on the same subject. Kids learn
best from segments which invite them to
join in, and <u>Sesame Street</u> is an active
show which does just that. Many times I
have marveled a the way Bern and Ernie,
roommates and best friends, have
pointed to the television camera and
talked directly to me, or my little
sister. I have smiled when she claps in
delight, believing they are talking
directly with her and can see her.

   The show has been improved by trhe
new method of carrying over several of
its plot lines from one day's episode
to the next, or longer, as with Maria's
pregnancy, which lasted on screen for a
life-like span of seven months. It
began with the couple's announcement to
the <u>Sesame Street</u> community in February
and culminated with the baby's birth at
the end of the season (Rachlin 55;
Seligmann). The idea is to reinforce
lessons, like counting to ten, in
subsequent episodes by repeating them

Dunham 13

over and over or continuing them
in a gradually changing but constant
process, as with Maria's pregnancy.

Nancy Diamonti agrees with this
set-up, and is angered by criticisms
that <u>Sesame Street</u> is not a good
teacher. "Sesame Street was never
disjointed. It was very consistent
all the time. They repeat a lot of
the segments. You might have numbers
and sounds and letters coming in short
bursts, but the people that are behind
it are always there. So I don't think
the criticism holds that it shortens
attention span, that it's not connected
to anything. That was the idea of
<u>Sesame Street</u>, to take a series of
"commercials" for learning, and then
the storyline is the neighborhood."

There is more to this show than
meets the eye, certainly. It is
definitely more than just a crowd of
furry animals all living together on
one street in the middle of New York

Dunham 14

City. Originally intended as an effort
to better educate underprivileged
youth, <u>Sesame Street</u> is a set in the
very middle of an urban development
on purpose (Hellman 52). As he sees
it, Jon Stone, one of the show's
founding writers and co-producers,
the program couldn't be "just another
escapist show set in a tree house or
badger den" (Hellman 52). Instead, the
recognizable environment gave something
to kids they could relate to. "And it
had a lot more real quality to it than,
say, Mister Rodgers. . . Kids say the
reason they don't like Mister Rodgers
is that its unbelievable" (Diamonti).

Its cast of characters also is
testimony to its racial and cultural
diversity. Strongly represented are
black, Asian, and Hispanic cultures,
while whites, surprisingly, are in the
minority (Hellman 52). I even remember
the cast included a woman of Native
American descent, named Buffie, and her

papoose, Cote. What better way to
educate kids about life around them
that through teaching them to relate to
all kinds of people? And what better
way to have them learn the importance
of diversity than to have it taught so
subtly; so stands the reasoning behind
Ray Charles singing a sincere, and
beautiful song "It's Not Easy Being
Green" (Rachlin 55).

The fact that the show is so
widely viewed around the world proves
its methods are working. From the
beginning in 1969, it was discovered
that kindergartens around the country
experienced incoming students who
watched <u>Sesame Street</u> already knew
their ABC's (Chira 13). A 1971 study by
the Education Testing Service showed
children who watched the show made
"cognitive gains two and a half times
greater than those of children who
didn't" (Hellman 52). So why all the
criticisms?

Dunham 16

Critics focus on whether television is a good teacher. Neil Postman, professor of communications at New York University, believes "all a good TV show does is make a kid want to watch more TV, just like a good book makes you want to read more books" (Rachlin 55). Another argument is presented by Ann-Marie Mott, preschool coordinator for the Bank Street College of Education in New York City. "We all respect the goals," she says, "but I don't think it's how children learn . . . They need to be actively involved. The experience should be very concrete, very active, child-initiated, in a stimulating environment filled with other children and adults" (Chira 13).

If these are the qualifications for an effective educational experience, what's the problem? One day, at age three, my sister came up to me and starting reciting numbers in Spanish, and when I asked where she

learned that, she replied, "Big Bird
told me." She was proud. I was amazed.
How could kids be more actively
involved in an educational program than
they are in viewing <u>Sesame Street</u>?

    Nancy Diamonti agrees. In response
to criticism of the program in
<u>Education Week</u>, which argued that
<u>Sesame Street</u> was a poor substitute for
quality daycare, or a quality home,
Diamonti says it missed the point:
"Having not been there when it started
in 1969, that's where [the author of
the article] lost track of the fact
that the program was not developed for
middle-class kids whose mothers were
home. It was. . . in place of NOTHING
[emphasis added]. . . because an awful
lot of kids in '69 were home alone.
There was not mandatory school for
kindergarteners. Most kids didn't go to
school until they were six, and they
weren't in daycare. . . The whole idea
was to put something on that attractive

Dunham 18

enough to keep them glued to the TV,
which was a better alternative to being
out on the street. . . That's the whole
section of the population the show was
meant for. As it turned out it was
loved by all kids. It was 'too
successful' because it was supposed to
narrow the gap between low
socioeconomic kids and middle class
kids."

Perhaps Keith Mielke, Vice
President for Research at Children's
Television Workshop, and Gerald Lesser,
professor of education and psychology
at Harvard, and advisor to <u>Sesame
Street</u>, sum it up best when they
emphasize the obvious: <u>Sesame Street</u> is
not meant to be a substitute for the
hands-on kind of learning available to
children in the classroom, but only as
a prepatory aid designed to ready them
for schooling ahead of time (Chira 13).
In view of all this, I'd say it's doing
a pretty good job.

Dunham 19

I see enough evidence of the
success of <u>Sesame Street</u> through
watching my sister, as I've described,
and other children I come in contact
with. When Jim Henson died, the second
grade class at Nancy Diamonti's
elementary school created watercolor
portraits of their favorite <u>Sesame
Street</u> characters which were
subsequently hung, along with a tribute
the teacher composed on the same size
paper, on the glass cases heading into
the school courtyard. "It was touching
because they felt so deeply about it
. . .they really talked a lot about how
important <u>Sesame Street </u>was to them,
and their characters. . ." She reflects
a moment and adds, "Jim Henson was part
of it, but not all if it. Joan Ganz
Cooney had a vision, an amazing
vision."

She certainly did.

Dunham 20

Works Cited

Chira, Susan. "Sesame Street at 20:
        Taking Stock." New York Times 15
        Nov. 1989: 13.

Diamonti, Nancy. Personal Interview. 5
        Nov. 1990.

Hellman, Peter. "Street Smart." New
        York 23 Nov. 1987: 48-53.

Loevy, Diana. "Inside the House That
Henson Built." Channels March 1988:
52-61.

"On Televison's Influence: More Sesame
        Street Defense." Education Week 10
        Oct. 1990: 28.

Rachlin, Jill and Burke, Susan. "Why
        Can't They Clone Big Bird?" U.S.
        News and World Report 31 July
        1987: 50-51.

Rainie, Harrison. "Now, Who Can Tell Us
        How to Get To Sesame Street?" U.S.
        News and World Report 28 May 1990:
        12-13.

Robinson, Ray. "Big Bird's Mother Hen."
        50 Plus Dec. 1987: 24-27.

Dunham 21

Rubin, Zick and Elton B. McNeil.
     <u>Psychology/Being Human</u>. New York:
     Harper, 1985.
Seligmann, Jean. "Birth Day on Sesame
     Street." <u>Newsweek</u> 15 May 1989: 71.
Wood, Daniel B. "At 20, Sesame Street
     Sets Pace for Children's TV."
     <u>Christian Science Monitor</u> 10 Nov.
     1989: 10.

ANNOTATED DRAFT

The annotated draft of Heidi's paper follows. The handwritten notes are from Heidi and include comments passed on by her reader. The typeset notes are from me and point out both strengths and weaknesses in the paper. What additional comments would you pass on?

To do for revision:

① *At the library: find more on criticisms of the program. Check ERIC database? Look for Zillerman study (p. 7) and other studies that support educational value of Sesame Street.*

② *Reorganize. Use question/answer structure? First explore criticisms of program, then respond to them?*

③ *Try to vary sources more.*

Dunham 1

Heidi Dunham

Professor Williams

English 401

20 November 1990

Is The <u>Sesame Street</u>

Education A Good One?

Title centered, without underline or boldface. Don't capitalize articles.

It is inconceivable that

[Jim] Henson died for lack of

caring for himself. He took such

good care of those most precious

to us. He and his creatures taught

our children about exit signs, the

rules of street crossing, how

babies are born, how to distinguish

near and far, and how to count.

They taught the joy of friendship,

the importance of perservering,

the grace of tolerance, and the

beauty of diversity. Everything

kids need to know, they learned

from the muppets. We can hope that

<u>Sesame Street</u> will be the first

bond of their generation. . . .

(Rainie p. 12)

remove abbreviation

Heidi chose a quote for her lead, a moving tribute to Jim Henson. Note how the long quote is indented, or "blocked," 5 spaces.

Dunham 2

And so continues a tribute to the
late Jim Henson, creator of the ever-
popular Muppet clan, a crowd in full-
scale play in the television series
<u>Sesame Street</u>. Harrison Rainie couldn't
have said it better than he did in the
passage above, which appeared in the
May 28, 1990 issue of <u>U.S. News and
World Report</u>. Now that Henson has
passed away, Kermit the Frog is without
his originator's voice, and millions of
devoted viewers of <u>Sesame Street</u> are
without the man who brought them into
his very special world. Fortunately,
and partly through Henson's own grace
and caring, <u>Sesame Street</u> will continue
to teach, and young children will
continue to learn from it.

Through the incredible dedication
of everyone involved with the program,
and the unique way the series is strung
together, <u>Sesame Street</u> has become one
of television's most popular shows.
~~Despite this known fact~~, there are

Dunham 3

, *however,*

those∧who argue ~~the other side,~~
~~claiming~~²that <u>Sesame Street</u> provides
an unsuitable education. After you've
heard the critics, see if you agree
with me that children who are such
dedicated viewers of this program
should be the true judges of its
success. In my opinion, they know best.

Add statistics on viewers from next page?

Strengthen the thesis statement.

The controlling idea, or thesis, doesn't have to appear in the first few paragraphs. Heidi's thesis works well here, cueing readers to her purpose and point of view.

Though I'm now eighteen years old,
I was once a great fan of the show, an
interest ~~that hasn't completely burned~~
I've retained
~~out.~~ You can still find me caught up in
a daily morning episode as I finish my
breakfast and prepare to begin the day.
As an adult, I view the silly skits and
furry characters with a different
perspective. I obviously don't watch to
learn how to tell time or tie my
shoelaces. Instead today I watch my own
sister as she is taught these same
things, and I am struck by the enormous
effects that the show has had on her.

from   I'm fascinated by ~~how much~~ *Mitzi's* delight
~~Mitzi has felt~~ watching <u>Sesame Street</u>

Dunham 4

over the years, and to realize how her
delight is most assuredly a reflection
of my own not too long ago. Most
important,
~~interesting of all, perhaps, is~~ she has
learned all along as she watches the
show, and it has captured her attention
from the start. While entertaining her,
it has also educated her.

Begun in 1969, the brainchild of
co-founder Joan Cooney, <u>Sesame Street</u>
is a children's educational television
show broadcast several times a day to
over 11 million homes in the United
States. ~~There are also over~~ *and* 80
foreign countries. ~~whose young gener-~~
~~ations benefit from the carefully~~
~~planned out series~~ (Rachlin 50).

*Add more
background
here?
Move to
preceding
page?*

Each <u>Sesame Street</u> program is a
combination of previously-recorded, and
new one to two minute segments, each
with a particular educational purpose.
The cast of characters who together
run the show run the gamut, from a
lovable, fuzzy orange and yellow

Dunham 5

striped worm named Slimy, ~~pet to~~ Oscar
the Grouch 's *pet* ~~who makes his home in a~~
~~trash can,~~ to live personalities such
as Gordon and Olivia, a married couple
residing on Sesame Street with their
adopted son Myles.

Some actors and actesses who
contribute to the show's success have
done so by merely remaining a part of
the series most of their professional
lives. Sonia Manzano, for instance, the
actress who plays Maria, the Hispanic
who runs the fix-it shop with her TV
husband Luis, has been her character
ever since her start as a teenager
living on Sesame Street seventeen
years ago (Seligman 71). Today,
Sonia's own baby plays the role of
Maria and Luis's child on the
program, a birth that coincided with
the show's twentieth anniversary, and a
focus of anticipation and celebration
for people of all ages across the
country.

Since the article was only one page, omit the page number from the parenthetical citation.

Dunham 6

Seeing a pregnant Maria on the
screen taught young viewers the basics
of fetal growth and development, and
introduced the process parents go
through when expecting a child. Valerie
Lovelace, research director for the
show, explained that "we especially
wanted to show that fathers have an
important role both before and after
birth, which reflects what's going on
in real life" (Seligman). In preparing
for their baby by attending birth
classes together and reading books on
child care, Luis and Maria showed kids
across the country what it meant to
become parents.

A nice blend of quotation with interview.

~~Another reason for the shows~~
~~success is the dedication with which~~
~~the producers plan the segments which~~
~~will be shown.~~ In response to criticism in recent years that the two minute
segments discourage lengthy attention
span among young children, many of the
segments have been lengthened up to

Cut this sentence. The ¶ isn't really about the dedication of the producers.

Maybe develop this criticism about the attention span of viewers using the information on p. 5.

Dunham 7

three times, allowing for a more drawn
out focus. (Rachlin p. 55) But some
would argue that this isn't altogether
necessary to a good show. A team of
serious researchers is dedicated to
observing children of different ages to
find out their interests and levels of
cognitive ability as a preliminary
measure to beginning any new idea on
the show. The findings help them to
decide the exact ways in which kids
will best benefit from television
taught learning, and the very areas in
which that teaching is most needed.

Clarify this. Does it belong here?

Find out more about this study. In addition to a seventeen-year
$1.2 million study which has just been
launched to study the long-term effects
of Sesame Street on its viewers, many

passive voice

smaller experiments have been done to
determine routes for daily programming
(Wood 10). These folk are serious
about what they're doing. Currently,
Children's Television Workshop employs
a staff of five full-time researchers

too glib?

Dunham 8

for the show who are ever on the move
to examine and evaluate the successes
of each "Street" episode by taping
children as they watch and asking
opinions of various educators (Wood
10). For example, when planning the
programming of Maria's pregnancy,
Lovelace and her colleagues spent six
months on a project, interviewing sixty
New York schoolchildren to determine
what they did and didn't know about
pregnancy (Seligman 71). As Lovelace
explained, "Most of the kids couldn't
define the word pregnant, so we had
to explain it. Neither was the word
'womb' understood by many; in fact,
most of the kids confused it with
'room'. This led researchers to
recommend eliminating use of the word
in future episodes (Seligmann 71).

Another nice quote from Heidi's interview. Use apostrophes to quote within a quote.

Many who have doubts about Sesame
Street worry about the rapidly-
shifting scenes in any give episode.
Claims Jerome L. Singer, professor of

Move this ¶ to page 4 to lump criticism together?

Dunham 9

psychology at Yale, "If this is
intended seriously to be an education
show, I question whether the fast pace,
the interruptions, the fragmentation of
presentation is sufficient. Unless
counting is demonstrated in a concrete
way, just knowing the names of numbers
doesn't mean anything." (Chira 13). ~~In response to this criticism,~~ University
of Massachusetts pyschology professor
Daniel A. Anderson ~~claims~~ *counters* that while ~~it~~
~~may be the case that~~ *Some* segments are
rather short, this ~~characteristic~~ may
~~actually~~ *help* ~~be a plus to the show's~~
~~success at~~ ~~maintaing~~ *maintain,* a child's interest.
He said that a recent study shows the
average child looks at and away from
Sesame Street 150 times over the hour,
and that (he) tends to zero in and focus
on those segments which interest (him)
most and which (he) is best able to
relate to and comprehend (Chira 13).

Nancy Diamonti, a local elementary
school principal and mother of three,

*Heidi
used the
masculine
pronoun
exclusively
when
referring to
an indefinite
person.
Revise to
avoid sexist
language.*

Dunham 10

remembers as I do a few of these <u>Sesame</u>
<u>Street</u> segments, recalling the
significance of what each meant and
taught. ~~As she pointed out, there was~~ *She cites*
one segment "that kids absolutely
loved. . .[It was on the manufacturing
process, and they went to a crayon
factory. Now they could have gone to
any kind of factory and bored people
silly but instead they went to a crayon
factory and kids were thrilled. . ."

In yet another instance, she
recalls, "kids are taught all kinds of
sequencing skills. . . all kinds of
problem-solving skills." ~~It is the one~~ *In this segment a*
~~in which the~~ baby screams out for her
bottle, and the scene switches
instantaneously back /at the cows on the
farm. As viewers we are taken through
the whole process, from cow to the
factory where the milk is pasteurized
and homogenized, to the bottle factory
where the bottles are filled, to the
milk truck making its delivery, and

*If the
interview
subject's
name is
mentioned in
text, it's not
necessary to
parenthetically
cite the
interview.
Include it
in "Works
Cited,"
however.*

Dunham 11

finally to the baby, who receives her
bottle, stops her crying, and sits up
giggling contentedly in her crib. ~~It is~~ *These*
~~this kinds of~~ *are the* lessons which <u>Sesame</u>
<u>Street</u> is well known for and ~~which~~ are
most beneficial to kids because they
are entertaining at the same time.

Studies, including one by Dolf
Zillerman and his co-workers in 1980,
have also shown that children respond
better to programs which grab their
attention and hold it there by
including humorous inserts between the
serious (Rubin 150). ~~In this study it~~ *Researchers*
~~was~~ discovered that while the average
college student would find this method
both illogical and be unable to relate
it to his learning, young kids in fact
benefit from it. A program such as
<u>Sesame Street</u>, where Cookie Monster*, demanding a cookie,*
may suddenly interrupt Grover
explaining the meaning of "near" and
"far" ~~demanding a cookie~~ is much more
attention-grabbing than a serious

*A common
example of
passive voice
in research
papers: Who
conducted it?*

Dunham 12

lesson on the same subject. Kids learn

best from segments which invite them to   *This study*

join in, and <u>Sesame Street</u> is an active   *seems*

show which does just that. Many times I   *impt.*

have marveled a̲t̲ the way Berṅ and Ernie,   *Try to find it*

roommates and best friends, have   *in the journals?*

pointed to the television camera and

talked directly to me, or my little

sister. I have smiled when she claps in

delight, believing they are talking

directly with her and can see her.

Producers ~~The show has been~~ improved *the show* by t̸he

new method of carrying over several of

its plot lines from one day's episode

to the next, or longer, as with Maria's

pregnancy, which lasted on screen for a

life-like span of seven months. It

began with the couple's announcement to

the <u>Sesame Street</u> community in February

and culminated with the baby's birth at

the end of the season (Rachlin 55;

Seligmann). The idea is to reinforce

lessons, like counting to ten, in

subsequent episodes by repeating them

Dunham 13

over and over or continuing them
in a gradually changing but constant
process, as with Maria's pregnancy.

    Nancy Diamonti agrees with this
set-up, and is angered by criticisms}
that <u>Sesame Street</u> is not a good
teacher. "Sesame Street was never
disjointed. It was very consistent
all the time. They repeat a lot of
the segments. You might have numbers
and sounds and letters coming in short
bursts, but the people that are behind
it are always there. So I don't think
the criticism holds that it shortens
attention span, that it's not connected
to anything. That was the idea of
<u>Sesame Street</u>, to take a series of
commercials for learning, and then
the storyline is the neighborhood."

    There is more to this show than
meets the eye, certainly. It is
definitely more than just a crowd of
furry animals all living together on
one street in the middle of New York

Haven't really developed this criticism yet.
See p. 9.

Block quote

Dunham 14

City. Originally intended as an effort
to better educate underprivileged
youth, <u>Sesame Street</u> is a set in the
very middle of an urban development
on purpose (Hellman 52). As he sees
it, Jon Stone, one of the show's
founding writers and co-producers,
the program couldn't be "just another
escapist show set in a tree house or
badger den" (Hellman 52). Instead, the
recognizable environment gave something
to kids they could relate to. "And it
had a lot more real quality to it than,
say, Mister Rodgers. . . Kids say the
reason they don't like Mister Rodgers
is that its unbelievable" (Diamonti).

Its cast of characters also is
testimony to its racial and cultural
diversity. Strongly represented are
black, Asian, and Hispanic cultures,
while whites, surprisingly, are in the
minority (Hellman 52). I even remember
the cast included a woman of Native
American descent, named Buffie, and her

Should this background info. come earlier in the paper? Maybe on p. 3?

Dunham 15

papoose, Cote. What better way to
educate kids about life around them
that through teaching them to relate to
all kinds of people? And what better
way to have them learn the importance
of diversity than to have it taught so
subtly; so stands the reasoning behind
Ray Charles singing a sincere, and
beautiful song "It's Not Easy Being
Green" (Rachlin 55).

The fact that the show is so
widely viewed around the world proves
its methods are working. From the *Kindergarten*
beginning in 1969, ~~it was discovered~~
teachers
~~that kindergartens~~ around the country
had
~~experienced~~ incoming students who
who
watched Sesame Street already knew
their ABC's (Chira 13). A 1971 study by
the Education Testing Service showed
children who watched the show made
"cognitive gains two and a half times
greater than those of children who
didn't" (Hellman 52). So why all the
criticisms?

Dunham 16

Critics focus on whether
television is a good teacher. Neil
Postman, professor of communications
at New York University, believes "all
a good TV show does is make a kid want
to watch more TV, just like a good book
makes you want to read more books"
(Rachlin 55). ~~Another argument is~~
~~presented by~~ Ann-Marie Mott, preschool [Move this info. by critics with other criticisms on p. 5?]
coordinator for the Bank Street College
of Education in New York City, [adds,] "We all
respect the goals," she says, "but I
don't think it's how children learn . . .
They need to be actively involved. The
experience should be very concrete,
very active, child-initiated, in a
stimulating environment filled with
other children and adults" (Chira 13).

If these are the qualifications
for an effective educational
experience, what's the problem? One
day, at age three, my sister came up to
me and starting reciting numbers in
Spanish, and when I asked where she

Dunham 17

learned that, she replied, "Big Bird
told me." She was proud. I was amazed.
How could kids be more actively
involved in an educational program than
they are in viewing <u>Sesame Street</u>?

Nancy Diamonti agrees. In response
to criticism of the program in
<u>Education Week</u>, which argued that
<u>Sesame Street</u> was a poor substitute for
quality daycare, or a quality home,
Diamonti says it missed the point:

Block quote

"Having not been there when it started
in 1969, that's where [the author of
the article] lost track of the fact
that the program was not developed for
middle-class kids whose mothers were
home. It was. . . in place of NOTHING

Uses square brackets to add clarifying information not in the original passage and ellipses to indicate words that have been omitted.

[emphasis added]. . . because an awful
lot of kids in '69 were home alone.
There was not mandatory school for
kindergarteners. Most kids didn't go to
school until they were six, and they
weren't in daycare. . . The whole idea
was to put something on that attractive

Dunham 18

enough to keep them glued to the TV, which was a better alternative to being out on the street. . . That's the whole section of the population the show was meant for. As it turned out it was loved by all kids. It was 'too successful' because it was supposed to narrow the gap between low socioeconomic kids and middle class kids."

Perhaps Keith Mielke, Vice President for Research at Children's Television Workshop, and Gerald Lesser, professor of education and psychology at Harvard, and advisor to <u>Sesame Street</u>, sum it up best when they emphasize the obvious: <u>Sesame Street</u> is not meant to be a substitute for the hands-on kind of learning available to children in the classroom, but only as a prepatory aid designed to ready them for schooling ahead of time (Chira 13). *Using this source too much?* In view of all this, I'd say it's doing a pretty good job.

Dunham 19

I see enough evidence of the
success of <u>Sesame Street</u> through
watching my sister, as I've described,
and other children I come in contact
with. When Jim Henson died, the second
grade class at Nancy Diamonti's
elementary school created watercolor
portraits of their favorite <u>Sesame
Street</u> characters which were
subsequently hung, along with a tribute
the teacher composed on the same size
paper, on the glass cases heading into
the school courtyard. "It was touching
because they felt so deeply about it
. . .they really talked a lot about how
important <u>Sesame Street </u>was to them,
and their characters. . ." She reflects
a moment and adds, "Jim Henson was part
of it, but not all if it. Joan Ganz
Cooney had a vision, an amazing
vision."

   She certainly did.

Heidi ends strongly with an anecdote that nicely ties the ending with the beginning and also reinforces the thesis.

Dunham 20

Works Cited

Double-space the "Works Cited" page. Indent the second and subsequent lines of each entry 5 spaces.

Chira, Susan. "Sesame Street at 20: Taking Stock." New York Times 15 Nov. 1989: 13.

Diamonti, Nancy. Personal Interview. 5 Nov. 1990.

Hellman, Peter. "Street Smart." New York 23 Nov. 1987: 48-53.

indent 5 spaces

Loevy, Diana. "Inside the House That Henson Built." Channels March 1988: 52-61.

"On Televison's Influence: More Sesame Street Defense." Education Week 10 Oct. 1990: 28.

Rachlin, Jill and Burke, Susan. "Why Can't They Clone Big Bird?" U.S. News and World Report 31 July 1987: 50-51.

Rainie, Harrison. "Now, Who Can Tell Us How to Get To Sesame Street?" U.S. News and World Report 28 May 1990: 12-13.

Robinson, Ray. "Big Bird's Mother Hen." 50 Plus Dec. 1987: 24-27.

Dunham 21

Rubin, Zick and Elton B. McNeil.

    <u>Psychology/Being Human</u>. New York:

    Harper, 1985.

Seligmann, Jean. "Birth Day on Sesame

    Street." <u>Newsweek</u> 15 May 1989: 71.

Wood, Daniel B. "At 20, Sesame Street

    Sets Pace for Children's TV."

    <u>Christian Science Monitor</u> 10 Nov.

    1989: 10.

APPENDIX C

□ ■ □

APA-Style Documentation

HOW TO USE APA STYLE

The Modern Language Association (MLA) author/page number system for citing borrowed material, described in the body of this text, is the standard for most papers written in the humanities, though some disciplines in the fine arts as well as history and philosophy may still use the footnote system. Confirm with your instructor that the MLA system is the one to use for your paper.

Another popular documentation style is the American Psychological Association (APA) author/year system. APA style is the standard for papers in the social sciences as well as biology, earth science, education, and business. In those disciplines, the currency of the material cited is often important.

I think you'll find the APA system easy to use, especially if you've had some practice with the MLA approach. Converting from one system to the other is easy. Basically, the APA author/year system cites the author of the borrowed material and the year it appeared. A more complete citation is listed in the "References" (the APA version of MLA's "Works Cited") at the back of the paper. (See the sample APA-style paper later in this appendix.)

The *Publication Manual of the American Psychological Association** is the authoritative reference on APA style. Though the section that follows should answer your questions, check the manual when in doubt.

Publication Manual of the American Psychological Association, 3d ed. (Washington, DC: APA, 1990).

Format of an APA-Style Paper

Page Format

Papers should be double-spaced, with 1½ inch margins on all sides. As always, use a fresh ribbon on your typewriter or printer and avoid fancy typefaces. (Macintosh users, take notice!) Number all pages consecutively, beginning with the title page; put the page number in the upper-righthand corner. Above the page number, place an abbreviated title of the paper on every page, in case pages get separated. As a rule, all paragraphs of text should be indented five spaces.

Title Page

Unlike papers in MLA style, APA-style papers often have a separate title page, containing the following information: the title of the paper, the author, and the author's affiliation (what university she is from). At the bottom of the title page, in uppercase letters, you may also include a *running head,* or an abbreviation of the title (fifty characters or less, including spaces). Repeat this shortened title at the top of each manuscript page, along with the page number. Each line of information should be centered and double-spaced.

Abstract

Though it's not always required, many APA-style papers include a short abstract following the title page. An *abstract* is essentially a short summary of the paper's contents, usually in about one hundred words. This is a key feature, since it's usually the first thing a reader encounters. The abstract should include statements about what problem or question the paper examines and what approach is followed; it should also cite the thesis and significant findings. Type the title "Abstract" at the top of the page. Type the abstract text in a single block, without indenting.

Body of the Paper

The body of the paper begins with the centered title, followed by a double-space and then the text. A page number (usually an abbreviated title and "3" if the paper has a title page and abstract) should appear in the upper-righthand corner.

You may find that you want to use headings within your paper. If your paper is fairly formal, some headings might be prescribed, such as Introduction, Method, Results, and Discussion. Or create your own heads to clarify the organization of your paper.

If you use headings, the APA recommends a hierarchy like this:

CENTERED UPPERCASE HEADING

Centered Lowercase

<u>Centered, Underlined, Upper and Lowercase</u>

<u>Flush left underlined</u>

<u>Indented underlined</u>

Reference Page

All sources cited in the body of the paper are listed alphabetically by author (or title, if anonymous) on the page titled "References." This list should begin a new page. Each entry is double-spaced; begin each first line flush left, and indent subsequent lines three spaces. Explanation of how to cite various sources in the references follows (see "Citing Sources in the Reference List").

Appendix

This is a seldom used feature of an APA-style paper, though you might find it helpful for presenting specific or tangential material that isn't central to the discussion in the body of your paper: a detailed description of a device described in the paper, a copy of a blank survey, or the like. Each item should begin on a separate page and be labeled "Appendix" followed by "A", "B", and so on, consecutively.

Notes

Several kinds of notes might be included in a paper. The most common is *content notes,* or brief commentary by the writer keyed to superscript numbers in the body of the text. These notes are useful for discussion of key points that are relevant but might be distracting if explored in the text of your paper. Present all notes, numbered consecutively, on a page titled "Footnotes." Each note should be double-spaced. Begin each note with the appropriate superscript number, keyed to the text. Indent each first line five spaces; consecutive lines run the full page measure.

Tables and Figures

The final section of an APA-style paper features tables and figures mentioned in the text. Tables should all be double-spaced. Type a table number at the top of the page, flush left. Number tables

"Table 1" "Table 2," and so on, corresponding to the order they are mentioned in the text. A table may also include a title. Each table should begin on a separate page.

Figures (illustrations, graphs, charts, photographs, drawings) are handled similarly to tables. Each should be titled "Figure" and numbered consecutively. Captions may be included, but all should be typed on a separate page, clearly labeled "Figure Captions," and listed in order. For example:

Figure Captions

<u>Figure 1:</u>   A photograph taken in the thirties by Dorthea Lange.

<u>Figure 2:</u>   Edward Weston took a series of green pepper photographs like this. This is titled "No. 35."

Citing Sources in the Text

1. WHEN THE AUTHOR IS MENTIONED IN THE TEXT

The author/year system is pretty uncomplicated. If you mention the name of the author in text, simply place the year her work was published in parentheses immediately after her name. For example:

Herrick (1992) argued that college testing was biased against minorities.

2. WHEN THE AUTHOR ISN'T MENTIONED IN THE TEXT

If you don't mention the author's name in the text, then include that information parenthetically. For example:

A New Hampshire political scientist (Bloom, 1992) recently studied the state's presidential primary.

Note that the author's name and the date of her work are separated by a comma.

3. WHEN TO CITE PAGE NUMBERS

If the information you're citing came from specific pages (or chapters or sections) of a source, that information may also be included in the parenthetical citation. Including page numbers is essential when quoting a source. For example:

```
The first stage of language acquisition of

children is called "caretaker speech" (Moskowitz,

1985, pp. 50-51), in which they model their

parents' language.
```

The same passage might also be cited this way if the authority's name is mentioned in the text:

```
Moskowitz (1985) observed that the first stage of

language acquisition is called "caretaker speech"

(pp. 50-51), in which they model their parents'

language.
```

4. HOW TO CITE TWO OR MORE AUTHORS

When a work has two authors, always mention them both whenever you cite their work in your paper. For example:

```
Allen and Oliver (1982) observed many cases of

child abuse and concluded that maltreatment

inhibited language development.
```

If a source has more than two authors but less than six, mention them all the first time you refer to their work. However, any subsequent references can include the surname of the first author followed by the abbreviation *et al.* When citing works with more than six authors, *always* use the first author's surname and *et al.*

5. HOW TO CITE A WORK WITH NO AUTHOR

When a work has no author, cite an abbreviated title and the date. Place article or chapter titles in quotation marks, and underline book titles. For example:

```
The editorial ("Sinking," 1992) concluded that the

EPA was mired in bureaucratic muck.
```

6. HOW TO CITE TWO OR MORE WORKS
BY THE SAME AUTHOR

Works by the same author are usually distinguished by the date; works are rarely published the same year. But if they are, distinguish among works by adding an *a* or *b* immediately following the date in the parenthetical citation. The reference list will also have these suffixes. For example:

```
Douglas's studies (1986a) on the mating habits

of lobsters revealed that the females are

dominant. He also found that the female lobsters

have the uncanny ability to smell a loser

(1986b).
```

This citation alerts readers that the information came from two studies by Douglas, both published in 1986.

7. CITING AN INSTITUTIONAL AUTHOR

When citing a corporation or agency as a source, simply list the date of the study in parentheses if you mention the institution in the text:

```
The Environmental Protection Agency (1992) issued

an alarming report on ozone pollution.
```

If you don't mention the institutional source in the text, spell it out in its entirety, along with the date. In subsequent parenthetical citations, abbreviate the name. For example:

```
A study (Environmental Protection Agency [EPA],

1992) predicted dire consequences from continued

ozone depletion.
```

And later:

```
Continued ozone depletion may result in widespread

skin cancers (EPA, 1992).
```

8. CITING INTERVIEWS AND LETTERS

Interviews and other personal communications are not listed in the references at the back of the paper, since they are not "recoverable data," but they are parenthetically cited in the text. Provide the initials and surname of the subject (if not mentioned in the text), the nature of the communication, and the date:

```
Nancy Diamonti (personal interview, November 12,

1990) disagrees with the critics of "Sesame

Street."
```

Citing Sources in the Reference List

All parenthetical citations in the body of the paper correspond to a complete listing of sources on the "References" page. The format for this section was described earlier in this chapter (see "Reference Page").

1. ORDER OF SOURCES

List the references alphabetically by author or by first key word of the title if there is no author. The only complication may be if you have several articles or books by the same author. If the sources weren't published in the same year, list them in chronological order, the earliest first. If the sources were published in the *same* year, include a lowercase letter to distinguish them. For example:

```
Lane, Barry (1991a). Writing . . .
Lane, Barry (1991b). Verbal Medicine . . .
```

2. ORDER OF INFORMATION

A reference to a periodical or book in APA style includes this information, in order: author, date of publication, article title, periodical title, and publication information.

Author. List *all* authors—last name, comma, and then first name along with an initial, if any. Use commas to separate authors' names; add an ampersand (&) before the last author's name. When citing an edited book, list the editor(s) in place of the author, and add the abbreviation *Ed.* or *Eds.* in parentheses following the last name. End the list of names with a period.

Date. List the year the work was published, along with the date if it's a magazine or newspaper (see "Sample References," following), in parentheses, immediately after the last author's name. Add a period after the closing parenthesis.

Article or Book Title. APA style departs from MLA, at least with respect to periodicals. In APA style, only the first word of the article title is capitalized, and it is not underlined or quoted. Book titles, on the other hand, are underlined; capitalize only the first word of the title and any subtitle. End all titles with periods.

Periodical Title and Publication Information. Underline the complete periodical title; type it using both uppercase and lowercase letters. Add the volume number (if any), also underlined. Separate title and volume number with a comma. If each issue of the periodical starts with page 1, then also include the issue number in parentheses immediately after the volume number (see examples following). End the entry with the page numbers of the article. Use the abbreviation *p.* or *pp.* if you're citing a newspaper or magazine; omit it if you're citing a journal.

For books, list the city of publication (adding the state or country if the city is unfamiliar; use postal abbreviations) and the name of the publisher; separate city and publisher with a colon. End the citation with a period.

Remember that the first line of each citation should begin flush left and all subsequent lines should be indented three spaces. Double-space all entries.

Sample References

1. A JOURNAL ARTICLE

Cite a journal article like this:

```
Blager, Florence B. (1979). The effect of

    intervention on the speech and language

    of children. Child Abuse and Neglect, 5,

    991-996.
```

2. A JOURNAL ARTICLE NOT PAGINATED CONTINUOUSLY

Most journals begin on page 1 with the first issue of the year and continue paginating consecutively for subsequent issues. A few journals, however, start on page 1 with each issue. For these, include the issue number in parentheses following the volume number:

Williams, John, Post, Albert T., & Stunk,

   Fredrick. (1991). The rhetoric of inequality.

   Attwanata, 12(3), 54–67.

3. A MAGAZINE ARTICLE

Maya, Pines. (1981, December). The civilizing of

   Genie. Psychology Today, pp. 28–34.

4. A NEWSPAPER ARTICLE

Honan, William. (1991, January 24). The war

   affects Broadway. The New York Times,

   pp. C15–16.

5. A BOOK

Lukas, Anthony J. (1986). Common ground: A

   turbulent decade in the lives of three American

   families. New York: Random House.

6. A BOOK OR ARTICLE WITH MORE THAN ONE AUTHOR

Rosenbaum, Alan, & O'Leary, Daniel. (1978).

   Children: The unintended victims of marital

   violence. American Journal of Orthopsychiatry,

   4, 692–699.

Fischler, Stanley I., & Friedman, Richard. (1979).

   Getting into pro soccer. New York: Franklin

   Watts.

7. A BOOK OR ARTICLE WITH AN UNKNOWN AUTHOR

New Hampshire loud and clear. (1992, February 19).
The Boston Globe, p. 22.

A Manual of Style (12th ed.). (1969). Chicago:
University of Chicago Press.

8. A BOOK WITH A CORPORATE AUTHOR

American Red Cross. (1979). Advanced first aid and
emergency care. New York: Doubleday.

9. A BOOK WITH AN EDITOR

Crane, R. S. (Ed.). (1952). Critics and criticism.
Chicago: University of Chicago Press.

10. A SELECTION IN A BOOK WITH AN EDITOR

McKoen, Richard. (1952). Rhetoric in the Middle
Ages. In R. S. Crane (Ed.), Critics and
criticism (pp. 260–289). Chicago: University
of Chicago Press.

11. A REPUBLISHED WORK

James, William. (1978). Pragmatism. Cambridge, MA:
Harvard University Press. (Original work
published 1907).

12. A BOOK REVIEW

Dentan, R. K. (1989). A new look at the brain
[Review of The dreaming brain]. Psychiatric
Journal, 13, 51.

13. A GOVERNMENT DOCUMENT

U.S. Bureau of the Census. (1991). <u>Statistical abstracts of the United States</u> (111th Ed.). Washington DC: U.S. Government Printing Office.

14. A LETTER TO THE EDITOR

Hill, Anthony C. (1992, February 19). A flawed history of blacks in Boston [Letter to the editor]. <u>The Boston Globe</u>, p. 22.

15. A PUBLISHED INTERVIEW

Personal interviews are usually not cited in an APA-style paper, unlike published interviews.

Cotton, Peter (1982, April). [Interview with Jake Tule, psychic]. <u>Chronicles Magazine</u>, pp. 24–28.

16. A FILM OR VIDEOTAPE

Hitchcock, A. (Producer and Director). (1954). <u>Rear window</u> [Film]. Los Angeles, CA: MGM.

17. A COMPUTER PROGRAM

<u>TLP.EXE Version 1.0</u> [Computer program]. (1991). Hollis, NH: Transparent Language.

SAMPLE RESEARCH PAPER
IN APA STYLE

Following is a great example of a paper that grew directly from the writer's experience. Dan noticed a connection between problem drinking and spouse abuse in the alcohol crisis intervention center where he worked. He noticed that women whose husbands were drinkers seemed to suffer chronic physical abuse. It was all brought home to Dan when a woman named Louise walked into the center, asking for help. Dan's research paper is, in part, Louise's story. But it's also an informative look at whether the connection Dan suspected is real and what can be done about it.

Dan's paper experimented with many of the approaches explored in this book. He wrote for reader interest—telling a story and bringing people to the page—and did so with a human voice. Yet he also managed to find and use authoritative sources to make the paper convincing. Notice how Dan blended the narrative and the exposition. How do you think it works?

Dan has offered this advice to writers of research papers: "Try to anticipate reader questions and present your information in a way that makes the piece flow in a sensible, easy-to-read manner. And I think, most importantly, do not give up your own personal voice in favor of that dry technical lecturer voice that runs rampant in most research papers. Don't be afraid to try something different."

Source: "Partner Abuse in Connection With Alcoholism" is reprinted with permission of Daniel C. Jaffurs.

1

Partner Abuse

*APA style
requires a
title page.
Double-space
and center
the title.*

Partner Abuse in Connection
With Alcoholism

Daniel C. Jaffurs
University of New Hampshire

Running Head: PARTNER ABUSE

*The
abbreviated
paper title,
to be used
in the
pagination.*

2

Partner Abuse

*In more
formal
APA-style
papers,
page 2 is
a one-page
abstract. It
was omitted
here, so the
text begins
on page 2.*

"A spaniel, a woman, and a walnut
tree--the more they're beaten, the
better they be" (An Old English
Proverb)

*The paper
opens with
a lead of
extended
dialogue.*

"How can I help you, Louise?"

"The man I live with said I had to
stop drinking or else he would throw me
out on the street," she answered with a
shaky voice and watery eyes. This was a
little hard for me to imagine. Louise
was sixty-nine years old and looked a
lot like someone's grandmother. Who
would throw their grandmother out on
the street? She reminded me of one of
those little old ladies who lives alone
in a large white house complete with
prize winning roses bushes and fourteen
siamese cats.

"Would he have done that?" I
asked.

Louise nodded her head with a
definite "yes," wispy gray hair waving

3

Partner Abuse

to and fro. "He told me that I had
fifteen minutes to find help, so I
called those AA people and they told me
to come here. Bob wouldn't give me a
ride, so they sent those folks who
brought me here."

She was referring to the
Alcoholics Anonymous Hotline that often
sent people in need of treatment to
where I worked--an Alcoholic Crisis
Intervention Center.

"Do you really think that you have
a drinking problem?"

"Sometimes I think maybe I drink
too much."

"Do you have any medical
problems?"

"My shoulder doesn't work real
well. I had it operated on about eight
years ago"

"I mean, do you have anything
wrong internally, like with your blood
pressure, or your liver maybe?"

4

Partner Abuse

"No, there is nothing wrong with
me," she answered firmly, with a wispy
wave of the head.

Well, there was something wrong
here. If Louise had a problem, it sure
wasn't showing. Alcoholism is a
progressive illness and there are
certain telltale signs that appear
depending on where the person is in the
progression.

Notice the shift from dialogue to explanation. The information in this paragraph is common knowledge and doesn't need to be cited.

Alcoholic drinking usually beings
with "relief drinking," (Maxwell, 1976)
drinking to calm nerves, gain
confidence, or just to feel better
after a bad day at the office.
Eventually, this leads to heavier
consumption, for "easing stress" (p.
83). Occasional memory lapses start to
occur and the alcoholic begins to lose
control over his or her drinking. While
dependence increases, so do memory
blackouts. Promises and resolutions
fail repeatedly, behavior becomes

5

Partner Abuse

grandiose and aggressive, and all
efforts to control drinking fail. If
the disease is allowed to continue
untreated, it will lead to physical
deterioration, loss of job and family,
and ending ultimately in insanity or
death (pp. 79–93).

It may take twenty years to
complete the progression, or it may
take as few as five or six. Nowhere in
this pattern could I find a spot for
Louise.

Most alcoholics don't live to see
sixty-nine. On a hunch I asked about
the man she lived with. Bob was sixty
and had been living with Louise for the
past ten years, about two years after
her husband died. During that time, Bob
had been to several detox centers and
was still actively drinking. He had
told Louise that she was the one with
the problem.

6

Partner Abuse

According to Maxwell (1976), it's
relatively common for the active
alcoholic to place blame for his
problems on others or anything at all
for that matter. This is known as the
"denial process" and is one of the
chief symptoms of alcoholism (p. 80).
Denial is also common among spouses in
that they are more apt to place blame
on themselves rather than an outside
influence (Kellerman, 1985 p. 7).

"Louise," I said, "I don't think
that there is anything I'll be able to
do for you. If you really feel that you
have a drinking problem, I can give you
some telephone numbers of people in AA
and Al-Anon and you can start to go to
meetings. In the meantime, I'll make a
call and see if I can't get someone to
take you home."

"I can't go back home. He won't
let me."

7

Partner Abuse

"What do you mean, he won't let
you?"

"He told me that if I come back,
he'll get a lawyer and a restraining
order and I'll be out on the sidewalk
like a bag lady."

"Would he really do that?"

"Yes. When he's drinking. . ." She
shook her head slowly and looked at the
floor, one hand clutching a mangled
kleenex and the other massaging her
sore shoulder.

She looked genuinely frightened of
going back home. Was there something
else going on here?

"Louise," I asked gently. "Does
Bob ever hit you?"

She looked at me with a pained
expression and I was almost sorry I
asked.

"He has before," she said
reluctantly. It was almost a whisper.
"But only when he drinks, and he hasn't

8

Partner Abuse

done it in quite a while. He's a nice
person when he doesn't drink." This
last was added almost as if it made
everything better, or at least more
excusable.

"Is that what happened to your
shoulder?"

She nodded and reached for another
kleenex.

I was noticing more of this kind
of thing showing up at the center. I
had been under the impression for some
time that alcohol was among the chief
culprits in partner abuse, but there
was very little substantiation of a
solid connection between alcoholism and
battering.

Violence prone marriages basically
fall into two groups. In the first,
partner abuse is due to personality
disorders such as extremely low self
esteem, severe depression, psychopathic
tendencies, and tolerance for

Dan establishes the focus of the paper.

9

Partner Abuse

frustration (Roy, 1982, p. 39). In the
second group, abuse stems from
conflicts with the relationship
(p. 39). These conflicts can include
anything from the mundane, such as an
argument over who was supposed to feed
the dog to more serious situations,
like unemployment and financial
difficulties. In either of these
groups, alcohol is considered to be
only a contributing factor, or
"trigger" that releases already
inflamed emotions (K. Kennet, personal
interview, April 18, 1985).

Other researchers (Gelles, 1972)
feel that either alcohol is used as an
excuse for deviant behavior, or that
men who are "potentially violent"
before entering into relationships with
women frequently experience negative
feelings, begin to drink, and then
become violent (Hanks & Rosenbaum,
1978).

Personal interviews are cited in the paper but not the "References."

10

Partner Abuse

In some cases, where a deviant
personality is present, the role of
alcohol could be considered a
"trigger," like throwing gasoline on an
already burning fire. I feel, however,

Dan's statement of thesis.

that alcohol abuse plays a much bigger
role in domestic violence than
presently believed.

For example, alcohol use was
reported by men in 50% of all first
cases of wife abuse, 56% of all
incidents of the severest battering,
and 58% of the last reported cases
before the women involved sought help
(Walker, 1984, p. 169).

In other correlations between
partner abuse and alcoholism, 80% of
battered women said they observed
incidents of violence in their home
when they were children--either they
were abused or they witnessed their
parents physically harm each other--and
in more than half of these homes at

11

Partner Abuse

least one parent abused alcohol or was
an alcoholic (Walker, 1984, p. 179).
Another study reported that in almost
all the cases where the parent had been
abused as a child, alcohol was involved
(Behling, 1978). This is not to say
that all alcoholics beat their wives
and children or that all batterers are
alcoholics, but the relationship
between both alcohol and violence is
too strong to ignore. Apparently,
physical abuse and alcoholism tend to
run in families, the values and
behavior of one generation passed on to
the next.

I also think it's important to
note that not all abuse is physical.
According to Kathy Kennet, "emotional
battering" can be as bad, or worse than
actual beatings (personal interview,
April 18, 1985). This can consist of
verbal abuse, placing blame on the
spouse--"It's your fault I'm like this"

12

Partner Abuse

or "If you were half the wife you're
supposed to be, this wouldn't be
happening"--and as in the case of
Louise, physical threats. The big
question now was, why did she stay with
him? This bit with the lawyers and
restraining orders was just excess
steam. It was he who should be out on
the street, not her.

"Louise, I can keep you overnight
here at the center, but tomorrow,
you're going to have to make some sort
of decision on how to deal with Bob."

"If I made him leave, where would
he go?"

"He doesn't seem to be worried
about that for you," I replied. "This
has been going on for what, ten years?
You really don't need this kind of
treatment."

"I just don't know. I keep hoping
this will get better. What should I
do?"

13

Partner Abuse

Dan is present throughout the paper, especially here. Is he too present?

I had a good idea. She should throw the bum out, but it was unlikely that she would do that. She was afraid to go home now, but come morning, things would probably change.

Gelles (1976) reports that there are three factors that come in to play concerning the actions of abused women. The less severe or frequent the abuse, the more the woman was struck as a child, or the fewer resources she had, the more likely she is to stay in the relationship (p. 659). And, in most cases, genuine love is involved (K. Kennet, personal interview, April 18, 1985).

Battered women also often think that they control their environment, minimizing any opportunity for the batterer to become violent (Walker, 1984). The majority of the women surveyed would avoid starting any conversations with the batterer, not

14

Partner Abuse

discuss anything that might lead to a
violent episode, keep the house
immaculate and the kids quiet. Almost
half of the women thought they could
control the batterer's behavior. It is
probably this sense of control that
gives women the hope that just maybe,
they can change their lives for the
better (pp. 78–79). This type of
rationale is also common among spouses
of alcoholics (Maxwell, 1982). They see
themselves as more sensitive,
responsible, and stronger for having
gone through a violent relationship
when actually, the reverse is true.
Batterers, like alcoholics, usually
keep control over their partners by
denying access to charge accounts,
savings accounts, cars, etc. Even
though he may make threats to leave the
home, or threaten to evict his wife,
his need for someone to lean on is

15

Partner Abuse

evidenced by the control exerted on the home environment.

Louise had told me that during the ten years she had lived with Bob, he managed to get his name on the deed to her house, had the only set of keys to their car, and gave her a bi-weekly allowance. She had given in on these things to alleviate further abuse, thus giving herself the impression that she was controlling the situation. In her efforts to control Bob, she had actually given him all the power but refused to realize it.

It was obvious to me that Louise had some feelings of love for Bob, and felt responsible for him. She was also afraid of what he might to do her when he drank. Not afraid enough, however, to not want to go back to him in the morning.

"When can I go home?" she wanted to know.

16

Partner Abuse

"Do you really think that's a good
idea? Do you think that things are
going to be any different?"

"Well, where else am I going to
go?"

"I called a place not too far from
where you live that provides shelter
for people in your position. Why don't
I call them for you and let you talk to
them?"

"Maybe I should call Bob first."

I had this feeling that if she
talked to Bob first she probably
wouldn't talk to the counselor at the
shelter. After a little not too subtle
persuasion, she reluctantly agreed to
contact the shelter.

The folks at the shelter were more
than willing to help Louise, but what
about Bob? What kind of services are
available for the alcoholic batterer?

According to the National
Institute of Alcohol Abuse, 35% of

Dan keeps weaving dialogue throughout. What's the effect?

17

Partner Abuse

those entering alcohol treatment
programs reported fighting as a common
occurrence when drinking. Six months
after treatment, violent behavior was
reduced by nearly half. Obviously,
treatment for alcoholism can reduce
violence. But according to Walker
(1984), the batterer needs more to
teach him to be non-violent, including
a program in assertiveness training,
anger management, and efforts at self-
control, all performed in a supportive
group setting (p. 71).

Probably the most important part
of treating the alcoholic batterer is
to treat the entire family, especially
the children, over one third of whom
suffer from some kind of anxiety
disorder (Rosenbaum & O'Leary, 1981,
p. 692). It is precisely these
disorders that are the root cause of
the generational cycle of abuse and
alcoholism described by Behling (1978).

A combined question-answer and problem-solution structure, with a narrative that ties it all together. Does it work?

18

Partner Abuse

While Al-Anon helps children and families of alcoholics, the issue of abuse isn't specifically addressed. It should be. There must also be education on domestic violence at all levels.

After talking to the people at the shelter, Louise called Bob and decided to go back home. I wanted to shake her and say, "Don't go!" but it was useless. I had done all that I could. The rest would be up to her. At least now she knew that there were options available.

Of all women who stayed at the shelter during the past year, 28% had gone back to their partners, according to Kathy Kennet (personal interview, April 18, 1985). However, the majority of that 28% eventually returned to the shelter and moved out of the abusive home environment.

Just about two hours after Louise left the crisis center, she called me

19

Partner Abuse

on the telephone and asked for the 24-
hour number to the shelter.

Thirty minutes later Bob called to
inform me that he held me personally
responsible for Louise leaving. It was
a good feeling.

*Is the ending
effective?*

20

Partner Abuse

References

Behling, Daniel. (1978, October).
<u>Comprehensive care clinic: Findings
relative to domestic violence and
alcohol abuse.</u> Paper presented at
NCA meeting, St. Louis, MO.

Gelles, Richard J. (1972). <u>The violent
home</u>. Beverly Hills, CA: Sage.

Kellermann, Joseph L. (1985). <u>Guide for
the family of the alcoholic</u>. Long
Grove, IL: Kemper.

Maxwell, Ruth. (1976). <u>The booze
battle</u>. New York: Ballantine.

Rosenbaum, Alan, & O'Leary, Daniel.
(1978). Children: the unintended
victims of marital violence.
<u>American Journal of Orthopsychiatry</u>,
<u>4</u>, 692–699.

Roy, Maria. (1982). <u>The abusive
partner</u>. New York: Van Nostrand
Reinhold.

Walker, Lenore E. (1984). <u>The battered
woman syndrome</u>. New York: Springer.

APPENDIX D

□ ■ □

Tips for Researching and Writing Papers on Literary Topics

Before I turned to English teaching as a profession, I had a background in science. I had written lots of research papers on science-related topics—lobsters, oak tree hybridization, environmental education—but felt totally unprepared to write a research paper on a book or a poem. What do you write *about?* I wondered. I paced back and forth all night before my first literature paper was due.

I know now—for a paper on any topic—not to waste time, staring off into space and waiting for inspiration, but to pick up my pen and simply start writing. I trust that I'll discover what I have to say. I also know that a paper on a literary topic isn't really so different from those papers I wrote for other classes. All good papers simply involve taking a close look at something, whether it's the mating habits of a fly or a short story by Franz Kafka.

MINE THE PRIMARY SOURCE

What distinguishes a paper on a literary topic from others is where most of information—the details—come from. When I wrote the book on lobsters, that information came largely from interviews and a variety of published sources. When I wrote about the manhood issues raised by the characters in two Wallace Stegner novels, most of that information came *from the novels*.

A research paper about a story, poem, essay, or novel will usually use that work more than any other source. Literary papers rely heavily on *primary sources*. In addition to the literary works, primary sources might also include letters or interviews by the author related to those works.

The emphasis on primary sources is obvious when you read the sample research essay at the end of this appendix about Franz Kafka's story "The Metamorphosis." The writer, Karoline, frequently wove lines, passages, and information from the short story into her essay, using the work to illustrate her points. If there's one key weakness in student papers on literature, it's that they don't mine the works enough. The writer should not stray too far from what's in the poem, story, novel, or essay she is writing about.

The emphasis on mining primary sources means that the research strategy for a literary paper is often a little different than that for other topics. First, remember that your most important reading will not be what you dig up in the library. It will be your reading of the work you're writing about. Be an activist reader. Mark up the book (unless it's a library copy, obviously) or the story, underlining passages that strike you in some way, perhaps because they seem to reach below the surface and hint at what you think the writer is trying to say. Use a journal. The double-entry notetaking method described in "The Third Week" (Chapter 3) is a great way to explore your reactions to your reading. Use fastwriting as a way to find out what you think after each reading of the work; explore your reaction, rather than staring off into space, trying to figure out what you want to write about.

How do you know what you think until you see what you say?

SEARCH STRATEGIES

Though your close reading of the work you're writing about should be at the heart of your research, you can do other research, too. Most literary topics can be seen from several other basic angles. You can look at the *author* or what *critics* say about the author and his work. You may also discover that the author or work you're writing about fits into other recognized *categories* or *traditions*. In the most general sense, the work might be classified as British literature or American literature, but it also might fit into a subclass, such as African-American or feminist literature, or align with a particular regional school, like southern writers. Each of these classifications is a subject by itself and will be included in reference sources.

Let's look at a few key library sources for a paper on a literary topic.

Researching the Author

Biography

In Karoline's paper on Kafka, she relied heavily on a biography of the author. She found a single book that proved useful, but a number of other reference sources could have provided her with helpful background information:

> *Authors' Biographies Index*. Detroit: Gale, 1984–present. *A key source to 300,000 writers of every period.*
>
> *Biography Index: A Cumulative Index to Biographical Material in Books and Magazines*. New York: Wilson, 1946–present. *Remarkably extensive coverage. Includes biographies, as well as autobiographies, articles, letters, obituaries, and the like.*
>
> *Contemporary Authors*. Detroit: Gale, 1962–present. *Up-to-date information on authors from around the world; especially useful for obscure authors.*

Other helpful sources by the Wilson company, the familiar publishers of *Reader's Guide,* include the following: *American Authors, 1600–1900, British Authors before 1800, British Authors of the Nineteenth Century,* and *European Authors, 1000–1900.*

Primary Bibliographies

It might be helpful to read additional works by the author you're researching. What else has he written? Biographies may tell you about other works, but they are often incomplete. For complete information, consult what's called a *primary bibliography,* or a bibliography *by* the author:

> *Bibliographic Index*. New York: Wilson, 1937–present. *The "mother of all bibliographic indexes" lists works that have been published by and about the author.*
>
> *Bibliography of Bibliographies in American Literature*. New York: Wilson, 1970. *Works by and about American authors.*

Index to British Literary Bibliography. Oxford: Clarendon, 1969–present. *Works by and about British authors.*

American Fiction: A Contribution Toward a Bibliography. San Marino: Huntington Library, 1957–present. *Entries on 11,000 novels, stories, and so on, indexed by author.*

Researching the Critics

What do other people say about your author and the work you're writing about? A thorough look at criticism and reviews is an important step in most research papers on literary topics, especially after you've begun to get a sense of what *you* think. Support from critics can be important evidence to bolster your own claims, or it can further your own thinking in new ways.

Several useful reference sources have already been mentioned. For example, so-called *secondary bibliographies,* or bibliographies *about* individual authors, are listed in the *Bibliographic Index* mentioned above. Check that. The most important index to check for articles about your author or her work is the *MLA International Bibliography,* mentioned in "The Third Week" (Chapter 3). This source is commonly available on CD–ROM. Other helpful references include:

Contemporary Literary Criticism. Detroit: Gale, 1973–present. *Excerpts of criticism and reviews published in the last twenty-five years.*

Magill's Bibliography of Literary Criticism. Englewood Cliffs, NJ: Salem, 1979. *Citations, not excerpts, of criticism of some 2,500 works.*

Book Review Index. Detroit: Gale, 1965–present. *Citations for tens of thousands of book reviews, including many obscure works.*

Current Book Review Citations. New York: Wilson, 1976–present. *Citations for reviews in about 1,200 publications.*

New York Times Book Review Index, 1896–1970. New York: Arno, 1973. *Great for a more historical perspective on literary trends; features about 800,000 entries.*

Researching the Genre or Tradition

What type of work, or *genre,* are you researching? A novel? A poem? Might it fit into some recognized category or tradition?

Another angle on your topic is to place your work or author in the context of similar works and authors. One place to begin is with general survey books, such as *The Oxford Companion to American or English Literature*. Other references are surveys of period literature, such as *English Literature in the Sixteenth Century*, as well as world literature, such as *History of Spanish American Literature* and *World Literature Since 1945*.

Within each of these broad literary landscapes are some smaller ones, each with its own reference sources. For example, within the broad topic American literature, there's a growing list of references to African-American literature. For example, *Afro-American Literature: The Reconstruction of Instruction* is a reference filled with essays on the place of African-American literature in literary history. Similarly, *American Indian: Language and Literature* lists 3,600 books and articles on American Indian literature and language.

Sheehy's *Guide to Reference Books* provides a helpful listing of sources that can help you place your topic in a larger context. But the best reference for research on a literary topic is this:

Harner, James L. *Literary Research Guide*. New York: MLA, 1989.

This amazing source reviews bibliographies, histories, indexes, surveys, and periodicals on every class and subclass of literature imaginable, from world literature to Chicano fiction. Buy the *Literary Research Guide* if you have to write a lot of papers on literature.

THE PERSONAL APPROACH

Reading imaginative literature can be a deeply personal experience. It should be. As you're reading a novel, poem, or essay, pay attention to what moves you. A character or idea that gets your attention is often the launching place for a good paper. Your emotional response is your way into the author's work.

I recently read several novels by Wallace Stegner and found myself in tears on several occasions. When I looked more closely at what passages I found so moving, I noticed they all had to do with a son trying to define his own manhood through his father. I began working on a paper that explored my response. I became interested in the question of how manhood is constructed and what Stegner's characters—and the author—suggested to me about that.

The first several pages of that paper (written in MLA style) follow:

Dealing With the Ax-Father

in Wallace Stegner's

Big Rock Candy Mountain

and Recapitulation

Three weeks before my father died, he invited
me to his shabby quarters at the back of his
antique and picture framing business. Like its
proprietor, the business was failing. I hadn't
spoken to my father in six months when he invited
me over that New Year's Day. I found his life
pathetic and could no longer bear to witness the
ravages of alcoholism--the pasty complexion, the
glassy eyes, and the way his hands trembled as he
brought a cigarette to his face. I was tired of
the old stories about his Tribune days, about the
house he would build on St. John or the book he
was going to write, because I no longer believed
them.

My father lived in two rooms at the back of
the store. A small bedroom was always darkened by
blinds, and a kitchen, which doubled as an office,
had aqua-colored tile walls, yellowed from a film
of grease and cigarette smoke. Dirty dishes and
used insulin syringes were scattered in the sink
and on the kitchen counter. An old Royal
typewriter, a machine I was to later use to
compose my first published essays, was perched on
a shaky typewriter table in the middle of the
room.

We sat together in that kitchen, facing a small television set, watching a football game, each of us clutching a beer. We didn't talk about the game; it was just a tactic to avoid eye contact. He was overcome by shame, and I, by pity. Yet I remember it as a rare moment, too, when we awkwardly reached for each other across years stained with anger and hurt. For the first time in years, it felt almost like I imagined it should be, like a man and his son sharing an easy moment.

I remember staring at the television screen, watching the football players move repeatedly from huddle to play, lining up against each other and then suddenly disassembling into jarring collisions and chaos, and it occurs to me now that my father and I had spent a good part of our lives engaged in a similar kind of skirmish. We played against each other until I didn't want to play anymore.

"Memory," said Bruce Mason, the narrator of Wallace Stegner's 1979 novel Recapitulation, "sometimes a preservative, sometimes a censor's stamp, could also be an art form" (265). Did my father really tell me, as I was leaving that New Year's Day, that he was sick and needed my help? Did I really see tears in his eyes when he said it? And if so, how could I leave and hope I would never see him again? What was that game we played, and why don't the injuries from it ever seem to heal?

In Iron John, Robert Bly describes the
"father-hunger" (99) of American men, an ache that
is especially acute since industrialization took
the father out of the home, away from his sons and
daughters, and transformed him into a remote,
seemingly irrelevant, and sometimes ridiculous
figure with his nose buried in a newspaper. This
creates its own special problems for daughters,
but for sons, the loss is profound. Set adrift
from a sense of masculine identity, we run aground
on the treacherous memory of our fathers. Bly
tells an African tale of a man and his son who go
hunting together. When the father captures a rat,
the son throws it away, an act that prompts the
father to hit him on the head with an ax. The blow
represents all the hurts inflicted on the son by
the father. Bly writes, "We can say for each of us
this father question has to be dealt with. Sooner
or later, we have to deal again with that side of
the father who hit us with an ax" (114-115).

It is this "father question" that is Wallace
Stegner's primary concern in two novels, The Big
Rock Candy Mountain, published in 1943, and
Recapitulation, a "trailer" to the earlier work
that was published more than thirty years later.
Because of his background, sensibilities and
motivations, Stegner is a writer who is especially
well equipped to guide us on an exploration of
what it means to be a man in an age when no one is
quite sure.

Reading As an Experience

You don't need to get this personal to write an effective research essay. But I wanted to share this with you to demonstrate that writing on a literary topic doesn't have to seem objective or dispassionate.

Reading is an *experience*. Explore that experience with the same feeling and curiosity you might use to write about something else important that happened to you.

SAMPLE RESEARCH PAPER ON A
LITERARY TOPIC

In the sample paper that follows—"Metamorphosis, the Exorcist, and Oedipus"—Karoline chose a less personal approach but one that is still effective. Through careful use of the primary text—Kafka's short story "The Metamorphosis"—along with just two other sources—a biography and a collection of Kafka's diary entries—Karoline showed how the author and his story merge. She remained behind the scenes in this paper, at least, much more so than I did in the excerpt from my paper on Stegner. But the paper still relays a sense of a purposeful writer, shaping and shaving the material, someone who has a clear sense of what she wants to say and who wants us to understand it.

Karoline's paper also uses MLA conventions.

Source: "Metamorphosis, The Exorcist, and Oedipus" by Karoline A. Fox. Reprinted with permission.

Fox 1

Karoline Ann Fox

Professor Dethier

English 401

15 December 1991

Metamorphosis, the Exorcist,

and Oedipus

According to Ernst Pawel, Franz

Kafka's "The Metamorphosis" goes beyond

"standard categories of literary

criticism; it is a poisoned fairy tale

about the magic of hats and the power

of hypocrisy . . . charting the

transmogrification of a lost soul in a

dead bug" (279). Kafka's tale is more

than a literary work. It is a

frighteningly realistic representation

of the most desperate and obsessing

fears of its author. Disguised behind

the all-too literal shell of the

character Gregor Samsa, Kafka attempts

to exorcise the demons of his haunted

childhood.

    In one of his many diary entries,

Kafka described writing as "the

Karoline's thesis is clearly stated in the lead. In a short essay such as this, it's helpful to state the thesis early.

Fox 2

revealing of oneself to excess;
that utmost self-revelation and
surrender . . ." (<u>Memory</u> 72), yet he
admits that this surrender fulfills "a
great yearning to write all my anxiety
entirely out of me, write into the
depths of the paper just as it comes
out of the depths of me . . ." (38). In
"The Metamorphosis," Kafka clearly
makes no attempt to hide his deepest
anxieties, but reveals them with
deliberate vindictiveness.

There is, for example, a striking
resemblance between Kafka's father and
Gregor's father in the story. Like
Herrmann Kafka, Mr. Samsa seems a
tyrannical giant, whose violence
overwhelms any sympathy for his
unfortunate son. In fact, Mr. Samsa's
first reaction to his son's condition
is to knot "his fist with a fierce
expression on his face as if he meant
to knock Gregor back into his room
. . ." (869). And even Gregor's kindest

*When citing
two or more
sources by
the same
author,
abbreviate
the titles.
Note that
Kafka's
name is
mentioned in
the text; it
doesn't need
to be
included
in the
parenthetical
citation.*

Fox 3

Karoline effectively weaves passages from different parts of the story into this paragraph. Cite only page numbers when it's clear from the text where borrowed material has come from.

intentions are misunderstood by his father, who "pitilessly . . . drove him back, hissing and crying 'Shoo!' like a savage," and ultimately sent him flying into his room "bleeding freely" (871).

Though Herrmann never abused the young Kafka, his son had a unnatural fear of the man. Remembering a time when his father punished Kafka by locking him out on a balcony, his son later wrote, "Even years afterward I suffered from the tormenting fancy that the huge man, my father, the ultimate authority, would come almost for no reason at all and take me out of bed in the night and carry me onto the [balcony], and that meant I was mere nothing for him" (<u>Memory</u> 10).

Kafka's view of his father as a rival for most, if not all, of his life indicates an oedipal complex, according to Pawel (15). Kafka's mother, Julie, was completely devoted to her husband but neglected her son, who was taken

Fox 4

care of by servants until old enough to
care for himself. Kafka did not take
out his anger for this neglect on his
absent mother but on the recipient of
her affection, Herrman.

Gregor, in "The Metamorphosis,"
shares this jealousy. He witnesses an
almost erotic reunion between his
parents as he saw "his mother rushing
toward his father, leaving one after
another behind her on the floor her
loosened petticoats, stumbling over her
petticoats to his father and embracing
him in complete union . . ." (881-882).
Yet his mother seems saintly, despite
her loosened petticoats, "with her
hands clasped around his father's neck
. . . she begged for her son's life"
(882). Gregor's mother is his angel of
mercy, and only she harbors hope that
he will one day become human again. She
refuses to remove the furniture from
his room, say ". . . when he comes back
to us he will find everything unchanged

Fox 5

and be able all the more easily to
forget what has happened in between"
(878).

Despite Kafka's idealized vision
of his mother, the author and his
mother were never very close. Julie
Kafka was always at Herrmann's beck-
and-call. As a boy of five, Franz saw
the birth of first one and then another
sibling as a threat to his monopoly of
what was almost non-existent maternal
attention. With the successive deaths
of his sibling rivals, Kafka suffered
from traumatic guilt which he fought
the rest of his life (Pawel 63).

He felt no such rivalry when three
more sisters were born, years later.
Instead, Kafka was happy to have the
companionship, and became particularly
fond of his youngest sister, Ottilie.
In "The Metamorphosis," Gregor also
has a younger sister for whom he is
willing to sacrifice a portion of his
salary so she can study violin at the

*Throughout,
biographical
information
about the
author
reflects
against
material in
his short
story, each
illuminating
the other.*

Fox 6

Conservatorium. It is Grete, who "in
the goodness of her heart" (873) brings
Gregor food and cleans his room.

Grete's compassion fades, however,
because the young girl can't endure her
brother's appearance, making Gregor
"realize how repulsive the sight of him
still was to her, and that it was bound
to go on being repulsive" (876). Grete
later abandons her good intentions
towards her brother but keeps up her
care, enjoying a kind of selfish
martyrdom.

Later, even that disappears and
Grete's rejection of her brother is
complete. When Gregor hears Grete play
the violin, he remembers his longing to
send her to the Conservatorium and,
weak from pain and near starvation,
crawls toward the sound of the music
"determined to push forward till he
reached his sister, to pull at her
skirt and so let her know that she was
to come into his room with her violin,

Fox 7

for no one . . . appreciated her
playing as he would appreciate it"
(887). Instead of seeing the affection,
Grete is horrified, saying ". . . we
must try to get rid of it" (888).

Like Gregor, Kafka felt himself
trapped within a hatefully repulsive
shell, writing "it is certain that a
major obstacle to my progress is my
physical condition. Nothing can be
accomplished with such a body" (<u>Memory</u>
37). He feels incapable of being loved
by anyone. Desperately, he tried to
conceal his need for affection with
indifference, claiming "the sorrows and
joys of my relatives bore me to the
very soul" (89) and "all parents want
to do is drag one down to them, back to
the old days from which one longs to
fill oneself and escape" (60). This
denial of his need for love led Kafka
to severe depression, suicidal self-
hatred, insecurity, self-pity,

hypochondria and serious physical
ailments (Pawel 191).

Even as a young man, Kafka put
himself down, insisting that he would
fail in every endeavor: "He sincerely
believed himself to be incompetent,
lazy, forgetful, clumsy, badly dressed,
incoherent" (Pawel 53). Admitting
"success . . . did not inspire
confidence; on the contrary, I was
always convinced . . . that the more I
accomplished, the worse off I would be
in the end" (Kafka, Memory 26).

This incessant self-doubt,
however, served as a safety net for the
Kafka. If he insisted he would fail, he
couldn't be held accountable when he
did. If he succeeded, then he could
enjoy his success without setting
unreasonable goals for himself. Kafka's
super-sensitive ego could never have
withstood the defeat of both failure
and wounded pride because he so

desperately sought approval of his
friends and his enemies alike.

Writing becomes the glue that
holds Kafka together. Again and again
he curses his incompetence at it,
arguing "God does not want me to write
while I, I have to write. And so there
is a constant tug-of-war" (Memory 7).
It was a tug-of-war in which he had to
participate, because Kafka clung to his
writing more than he did to life
itself: "The novel is me, my stories
are me . . . It is through my writing
that I keep a hold of life" (Memory
viii).

Not surprisingly, Kafka's family
did not approve of his writing. When he
wrote his father about his plans to be
a writer, it's likely that the young
author found some pleasure in his
father's disappointment. But his father
never read it. His mother did not give
it to him, thinking that her son would
outgrow his interest in writing (Memory

Fox 10

ix). Julie Kafka's lack of understanding left her son embittered, and
he later wrote in his diary a dialogue
between himself and his mother which
ended, "Certainly, you are all
strangers to me, it is only blood that
connects us, but that never shows
itself" (<u>Memory</u> 91).

Kafka wrote that "what we need are
books that affect us like some really
grievous misfortune, like the death of
one whom we loved more than ourselves,
as if we were banished to distant
forests, away from everybody, like a
suicide" (<u>Memory</u> 7). Of "The
Metamorphosis" he said, "[T]he more I
write, the more I liberate myself"
(<u>Memory</u> 61). This liberation came from
his ability to put his life into his
story and exorcise the demons of his
childhood. Paradoxically, by doing so
he was able to hold onto that life.

"The Metamorphosis" embodies those
conflicting sentiments. In it, we see

Fox 11

more than the dried and withered empty
shell of a life. We see a man, Kafka,
lying in the darkest corner of a filthy
room, unable to move into the light and
accept the love he so desperately needs
in order to remain alive.

Karoline restates her thesis but in a fresh way.

Fox 12

Works Cited

Kafka, Franz. <u>I Am a Memory Come Alive</u>.

Ed. Nahum N. Glatzer. New York:

Schocken Books, 1974.

———. "The Metamorphosis." <u>Fiction 100</u>.

Ed. James Pickering. New York:

Macmillan, 1988.

Pawel, Ernst. <u>The Nightmare of Reason</u>.

New York: Farrar, 1984.

Use three dashes to show another work by the author in the preceding citation.

Karoline used just three sources, but vigorous use of the primary source—the Kafka short story— throughout the paper helped make it meaty.

Index

NOTES

NOTES

NOTES

NOTES